Archaeology and World Religion

Archaeology and World Religion is an important new work, being the first to examine these two vast topics in conjunction with each other. The volume explores the relationship between the two, and the contribution archaeology can make to the study of what are today termed 'World Religions', namely Buddhism, Christianity, Hinduism, Islam and Judaism. This work is the definitive text for this growing area of archaeology.

Divided into two parts, it first surveys each of the religions in question and then goes on to address the important themes of ethics, gender and death. The contributors consider a number of questions: can religious (sacred) texts be treated as historical documents, or do they merit special treatment? Does archaeology with its emphasis on material culture dispel notions of the ideal/divine within religious texts and what are the implications of this possible conflict? Does the study of archaeology and religion lead to differing interpretations of the same event? In what ways does the notion of a uniform religious identity exist, the ideal Muslim or Christian, for example, and is this recognisable in the archaeological record – through diet, dress, sacred buildings, burials, art and iconography, landscapes and personal possessions?

Clearly written and up to date, this volume will be of special significance to anyone interested in archaeology and religion and will be an indispensable research tool for academics and specialists in these fields.

Timothy Insoll is Lecturer in Archaeology at the University of Manchester.

Contributors: Anders Bergquist, Dilip Chakrabarti, Robin Coningham, Rachel Hachlili, Timothy Insoll, Paul Lane, Rachel MacLean and Mike Parker Pearson.

Archaeology and World Religion

Edited by
Timothy Insoll

London and New York

First published 2001
by Routledge
11 New Fetter Lane, London EC4P 4EE

Simultaneously published in the USA and Canada
by Routledge
29 West 35th Street, New York, NY 10001

Routledge is an imprint of the Taylor & Francis Group

Typeset in Baskerville by
Florence Production Ltd, Stoodleigh, Devon
Printed and bound in Great Britain by
Biddles Ltd, Guildford and King's Lynn

British Library Cataloguing in Publication Data
A catalogue record for this book is available from the
British Library

Library of Congress Cataloging in Publication Data
Archaeology and world religion / edited by Timothy Insoll.
     p. cm.
   Includes bibliographical references and index.
   1. Archaeology and religion.   I. Insoll, Timothy.
   BL65.A73 2001
   200'.9–dc21   00–059239

ISBN 0–415–22154–4 (hbk)
ISBN 0–415–22155–2 (pbk)

Contents

Figures

Tables

Contributors

Bergquist, Rev. Canon Dr Anders, St Albans Cathedral, St Albans, Hertfordshire, AL1 1BY.

Chakrabarti, Dr Dilip, Lecturer, Department of Archaeology, University of Cambridge, Downing Street, Cambridge, CB2 3DZ.

Coningham, Dr Robin, Senior Lecturer, Department of Archaeological Sciences, University of Bradford, Bradford, BD7 1DP.

Hachlili, Professor Rachel, Chair of the Department of Archaeology, University of Haifa, Israel.

Insoll, Dr Timothy, Lecturer in Archaeology, School of Art History and Archaeology, University of Manchester, Oxford Road, Manchester, M13 9PL.

Lane, Dr Paul, Director, British Institute in Eastern Africa, PO Box 30710, Nairobi, Kenya.

MacLean, Dr Rachel, Honorary Secretary, British Institute in Eastern Africa, 10 Carlton House Terrace, London, SW1Y 5AH.

Parker Pearson, Dr Mike, Reader, Department of Archaeology and Prehistory, University of Sheffield, Northgate House, West Street, Sheffield, S1 4ET.

Acknowledgements

This volume initially took shape during a conference organised and held at St John's College, Cambridge, in April 1998, and I would like to thank the Master and Fellows of the College for generously sponsoring the conference, thus making the whole project feasible. Support for this project has also subsequently been provided by the School of Art History and Archaeology at the University of Manchester for which I am grateful. A debt of gratitude is also owed to the referees who looked at the papers, often at short notice, and to Vicky Peters at Routledge and the assessors of the original proposal for making the volume more cohesive. Thanks are also offered to my family for all their support over the past two years as this volume has taken shape, and to Rachel MacLean and Siân Jones for comments on Chapter 1. Finally, I would like to thank the students who have taken my MA course in the Archaeology of Religion at the University of Manchester for stimulating my thinking on the subject and for much lively debate.

Every effort has been made to trace copyright holders. The editor, authors, and publisher would like to apologise in advance for any inadvertent use of copyright material, and thank the following individuals and organisations who have kindly given their permission to reproduce copyright material. For Figure 1.3, the executors of Professor G.D.B. Jones, and for Figure 1.7, the University of Manchester. Figures 2.2, 2.3, and 2.4 have been reproduced courtesy of the Department of Ancient History and Archaeology, Allahabad University. Figure 4.4 is reproduced courtesy of the Archaeological Exploration of Sardis, and Figure 4.7 courtesy of the Israel Antiquities Authority. For Figures 7.1 and 7.2 thanks are also owed to David Kelsall, Archivist of St Albans Abbey and The Cathedral and Abbey Church of St Alban.

Chapter 1

Introduction

The archaeology of world religion

Timothy Insoll

Definitions and objectives

The archaeology of world religions is a vast subject, and one which it might seem foolhardy to attempt to consider within the confines of an edited volume composed of nine chapters, three of which are considerably shorter commentaries. However, this volume does not claim to be universal, rather it aims to examine the relationship between, and the contribution archaeology can make to the study of, what are today termed world religions, through focusing upon the examples of Judaism, Islam, Christianity, Hinduism, and Buddhism. This raises a couple of questions. First, why world religions in particular? Although there is no shortage of archaeological studies of elements of world religion in 'mainstream' archaeological literature there appears to be a gap with regard to an overall consideration of archaeology and world religion (a notable but dated exception is a namesake volume [Finegan 1952] which attempts to be all-inclusive but is now rather dated). There is also a certain imbalance in the mainstream literature (the focus, at least, of this introductory chapter) in favour of Christian archaeological remains (see for example Frend 1996, Platt 1987, Blair and Pyrah 1996), probably a reflection of the bulk of work having been undertaken in Europe, which is also the centre of many of the relevant archaeological journals and publishing houses. Thus applicable studies of Islamic, Hindu, Buddhist, or Jewish archaeology or archaeological material tend to be confined to specialist journals and other publications, though to be fair this imbalance has begun to be rectified of late (see for example Barnes 1995, Insoll 1999a).

Second, it could be asked why these religions in particular? The examples chosen are certainly not meant to be exclusive, but merely reflect the interests and specialisations of the contributors to the volume. Third, what constitutes a world religion? This is in fact something which is frequently neglected in the literature. Is it number of adherents? Is it geographical spread? Is it length of time in existence? Is it unity in practice and doctrine? Is it Universality, or consideration by their adherents to be proper to all mankind? (Sopher 1967). Is it the existence of a notion of salvation, or because they rest on a basis of written scripture? (Bowie 2000: 26). Is it all, some, or none of these, or many other criteria which could be listed? Answers to these questions are elusive, as they are, indeed, to answering the question of what is religion itself, an issue which has been the subject of 'seemingly endless debate' (Clarke and Byrne 1993: 6). One could turn to the simplistic definitions of religion listed in major dictionaries (see for example Renfrew [1994: 48] for such an application), but such definitions are by their very nature so general as to be of little use.

No answer is to be provided here, though having said this, Durrans' (2000: 59) recent definition of religion is as useful as any other, 'a system of collective, public actions which conform to rules ("ritual") and usually express "beliefs" in the sense of a mixture of ideas and predispositions'. Likewise, to endeavour to neatly differentiate religion from one of the archaeologist's favourite categories, that of ritual (see below), is a major undertaking. Indeed, to attempt a definition of either world religion or religion/ritual itself is beyond the confines of this introductory chapter, and of the volume. This might be taking the easy option, but the author is unapologetic for this, and it is merely noted that with regard to the examples chosen, geographical spread and thus an extensive archaeological legacy tie these five religions loosely together as much as anything else. Archaeology is the concern, and is witnessed by the material record of Judaism in Israel and the Diaspora, Buddhism in south and south-east Asia, and more recently, elsewhere in the world, Hinduism likewise, Islam within the borders of the Muslim world as usually defined from Morocco in the west to Indonesia in the east, but also, increasingly, worldwide, and finally, that of Christianity similarly spread across the continents.

Definitions aside, what then does this chapter attempt to achieve? First, a possible structure of study for the archaeology of world religion will be considered. Whether the archaeological study of world religion can draw upon methodologies and concepts developed elsewhere in the study of religions, notably the broad field encompassed by history of religions, or whether there is little to be gained from adopting explicit theoretical approaches from such sources. Second, the approaches which have been adopted to the archaeology of world religion will be briefly outlined, again with the proviso added that within the limits of circa 10,000 words this cannot be considered exhaustive. This section will essentially be divided into two parts – what could be termed negative aspects regarding archaeology and its application to the study of world religion, and in contrast, the positive aspects as well. Finally, the papers themselves will be introduced, and the perceived similarities and differences in how they might be approached by archaeologists will be examined.

An approach to the archaeology of world religion?

Archaeological approaches to religion are remarkably piecemeal, at least in the UK, ad hoc almost, with the subject being considered as and when necessary, with few serious attempts at examining approaches to the archaeological study of religion overall. Conferences, for example, have been occasionally organised with archaeology and religion as their focus, the Sacred and Profane meeting in Oxford (Garwood *et al.* 1991) being notable, or the conference held in Cambridge in 1998 from which these papers emerged being another (see Insoll 1999b). Other examples of approaches to archaeology and religion within the 'mainstream', outside of a conference format, vary, with one of the most famous of these being Christopher Hawke's 'ladder of inference', whereby ritual/religion was placed as one of the most inaccessible rungs in the interpretative process, compared to, for instance, economy (see also Parker Pearson in this volume). The realisation that religion/ritual might be of importance to archaeologists in general is sometimes accredited to proponents of the 'New Archaeology' (see for example Demarest 1987). David Clarke (1968), for example, was influential in this respect, seeing religion 'as a distinct information subsystem' (P. Lane pers. com.), as important as economy or social organisation in maintaining equilibrium in systems/cultures. More recently Renfrew (1994) has approached the archaeology of religion within the framework of cognitive archaeology (Renfrew and Zubrow 1994). He draws upon the ideas of, among others, Rudolf Otto (1950) and his notion of the numinous, of religious 'essence' (discussed in greater detail below), before considering how religion/ritual might be recognised in archaeological contexts.

However, Renfrew's approach towards religion is general, as the title of his paper, 'the archaeology of religion', implies. The components of religion, world religions, for example, have been little considered in terms of archaeological approaches that might be employed to further their study. This lacunae in approaching world religions is apparent in the work of other archaeologists who have approached religion/ritual from a theoretical, or what could be termed a 'dedicated', perspective. The Sacred and Profane conference referred to previously (Garwood *et al.* 1991) is heavily focused towards prehistory and 'ritual' rather than protohistorical or historical archaeology as might fall within the domains of the study of world religion. In fact, prehistory would in general appear to be the slightly more favoured partner when it comes to devoted mainstream archaeological research and publication directed at investigating religion/ritual (see for example Gimbutas 1989, Gibson and Simpson 1998, Green 1991, Burl 1981).

A further and well-known example of a dedicated mainstream consideration of religion is provided by the *Sacred Sites, Sacred Places* volume

(Carmichael *et al.* 1994), one of the volumes in the One World Archaeology series derived from the World Archaeological Congress. Coverage in this is more even than in the *Sacred and Profane* volume previously considered, yet besides the introductory papers (see for example Hubert 1994), the ensuing case studies are particularistic in focus, a further characteristic of relevant research discussed below. This weakness in archaeological theory towards the investigation of religion in general is something remarked upon by Garwood *et al.* (1991: v) who refer to it as an 'extraordinary neglect . . . which must be addressed'. These are admirable sentiments and even today, too often, material that is unusual or eludes interpretation is placed within that convenient catch-all interpretative dustbin of ritual. A practice which is easy to justify as the necessary debate over the terminology, methodology and theory of archaeology and religion/ritual has still to be seriously initiated.

Anthropology, in contrast, would appear to be more mature in its theoretical approaches to religion, a debate which has continued for some years and a process charted, in part, by Parker Pearson (this volume). Anthropology also benefits from several convenient summaries of approaches to religion which have been employed within the discipline (see for example Evans-Pritchard 1965, Saliba 1976, Morris 1987, Bowie 2000). This debate is something which archaeology has lacked to date (Insoll forthcoming). Yet this does not mean that anthropologists over the course of the past 150 years or so have worked out the perfect methodological and theoretical approaches to religion, they have not. The excesses of the early evolutionary approaches to religion, exemplified by, for example, Frazer (1890), Spencer (1876), and Tylor (1871) might be past, and a much more mature approach in evidence, but a dichotomy still appears to exist. To quote Morris, anthropology texts 'largely focus on the religion of tribal cultures and seem to place an undue emphasis on its more exotic aspects' (1987: 2). So-called tribal religions are thus split up into phenomena – myth, witchcraft, magic and so on – whereas in contrast, as Morris also notes (ibid.: 3), world religions are treated according to a quite different theoretical framework whereby they are treated as discrete and distinct entities, such as 'Buddhism' or 'Islam'. Admittedly, anthropological approaches to the study of religion are more complex that this, as Parker Pearson indicates below, but the important point is that even after many metres of bookshelves-worth of relevant material have been published and much introspective disciplinary soul-searching completed, an ideal approach has yet to be adopted, and in all probability never will.

Where then does this leave the archaeology of world religion as regards theoretical perspective? Put simply, there is not one. As already indicated, archaeological studies of religion with an explicit theoretical focus are few and far between, whereas innumerable studies of actual material exist in both mainstream and more specialised media. These are studies completed

Figure 1.1 The Wailing or Western Wall in Jerusalem, with above it the Dome of the Rock – the foci of pilgrimage in two world religions, and also the focus of much controversy (photo T. Insoll)

at a variety of levels, local, regional, focusing upon component parts of religious practice such as pilgrimage (Figure 1.1), or at the total religious scale (Rodwell 1989, Gilchrist 1994, Graham-Campbell 1994, Frend 1996, Insoll 1999a), but lacking a common theoretical approach. Even within this volume, edited by one person with fairly clear views as to the desired end product, the disparity in approaches is readily apparent. Yet this is not necessarily a bad thing, and it is not the presumption here to try and develop a theoretical approach for the archaeology of world religion. This is patently an absurd proposition, but it is possible, perhaps, to point to a few useful avenues of investigation, which other better qualified scholars might then explore.

Primary amongst these would appear to be the acknowledgement that a useful source of material which might be drawn upon to begin to consider relevant approaches exists within the fields of study encompassed within history of religions, comparative religions, or what is sometimes rather forbiddingly referred to in its untranslated (and untranslatable) German as *Religionswiffenschaft*. This is defined by Hinnells (1995: 416) as the academic study of religion apart from theology, and was introduced by Fredrich Max Müller (1823–1900). In many ways the certain degree of untranslatability of *Religionswiffenschaft* into English reflects the dichotomy of archaeology as a discipline in itself, with *Religionswiffenschaft* as a term in German covering both science and humanities, a meaning largely lost in translation (Hinnells ibid.). This multi-disciplinary aspect of what we might refer to as history of religions might be useful as it draws in many different aspects of research, conveniently defined by Saliba (1976: 25) as, 'the study of the origin and development of religion – embracing all the world's religions past and present in one single field, as one whole phenomena evolving in time'. This idea of unity is exciting and might help in breaking down many of the particularities all too often evident in relevant archaeological research, and thus help us to move beyond merely description or the listing of facts. These are faults not unique to archaeology but something remarked upon by Evans-Pritchard with regard to comparative religion itself, a discipline which he stresses, 'must be comparative in a relational manner if much that is worthwhile is to come out of the exercise. If comparison is to stop at mere description – Christians believe this, Moslems (sic) that and Hindus the other . . . we are not taken very far towards an understanding of either similarities or differences' (1965: 120).

Within the history of religions, study is encompassed under a number of sub-disciplines, psychology of religion, philosophy of religion, sociology of religion, phenomenology of religion, history of religion (lacking plural). Why not archaeology of religion as well? Demarest refers to archaeology and the study of religion maintaining 'a close but uneasy relationship' (1987: 372); should archaeology be further integrated within the study of religion forming perhaps another component part of history of religions-type approaches or is it too much to see archaeology reduced to a micro-category and subsumed within a macro-heading such as history of religions? It depends upon personal preference, yet Bergquist (this volume) is, according to this author at least, quite correct when he stresses that archaeology really ceases to be a discipline in itself and becomes a 'set of techniques that may be placed at the service of a whole range of disciplines – economic history, demography, anthropology, history of religions etc.' (below). To investigate phenomena such as religion – world religion, archaeology does not really take the ascendancy but forms part of a battery of techniques applied to understanding such complex phenomena.

Thus the over-arching framework of history of religions appears to offer a multi-disciplinary superstructure under which to labour as archaeologists. Or does it? This author is always wary of deriving too much inspiration from one source, and elsewhere has advocated a 'mix and match' approach (Insoll 1999a: 12–13), without trying to bang the theoretical drum of one stance or other too loudly. Yet history of religions under its umbrella encompasses a wealth of relevant ideas and methodologies which might benefit archaeology. Sharpe (1986: 45), for example, makes the important point that one of the fundamental prerequisites of *Religionswiffenschaft*, something which existed from its very beginnings, was the insistence by Müller that accuracy should be employed not only 'with regard to dead traditions, but sympathy with regard to living traditions' as well. Similarly, all religions should be taken seriously, 'not merely as objects of study, but as *religions*' (ibid.: 159).

This notion of the position of the observer, the researcher, the archaeologist, would appear all-important but little discussed as regards archaeology and religion. The controversies, biases, and general opportunities for misuse of archaeological data of a religious nature (and of various other forms, not the focus of discussion here) is all too well known, and is indeed considered with reference to a couple of case studies later. Thus this notion of sympathy, neutrality, and of being free of value-judgements on the part of the researcher is of critical importance, or should be to the archaeologist involved in the investigation of religion, even if it is not always possible to achieve (see below). We are not largely (though this is also discussed later) what could be termed 'theological archaeologists', attempting to 'express or articulate a given religious faith' as part of 'an attempt to state and defend the fundamentals of his faith for his fellow believers' (Byrne 1988: 3), but this does not preclude, as far as is possible, a sympathetic approach to the archaeological study of religion.

But is this notion of stance, of faith, really of such importance? Elsewhere, the author has suggested that being a believer or adherent of the faith or belief system being studied could be a hindrance as 'one cannot see the complete whole through being detached from it' (Insoll 1999a: 7). Equally, the existence of the converse position was also stated, that something could also be lost by being an adherent of the said faith or belief system, by making it difficult to question established doctrine or practice. These are issues which the author had to grapple with in connection with a recently completed study (ibid.). It is also something which has been considered by Hubert (1994: 12) who, rightly, makes the point that religion, in England (the focus of her study), has become compartmentalised, and that notions of the sacred have changed both with regard to the 'concept of sacredness of the land as a whole' and even in how churches 'are treated less and less as sacred places'. Such issues could have an obvious effect upon the role of the archaeologist, a product of this social milieu, as interpreter of religion, whose understanding of the sacred might be fundamentally different from that imbued in the material culture which they study.

Practical issues also arise when the notions of faith and archaeology are considered. Heinrich Harrer, for example, recounts the difficulties he had in getting his Buddhist Tibetan workmen to build dykes as, 'there was an outcry if anyone discovered a worm on a spade. The earth was thrown aside and the creature put in a safe place' (1955: 238). It is not so much the specific example that is important here (but could be to someone

engaged in archaeology in Tibet), rather the general ideas are of relevance, that faith can impinge upon archaeology and religion in many
ways, both theoretically and practically. Similar factors can underpin the
varying significance of monuments. Consider for example the role of
Masada, the site of the Zealots' last stand against the Romans in 73 CE,
whose importance to national identity (interwoven with aspects of religious
identity as well) is of such significance in Israel (see Yadin 1966, Zerubavel
1995). This notion of the varying importance of monuments, in this case
directly influenced by issues of faith, can be clearly seen when the issue
of varying levels of access is considered. Bergquist (this volume) describes
the complex negotiations which had to be completed to gain permission
to complete a survey of the traditional Tomb of Christ. But as convoluted
as these negotiations were, research was allowed to finally take place here
and elsewhere in the Church of the Holy Sepulchre (see also Gibson and
Taylor 1994). In contrast investigation of the Holy Places of Islam, those
in Mecca and Medina would not be possible, if indeed, it was desired (see
below). Though the Temple Mount, on which sits the third most holy site
in Islam, the Dome of the Rock, has been the scene of some research and
much controversy (Anon 1996, Walker 1996) (Figure 1.1).

These are complex issues and many other dimensions to them exist
than those briefly touched upon here, but at this juncture it is profitable
to observe that we appear to be flailing around somewhat, and it might
be useful to search deeper within the component parts of history of religions for more precise ways to approach the archaeology of world religion.
The psychology of religion, defined by Hinnells (1995: 394) as the application of 'the theories and methods of psychology to the study of religious
phenomena' would appear to be of little relevance. Similarly, the sociology of religion, concerned as it is with the 'notion of rationalisation'
(Morris 1987: 69), as exemplified in the work of scholars such as Durkheim
(1976) and Weber (1963) with their emphasis upon empirical questions as
to the social implications of 'what kinds of people hold what kinds of
beliefs under what kinds of conditions' (Hinnells 1995: 486) does not appear
to offer much of a way forward either. The same could be said of philosophy of religion. Whilst conventional history of religion, more a collection
of facts and collation of dates and events in a manner reminiscent of the
type of descriptive approach bemoaned by Evans-Pritchard, referred to
earlier, is also inappropriate. This leaves phenomenology of religion.
However, one does not want to fall into the trap of what Sharpe describes
as misdefining and reducing phenomenology to a simplistic level, 'that it
means little more than the "sympathetic study of religion" – an assumption which is not false, but which is scarcely appropriate' (1986: 221).
Having acknowledged this, it is possible that phenomenology of religion
might offer some potential for the archaeologist interested in world religion,
and phenomenological approaches have certainly been used successfully

by archaeologists investigating aspects of prehistoric ritual/religion (see for example Tilley 1994).

It is precisely with regard to the notion of the sympathetic study of religion that archaeologists might profit, through following neither the agenda of theologically driven religious fundamentalism, nor atheism or agnosticism, the latter an approach to religion likened to 'a blind man judging a rainbow' (De Vries 1967: 221 cited in Saliba 1976: 145). Otherwise, elements of phenomenology of religions are equally of little practical use to the archaeologist interested in world religion or religion in general. The emphasis of scholars such as Mircea Eliade (1969) upon looking at religions from the perspective of the 'detached within' (Saliba 1976: 34), of 'introspection' or 'internalisation' is admirable perhaps, certainly idealistic, and equally little achievable. The utilisation of *epoché*, emphasising 'the need to abstain from every kind of value judgement – unconcerned with questions of truth and falsehood' (Sharpe 1986: 224), is equally commendable and equally unachievable, for the interpretative process cannot fail to include value judgement (see for example Bowie 2000: 11), and these are well-worn paths down which we need travel no further for our purposes here.

A further useful element which can be drawn from the work of one of the early proponents of history of religions is the concept that at the core of religion, world religion or otherwise, there is an irreducible, a 'numinous', a Holy element (Otto 1950). This is something which archaeologists will similarly fail to approach, regardless even of advances in cognitive archaeology. Why? Because as Sharpe (1986: 164) notes, it is irreducible, it 'can be discussed but cannot be defined'. This is the essence of religion, the search for which has been the focus of so much effort. It is something which has perhaps existed from as early as the Middle Palaeolithic (see for example Trinkhaus 1983, Parker Pearson 1999: 148–9), and less controversially for the Upper Palaeolithic (Lewis-Williams and Dowson 1988, Dennell 1983, Bahn and Vertut 1988).

Although it might be materially elusive, and equally the very suggestion of the existence of the numinous has been criticised by some for the lack of evidence (Sharpe 1986: 165), it does provide a starting point for a required conceptual framework. Such a concept acknowledges the sacred element in religion, something often abstracted in archaeological studies, and allows study to move beyond merely cataloguing religious buildings and artefacts and thinking that this is the sum total of the archaeology of religion. Yet academic minds, including archaeological ones, could well be sceptical about the existence of this numinous element. To quote Sharpe (1986: 234) again, its existence 'is one which *homo religiosus* himself at once understands, but one which the academic mind has always regarded with some doubt, feeling that here he is invited to embark upon a hazardous voyage upon a metaphysical ocean'. The reader is not here invited to undergo such a voyage, but ultimately we have to recognise that religion is bigger than archaeology. To begin to approach religion the archaeologist should perhaps recognise that it is not a subsystem, solely a social manifestation, or something which can be conveniently compartmentalised; it can and frequently does act over the whole of life, meaning the archaeology of religion, of world religion, is a complete archaeology which can influence all facets of material culture and the archaeological record.

Negative approaches to archaeology and world religion

In search of proof

Thus having considered something of possible theoretical approaches to the archaeology of religion in general, and to world religions in particular, it is useful to move on to look at examples of approaches that have been adopted. The first group of examples can be classed as negative ones, exemplified by what can be termed 'prove it or not' research. This is material that might well fall within what Rahtz (1991: 44) defines as 'the "dubious" end of the motivation scale'.

A useful example of such approaches, not least because it has in part been recently reviewed with some regard to more recent research in the United States (Silberman 1998), as well as elsewhere (Bartlett 1997a), is provided by Biblical archaeology. It is possible to chart over time the changing use of archaeology as a means of proving or disproving Biblical events, usually, but not solely (see Whitelam 1996), with a Christian focus (Figure 1.2). According to Yamauchi (1972), whose work could hardly be classed as unbiased, archaeology began to be used in Biblical studies on a large scale as a reaction to the Biblical criticism prevalent in the latter half of the nineteenth century, especially in Germany, as exemplified by the Tubingen school. Thus Biblical scholars, from the early twentieth century, and especially in the US, 'welcomed the positive results of archaeology', though 'at times they abused such results by glossing over problems and by claiming more "proof" than the evidence justified' (ibid.: 24). Such overt approaches to the use of archaeology as a means of furnishing texts, combating criticism, and making scriptures 'better respected' (Unger 1962a: 26) was followed by the application of archaeology in a more conservative manner by scholars such as W.F. Albright (see for example Bartlett 1997b for a discussion of this). Whilst today a further change has occurred with Biblical archaeology largely being subsumed within Near Eastern archaeology, and evincing a rationale defined by Silberman (1998: 185) as 'devoted to the archaeological excavation of the lands of the Bible without being committed, as an institution, to any particular religious understanding, national interest or historical ideology'.

Figure 1.2 Concrete proof? A 'Christian' millstone in the remains of a Coptic monastery, Aswan (Egypt) (photo T. Insoll)

This then would appear to be the broad framework of how archaeology has been used within Biblical studies over the years. It is useful, however, to look in a little more detail at the application of archaeology within this field to see just how closely it has been tied to the requirements of proving scripture or religious events. Yamauchi (1972: 26), for example, mentions that his book is 'written by one who is committed to the historical Christian faith, seeks to summarise, albeit in selective fashion, the archaeological evidence and its bearings upon the Scriptures'. This emphasis upon selectivity is a problematical feature, emphasis upon proof might be evident, but if the evidence contradicts the asserted viewpoint, then it is just discounted. Practical examples of this abound, again largely related to Biblical archaeology. The search for Noah's Ark by the French industrialist and amateur explorer, Fernand Navarra, provides a notable instance. The background to this is related by Bailey (1977: 137) who describes Navarra's 'wood-retrieving expeditions' to Buyuk Aghri Daghi in Turkey, often identified with Mount Ararat. On one of these expeditions part of a hand-hewn beam was recovered which was analysed by various questionable methods, including the degree of 'lignification' evident, apparently giving a date of *c.* 3000 BCE. However, once samples were submitted for C14 dating at various laboratories, three of the dates obtained were actually found to cluster around the eighth century CE. More wood was recovered on a second expedition again giving similar C14 dates. These results, as Bailey notes (1977: 143), were ignored 'completely' by Navarra, whilst others argued that this young wood had been used for later repairs to the Ark, thus explaining its age.

As noted, this is far from an isolated instance. The interpretation of archaeological evidence for the Biblical Flood provides another case study. Keller (1965: 51), for example, in a book entitled *The Bible as History. Archaeology Confirms the Book of Books*, giving an idea of perspective, mentions the clay deposits found beneath Ur and at other sites in Mesopotamia (Iraq). These are described as allowing the delimitation of the flood area as some 400 miles by 100 miles. This is interpreted as 'a vast catastrophic inundation, resembling the Biblical Flood which had regularly been described by sceptics as either a fairy tale or a legend, had not only taken place but was moreover an event within the compass of history', something which had also taken place 'about 4000 BC' (ibid.). Needless to say, such claims are unsubstantiated and more neatly slot into a long tradition of scholarship on the Flood (see for example Cohn 1996). Similarly, the application of archaeological, or rather associated radiometric dating techniques to try to prove the authenticity of the Turin Shroud is another extremely well-known example of such approaches. With the Sindonologists, the 'near fanatical' (Gumbel 1998) scholars of the shroud staunchly disbelieving the radiocarbon dates obtained by three independent laboratories indicating that this was unlikely to be Christ's shroud (see Bortin 1980), this is a subject of which published claims by both supporters and opposers of the shroud continue to appear regularly in print (see for example Picknett and Prince 1994, Hoare 1994, Wilson 1998).

Essentially, this appears to be a no-win situation for archaeology, proof is sought using archaeological methods and data, but contradictory evidence is discounted (issues also considered by Bergquist in this volume). Alternatively, evidence might be massaged to fit a theory. Rahtz, for example, discusses how within the study of Christianity in Britain between the fourth and eighth centuries there is much debate over whether relevant sites – temples, cemeteries and so on – are Christian or 'pagan'. To quote Rahtz (1991: 45), 'it so happens that the archaeologists concerned (and indeed most of those who study undoubted *churches* and their surroundings) are themselves Christians. This has, perhaps understandably, caused them to lead towards a Christian interpretation of borderline cases which is not always fully warranted by the evidence' (original emphasis).

But to return to broader considerations of the use of archaeology in Biblical studies. Here, it is worth noting that Yamauchi, having been singled out for attention above, is not overly extreme. A more overt view of the application of Biblical archaeology is provided by M.F. Unger (1962a, b) who in his two-volume consideration of archaeology and the New and Old Testaments sees archaeology as a means of illustrating and explaining scripture and also of supplementing and authenticating it. The negative aspects of the use of archaeology are very much evident in the fundamental believer's perspective employed, which hardly bodes well for the posited archaeological interpretations. This is exemplified by the statement that the New Testament is 'beyond doubt the most important document in the world . . . no other religious writings – the Vedas, the Koran (sic), the sacred scriptures of Taoism, Confucianism, or Buddhism – can compare with the New Testament' (ibid.: 17). A believer in a particular faith is undoubtedly going to hold views over the pre-eminence of their particular beliefs and this is hardly something peculiar to Christianity, but it is unfortunate that archaeology is frequently utilised for such purposes in the pursuit of what is best termed theological archaeology, as defined earlier (Figure 1.3).

This is not to say that all studies concerned with archaeology and the Bible are methodologically flawed. Many of great merit, utility, and worthiness similarly exist. An example of just these is provided by Kathleen

Figure 1.3 The role of archaeology? Apse or mihrab? Souk el-Oti (Libya) (photo G.D.B. Jones)

Kenyon's study, *The Bible and Recent Archaeology* (1978). Kenyon has in fact been described by Bartlett (1997b: 9) as 'professionally independent of the Bible'. Kenyon is certainly realistic in her expectations as to how far archaeology can contribute to Biblical studies, acknowledging that much will be elusive concerning the 'sites and places traditionally associated with the events recorded in the Gospels ... for in the main these events are of a nature unlikely to leave material evidence' (1978: 99). Numerous other studies could be cited as well, the volumes edited by Winton Thomas (1967), for example, or more recently by Bartlett (1997a). The latter scholar sensibly emphasises that 'we cannot demonstrate the "truth" of the Bible simply by setting certain passages of it alongside archaeological discoveries' (1990: 6).

Biblical archaeology has thus come of age, or alternatively, been subsumed within a broader field of study, that of Near Eastern archaeology. Yet these older-style approaches with an emphasis upon proof persist, as a brief search through the Internet will indicate. Besides apparently academically serious sites such as *www.bibarch.com*, which answer questions such as 'can we prove the Bible true?' in a realistic manner, other sites are more reminiscent of the 'proof' school of archaeological use. For example, *http://ds.dial.pipex.com/goodnews/lighta.htm*, where, 'with your Bible in hand, you are invited to examine the evidence to see whether the work of the archaeologist confirms or denies God's word'. Similarly, one could ask how much things have really changed when one looks at journals such as *Biblical Archaeology Review*, where the adverts, if anything, are an indicator of the type of audience being addressed. This is exemplified, for instance, in the Sept/Oct issue for 1996 (22/5), where on an inside page we are informed that the 'House of Fabergé presents "The Nativity". A limited masterpiece ... richly accented with 24 carat gold.'

Are such approaches emphasising the use of archaeology as a means of proving/assessing/disproving religious texts, events etc. peculiar to Biblical archaeology, and at that, usually of a Christian slant? In short, they are not, but they are much more ubiquitous within this field of study. Relevant studies with regard to Judaism are usually also classified within Biblical archaeology, and the use of archaeology for such purposes certainly exists. Similar approaches have been employed with regard to the other world religions considered in this volume. Events and people associated with the Mahabharata, the great Hindu epic, have been the focus of archaeological study (see for example Chakrabarti 1999 and Lad 1983). The Qur'an, by contrast, has apparently not been the object of similarly focused, dedicated, archaeological studies, one reason being, as this author has noted elsewhere, that from a Muslim believer's perspective, 'the truth is already revealed and material culture, and therefore archaeology, cannot confirm or deny the faith of believers' (Insoll 1999b: 231). However, the Qur'an and related sources have been the focus of historical analysis which has drawn on aspects of material culture as well (see for example Crone and Cook 1977, Crone 1987, Wansbrough 1977). Relevant work utilising archaeology for illuminating Buddhism is reviewed by Coningham (this volume), and here it can be seen that the emphasis would appear to be on examining sites associated with the Buddha himself, sometimes within the framework of acquiring sacred relics.

Archaeology, controversy, and world religion

If the use of archaeology in an unsubtle way, usually from a believer's perspective (predominantly a Christian one), as a means of supporting sacred texts and events has been one of the major negative uses of the discipline in the study of world religion, the generation of controversy in many other ways through the use of relevant archaeological data has been another. Perfectly respectable research results can be misused or misinterpreted, and often through no fault of the archaeologists themselves, though ignorance, prejudice and bias on the part of archaeologists can be a contributing factor. Numerous well-documented instances exist of how such sensitive issues involving archaeology and world religion can be pulled into the full glare of the media.

A notable example involves the issues surrounding the treatment of human remains in various areas of the world (Figure 1.4). In Israel, for example, the desecration, or perceived desecration, of Jewish burial sites became a political issue following direct intervention by Orthodox Jewish groups to try to halt archaeological excavations over recent years. This was attributable to two main factors. First, the Jewish belief, and thus associated teaching in the Yeshiva religious schools, that 'graves are sacred and all disruption is forbidden' (Faulkner 1998). Second, the fragile political coalition on which the Netanyahu government rested and which relied upon the Ultra Orthodox parties for support. Thus images of Israeli police and Orthodox Jewish protesters clashing at archaeological sites became all too familiar in the media, culminating in the curtailing of archaeological excavation.

These are issues which have also been a factor within the UK, as exemplified in the controversy over the Jewbury excavations in York, events recounted by Rahtz (1991), and also considered from the perspective of ethics by Bergquist (this volume). At this site prior to the building of a Sainsbury's supermarket in the early 1980s, a Jewish cemetery dating from the twelfth century was unearthed. This was initially discounted as such by the Rabbinical Court on the basis that Jews 'were never buried north–south or with coffin nails' (ibid.: 47). Thus the skeletal remains were duly removed for analysis, but the resulting publicity, outcry by Jewish groups and various other circumstances led to an about-face by the Jewish authorities and a recognition that these were in fact Jewish remains. A complaint was subsequently made to the Home Office (the ministry

Figure 1.4 An eleventh-century Muslim burial in Denia (Spain) (photo T. Insoll)

ultimately responsible for such matters), and an order made that these remains should be returned to the Jewish community. These were immediately returned and subsequently reinterred in a special area of the Sainsbury's car park. Fortunately for archaeologists this was not a completely wasted exercise as some useful data on Jewish burial practices were also obtained from the excavations (see Lilley *et al.* 1994).

Positive approaches to archaeology and world religion

Heresy

Thus far the impression might be that the relationship between archaeology and world religion is merely one of narrow research aims, with these lacking any methodological or theoretical framework, the whole dogged by misuse for explicit political or religious ends. This, however, is not correct. Archaeology is increasingly contributing to our understanding of world religion in many ways. Primary amongst these is the contribution archaeology is making to our understanding of heresies, either as offshoots, or otherwise, of world religions. Two examples of heresies are provided by Manichaeism and Donatism which, as Frend notes (1999: 185), are dissenting movements, 'at last able to speak for themselves thanks to archaeology'. Documents and other records associated with heresies could, and frequently were, destroyed by the keepers of 'orthodoxy', through the perceived heretical nature of the movements which produced them. Thus it is primarily to archaeology that a debt is owed for the information gained on these movements. As Teague notes in relation to a study of the Mediaeval Cathar or Albigensian heresy of south-western France, what we see with regard to (in this instance) the Western church, is a 'survivors' record in the historical legacy – the church actively sought out and destroyed offensive people and material, 'even posthumously' (1989: 130).

Possibly less persecuted, but also known to us through archaeological research, are the Manichaean communities of the oases of central Asia who were present in the region from the third to fourteenth centuries CE (Teague 1989: 133). The sites, which were the former homes of these communities in Chinese Turkestan, were the subject of various controversial expeditions during the heyday of the Imperial era at the end of the nineteenth and beginning of the twentieth centuries (see Hopkirk 1986, Frend 1999: 183). These resulted in a wealth of material being uncovered, illuminating many aspects of life and belief (see for example Stein 1903, 1912, Von le Coq 1928). Paintings, manuscripts, shrines, burials, everyday items, all aspects of material culture were preserved often in an 'as left' situation, as this description of the Manichaean Shrine K at Karakhoja by Albert Von Le Coq indicates: 'We found on the threshold the dried-up corpse of a murdered Buddhist monk, his ritual robe all stained with blood. The whole room, into which the door led, was covered to a depth of about two feet with a mass of what, on closer inspection, proved to be the remains of Manichaean manuscripts' (1928: 61).

It is these documents from central Asia in 'Latin, Greek, Coptic, Middle Iranian, Parthian, Sogdian, Old Turkic and Chinese' (Klimkeit 1982: 1) which especially have shed much light on the doctrines of what is, after all, a dead religion (similar documents have also been recovered from Egypt, as exemplified by the spectacular Nag Hammadi library from Upper Egypt [see Frend 1999: 184]), doctrines described by Klimkeit (1982: 9) as being typically Gnostic, maintaining 'a strict dualism between matter and spirit' (and see Lieu 1984). Supplementary to this new information gained on Manichaeism, the excavations in the central Asian oases also provided material on other religious communities. As Sims-Williams (1990: 47) notes, prior to these excavations, 'the erst-while existence of significant communities of Sogdian-speaking Christians was hardly suspected' in the region. But lectionaries, psalters, even the remains of a possible monastery at the site of Balayïq were all uncovered, indicating their former presence. Similarly, much new information on Buddhism in the region was also gained from the archaeological evidence, Buddhist communities having co-existed in many instances with Manichaean ones.

The 'unexpected'

In fact, this is a further area in which archaeology has made a significant positive contribution to our understanding of world religions, namely, through signalling the existence of the unknown or the little-expected. Examples abound. Selected ones illustrating this include the remains of churches and Christian cemeteries which were recorded in north-eastern Saudi Arabia. These provided evidence for 'extensive Christianisation of the Arabian peninsula and Gulf Coast between the fourth and seventh centuries' (Hammond 1994), evidence which conflicted somewhat with the usually held view that these churches merely served as 'short-lived seafarers' chapels' (ibid.). A similar case is provided by the material remains (inscriptions, gravestones) of the Jewish community of Kaifeng in China which have been reported. Though here, unlike the Saudi example, descendants of the original community remain. Archaeological evidence attested to the presence of a Jewish community in this Chinese town, a community which had been established during the Sung Dynasty (960–1126), and which, as was noted, is still represented by a few descendants of the original community, but by people who have lost all knowledge of Hebrew, of relevant religious practices, and of Jewish sacred texts (Poole 1998).

Likewise, as with the Saudi example, the evidence from China was deemed newsworthy as the sources from which the material was drawn show, being respectively, *The Times* and the *Independent on Sunday*. This again indicates the abiding interest which exists in both archaeology and world religion, either singularly or in combination. The final example which has been chosen illustrating this facet of the relationship between archaeology and world religion relates to the unexpected discovery of a church dating from the twelfth to thirteenth centuries at Tuneinir in Syria, close to the Iraqi border. This example, albeit from an area where Christian remains are perhaps to be expected, though maybe not from such a late date, indicates the degree of information on world religions which can be unexpectedly recovered through archaeology. Excavation of this structure delimited features usual to a church such as the apse and altar footings, but also a wooden mould used for the manufacture of Eucharistic bread, and an area of discolouration on the plaster floor in the nave interpreted as stains left by dripping candelabra (Fuller and Fuller 1994). In other words, a full picture was obtained of this unexpected ecclesiastical structure. The dimensions to which archaeology can contribute to our understanding of world religion are thus varied.

Syncretic traditions and popular religion

A further area of importance to which archaeology can make a significant contribution in understanding world religions is in assessing the development of religious syncretism, co-existence, adaptation, and the development of popular religious traditions. Quite what exactly is meant by syncretism and how useful it is as a descriptive device has recently been the subject of some debate both in anthropology and the study of religions (Stewart and Shaw 1994). Initially a term, as Shaw and Stewart note (1994: 1), which had pejorative connotations implying 'inauthenticity' or 'contamination' of supposedly 'pure' traditions, it is now again seen as being a term with utility. Debate aside, syncretism is conveniently defined by Van der Veer (1994: 208) as 'a process of religious amalgamation, of blending heterogeneous beliefs and practices'. Whether one uses the term 'syncretism', or 'creolized', or 'fragmented' (ibid.: 2), the existence of such phenomena cannot be denied in any world religion. They are expressed in the adaptation of religion to suit local circumstance, perhaps integrating pre-existing or new religious elements with those derived from world religions, to create popular religious tradition and practice, and thus render the idea of an untarnished, somehow pure world religion as a myth. Because, again to quote Shaw and Stewart, 'all religions have composite origins and are continually reconstructed through ongoing processes of synthesis and erasure' (1994: 7). Archaeology is well-suited to investigating such phenomena, of processes of adaptation, evolution, and change, and this is a theme much evident in the papers in this volume.

Case studies of where archaeology has been used to investigate the development of syncretic traditions and of popular religious practices are reasonably numerous, and increasingly more so. Eaton (1993), for example, has integrated archaeological evidence within a recent study looking at the acceptance of Islam in Bengal. Essentially, Eaton successfully succeeded in turning established thinking about the spread of Islam in this region on its head. Instead of models invoking Muslim immigration, conversion by the sword, or acceptance of Islam because of patronage or as a way of escaping the Hindu caste system, he proposed a more mature three-phase conversion model of 'inclusion', 'identification' and 'displacement'. A model which allowed for gradual religious change, and importantly, assimilation of older elements within the process as well. Of significance for our purposes here, he presents archaeological evidence attesting to all three phases, exemplified by the fusion within the 'inclusion' and 'identification' phases of local Hindu and Muslim notions of god, as indicated through inscriptions (ibid.: 275). This interplay of different religious elements is also something which has been explored through material culture by Ovsyannikov and Terebikhin (1994) amongst the Samoyed clans of the Arctic regions of the former USSR. Crosses were fundamental in the propagation of Christianity in the region, with wooden crosses functioning in a variety of roles, as grave and territorial markers, and as places of worship. Yet traditional religion co-existed alongside Christianity, as attested by the continuing practice of leaving offerings in sacred groves. As the authors note, 'side by side with adherence to the official Christian religion, pagan religio-mythological patterns continued to function' (ibid.: 80).

Conversion, continuity, and identity

Archaeology is well-suited to investigating such phenomena, as it is for examining all the intricacies of religious conversion, a process often thought of in simplistic terms but which archaeology can indicate to be anything but. Lane (this volume) examines such notions with regard to Romano-British conversion to Christianity, and rightly signals that this is by no means clear-cut. As Potter and Johns (1992: 209) note, 'the dividing line between Christian and pagan was a tenuous one'. A break with old traditions might be evident. Rodwell for example, describes a fourth-century CE ritual deposit of pagan sculptures found beneath the crypt of Southwark Cathedral in London as 'deriving from a liturgical "cleansing" of the site' (1993: 92). The pattern is also evident in the conversion of the Wallbrook mithraeum into a church, again with evidence for the deliberate destruction of the figures of the old Gods (ibid.). Similarly, one of the long-standing interpretations for the abandonment of the Zoroastrian fire-temple at Surk Khotal in Afghanistan was because of the conversion of King Kanishka to Buddhism in about the second century CE, and thus, 'the rapidity with which Buddhist missionaries were able to win converts among his subjects may help to account for the sudden abandonment of so important a Zoroastrian site' (Talbot Rice 1965: 144) (Figure 1.5).

Equally, continuity might be displayed, and again examples can be drawn from material which relates to Christianity, indicating, as was noted earlier, that this is a better investigated area within mainstream archaeology, the primary area from which the case studies are drawn. An example of this is provided by recent excavations in the Basilica of Dor some 30 km south of Haifa in Israel. Here, it was found that this ecclesiastical structure which dated from the fourth century had been built directly over a pagan temple, a process involving integrating and remodelling older elements, whereby the cella became the nave, the stoa was replaced by external aisles, and the adyton, 'the subterranean "holy of holies"' (Dauphin 1997: 157) was remodelled into a cistern. Likewise at Dvin in Armenia a 'three-aisled pagan building of the third century was converted early in the fourth to serve as its first cathedral' (Talbot Rice 1965: 229). Burial

Figure 1.5 Re-used Buddhist sculpture in a wall of the Muslim citadel, Daulatabad (India) (photo T. Insoll)

provides a further category of archaeological evidence which can inform on aspects of religious continuity. On the Isle of May in the Firth of Forth (Scotland) where excavation unearthed a variety of Christian burials from the Middle Ages, some of which contained white quartz pebbles, artefacts whose presence was interpreted as indicating pre-Christian beliefs 'carried over into the Christian era, that these pebbles were a token for entry into heaven' (Yeoman and James 1999: 194). The continuity in use of burial mounds for early Anglo-Saxon Christian burials in England is also some-thing which has recently been examined (see for example Williams 1998, Semple 1998). In this instance archaeology indicated that the adoption of churchyard burial was more gradual than previously thought.

Yet it should be noted that what one scholar might interpret as 'conti-nuity' could easily be interpreted by another as indicating a 'break' with the past through the re-use or conversion of sites associated with former religions. Less subjective perhaps is how newly found religious identity can be signalled in material culture, something amenable to investigation by archaeology. At Aksum in Ethiopia, the new Christian identity of the king, Ezana, was found to be indicated on coinage by the disc and crescent symbol being replaced by the cross half-way through his reign in the fourth century (Munro-Hay 1991: 190, Phillipson 1998: 113). An overt symbol

of religious change was thus being used, albeit in limited contexts in this
initial phase of Christianisation, but something which was immediately
recognisable through archaeology. Other ways in which religious identity
can be signalled in material culture and how these can be approached by
archaeologists are considered elsewhere in this volume, as by MacLean
with regard to gender and world religion for instance.

However, the examination of dietary change as a possible signifier of
religious identity is another area which it is worth briefly considering within
this introductory chapter. This is a field in which archaeology can again
make a significant positive impact. Faunal and botanical remains can be
structured as much, if not more, by religious or ritual considerations as
by economic ones (e.g. Ryan and Crabtree 1995). As Grant (1991: 110)
notes, 'the religious, the symbolic and the economic are all inextricably
combined', and she subsequently indicates this with regard to the development of Christian traditions of dietary abstinence in mediaeval England.
It is also a vast field with many hidden pitfalls for the archaeologist
attempting to differentiate religious groups or look for clear-cut markers
of religious identity in their faunal assemblages (see Coningham and Young
1999). Simoons (1994) provides ample examples of the complexity which
exists. If we consider one well-known example, that of pork prohibition,
this can be found to exist amongst perhaps unexpected groups, Christians
in Ethiopia or Zoroastrians exposed to Islamic influence in Iran for example
(ibid.: 41, 44). This complexity, certainly as regards the pig prohibition, is
something also indicated archaeologically, not only in Islamic sites (Insoll
1999a: 96–7), but on Jewish sites also. Meyers (1996: 8), for instance,
describes how simple correlations between the presence and absence of
species and religious groups is not always supported by archaeological
evidence in Israel, where pig remains were found in 'urban areas of mixed
Jewish and Christian populations' dating from the third century CE.

In the instance just described, religious differentiation through the
analysis of faunal remains was impossible, yet this is not always so. A
classic study illustrating just what can be achieved is provided by Ijzereef's
(1989: 47) analysis of faunal remains from an area of Amsterdam inhabited by Portuguese Jews in the seventeenth to eighteenth centuries. This
clearly indicated differences between Jewish and non-Jewish households.
The main criterion employed was the percentage of pig bones found,
ranging from zero – interpreted as Jewish, to between one to five per cent
– interpreted as non-Kosher Jewish or Jewish houses with non-Jewish resi-
dents as well, to over five per cent being interpreted as representative of
non-Jewish households. However, identification was not based upon this
criterion alone. The religious identity of the various households was further
supported by other aspects of the data. This included correlations with
the pig data of an absence of hind limb bones of cattle and sheep in Jewish
houses, an indicator of Kosher slaughter patterns (the presence of the

sciatic nerve which is difficult to remove renders these elements non-Kosher). Similarly, there was a high percentage of chicken bones, often with a lead Kosher seal attached to the sesamoid bones in the leg found in Jewish houses, along with an absence of eel remains, a further impure species (ibid.). Ijzereef provides an excellent example of a study which indicates the positive use of archaeology in furthering our understanding of world religion.

Thus the relationship between archaeology and world religion can be seen to be not only defined in terms of the negative. Negative images might abound, but the positive contributions archaeologists can make to the study of world religion are of greater significance, as has been briefly signalled. Heresies, the unexpected, the development of syncretic or popular religious traditions, continuity and discontinuity, and methods of signalling religious identity, all can be explored through archaeological evidence. These are but a few dimensions of study and others exist, but it is now necessary to move on to consider the papers themselves by way of introduction.

The individual chapters

As was noted at the beginning of this chapter, the contributions cover a wide range of material, disparate both in terms of geographical range and chronology. Does this diversity render them really amenable to consideration within a volume such as this? It is certainly true that they differ immensely, and this is something immediately apparent in the papers. Islam, for instance, is sometimes classified as more homogeneous than, say, Christianity, a notion which is similarly frequently criticised (see for example Rosander 1998: 2–3). Debatable as that particular example might be, it would certainly appear correct to say that Islam is more easily definable than Hinduism, but at the same time this difference does not mean one is a 'higher' religion and the other a 'lower' one (see Bowie 2000: 25–6 for a discussion of these issues). This is patently not the case, but differences obviously exist. In fact the definition of Hinduism and the debate over when it actually began to be defined as a religion is considered by Chakrabarti (this volume). These are also issues examined by Flood (1997: 6) who makes the point that 'part of the problem of definition is due to the fact that Hinduism does not have a single historical founder, as do many other world religions'. Hinduism is thus often loosely defined, as by Chakrabarti, and again to quote Flood it certainly exists as a definable entity but one with 'fuzzy edges' (ibid.). It is this element of 'fuzziness' which perhaps sets Hinduism slightly apart, though again, to further complicate matters, it could be argued that all the world religions considered here become more difficult to define at their outer edges, conceptually rather than geographically speaking.

Figure 1.6 Requests written on wooden tablets. The archaeology of the future? Kiyomizo-Dera Temple, Kyoto (Japan) (photo T. Insoll)

However, the difficulties in defining world religion have already been outlined at the start of this chapter where it was emphasised that one of their vague defining criteria was their wide geographical spread and ensuing extensive archaeological legacy. Another similarity which exists is in the categories of evidence which can indicate their presence archaeologically: sacred structures (churches, mosques, synagogues, temples), sacred land-scapes (associated with pilgrimage for example), tombs and other funerary monuments, as well as amulets and other types of more personal items possibly imbued with a religious dimension (Figure 1.6). These are but a few of the categories of material culture ubiquitous to the five world reli-gions considered in this volume, and the recognition of these categories of material is something which is examined in some detail in the indi-vidual chapters.

Yet as Lane (this volume) notes, the identification of a religion in the archaeological record should not be achieved merely by crossing off such elements on a 'checklist'. As has already been discussed, the notion of reli-gion varies and the 'pure' world religion amenable to such an approach does not really exist. Realities impinge upon ideals, popular religion expunges the orthodox, and the ideal suite of material culture reducible to simple formula, for example, Christianity = a church + x + y, Judaism

= a synagogue + x + y, Islam = a mosque + x + y, a suite of material culture which can be rolled out as a supposed aid to recognition, cannot ever be assumed to exist. These are issues which are considered at greater length within the chapters, but it is essential to re-emphasise that diversity exists within each of the world religions under consideration. However, at the same time the existence of the categories of material just described does indicate certain broad similarities in the categories of archaeological remains shared between our five religious traditions which as much as anything else make them amenable to consideration within one volume.

Thus the contributions consider a wide range of issues and a mass of material. Chakrabarti indicates, as has been noted, the diversity of Hindu belief and practice and the difficulties in assessing this through archaeology. He argues that it is better to examine the archaeological record in its entirety for categories of evidence which can be interpreted from the perspective of later Hinduism, rather than setting out with 'checklist' in hand. Chakrabarti places the archaeology of Hinduism in context across time and space in Indian archaeology rather than focusing upon Indus Valley or Harappan sites, with a pinch of Aryan Indo-European pepper added as well, the usual recipe concocted for the origins of Hinduism. Rather, evidence is sought and convincingly interpreted from as early as the Upper Palaeolithic. Archaeology can be seen to provide data wholly absent from texts, and one of the most interesting conclusions drawn is that the Brahmanical framework of Hinduism does not appear until circa 300 BCE, at approximately the same time as Buddhism assumes a pan-Indian character. The importance of sacred sites and landscapes, and the immense continuity in their use is also emphatically signalled, further emphasising the deeply embedded roots of Hinduism.

Whereas Chakrabarti signals the lack of use of archaeology in the investigation of Hinduism, Coningham indicates how it has been misused in the study of Buddhism. He describes how it has been seen as a poor cousin to texts for example, and applied haphazardly for the clearance of monuments, with crucial aspects of archaeological evidence such as faunal remains very rarely analysed. Coningham also considers the archaeology of Buddha himself, thus taking an angle which is lacking in the other papers where religious figures are not considered. It is shown how the archaeological evidence post-dates the Buddha by a couple of centuries, and also to a certain extent indicates the inadequacy of archaeology as applied to looking at early Buddhist sites. Similarly, Coningham also outlines the complexities involved in defining a Buddhist archaeology based upon a limited typology of monuments, and further undermining the checklist-type approach to the archaeology of world religion. The concept of fuzzy borders also recurs, as the fact that Buddha need not only be venerated by Buddhists is stressed, as is the notion that Buddhist sites can be important to other religious groups, a circumstance which can hardly be

Figure 1.7 Pilgrims at a Jain temple, Gujarat (India) (photo M. Ramsden)

said to be specific to Buddhist sacred places but something which also exists between other of the religious traditions under consideration here (see for example Lahriri 1999, Rao 1999) (Figure 1.7).

Hachlili, by contrast, looks in detail at various categories of evidence which might be considered an archaeology of Judaism, thus presenting a structure somewhat similar in approach to that adopted by this author with regard to Islam. Archaeological evidence is also considered from a precise time period, that of the Second Temple Period to the end of Late Antiquity (late second century BCE to seventh century CE). The utility of examining certain types of evidence is emphasised; synagogues and burials for example, whereas the irrelevance of others is also clearly demonstrated, the traditional domestic environment being the most notable. This author finds that a broader range of categories can be considered within the archaeology of Islam in his chapter, but stresses that checklists are again inappropriate. One of the primary conclusions drawn is that an 'ideal' exists but that this ideal is elusive in the archaeological record short of extremely good preservation. Lane also considers such ideas in some detail, and tellingly indicates the inapplicability of assessing the archaeology of Christianity via a list of identifying traits through, for example, the case study referred to previously which considers the Christianisation of Roman Britain. The importance of recognising that complexity in religious conversion exists is stressed, as is the fact that elements of pre-existing belief and practice can strongly influence the character of world religion. Furthermore, the effectiveness of archaeology in assessing such issues is apparent in Lane's chapter, and this is again a theme which is of relevance to all the world religions.

The three shorter commentary sections look at general themes rather than the religious traditions themselves. Bergquist examines the ethics of archaeology and world religion, and in this respect it is worth noting that as an Anglican clergyman (as well as a former archaeology student) he brings a most interesting perspective to the material he considers. Bergquist explores various important concepts such as the fact that the 'sacred' is graded according to a hierarchy, but that too often this is forgotten, and sacrality is thought of as being of one uniform level. Similarly, the plurality of meanings and interpretations inherent in religious artefacts according to the observer is also discussed, as is the notion that religions are subject to historical process, meaning that they too are subject to adaptive change, and thus what might be considered ethical in their study also varies over time. MacLean considers the role of gender in the archaeology of world religions. She indicates that it has been a much neglected subject, which is surprising considering, equally, as she illustrates, the numerous possibilities for research which exist in this area. MacLean rightly indicates that religion is not free of gender considerations, though all too often it could be thought that it was solely a masculine prerogative, something, consciously or subconsciously reinforced in archaeological interpretation as well. Finally, Parker Pearson, in a thought-provoking, and perhaps controversial commentary, examines the historical context of world religion largely as this pertains to death and the commemoration of the dead. He brings a fresh prehistorian's view to the study of world religion and places the development of the world religions within their broader context, the self-acknowledged 'big picture'.

In summary to this introductory chapter, it has to be acknowledged that only a selective consideration has been provided, in part, ultimately, because the issue of space constrained what could be said. Having made this point, it is also useful to reiterate that various themes of past and present research in archaeology and world religion have been outlined, but what of the future? This issue is considered in the individual chapters and it is not necessary to be pre-emptive. But essentially things are looking much better than they did and this can only be helped by the fact that the archaeology of religions in general is now a growing area of interest.

References

Anon. 1996. Riot Tunnel Fails to Excite Experts. *Times Higher Education Supplement* (1 Oct.).

Bahn, P. and Vertut, J. 1988. *Images of the Ice Age*. Oxford: Facts on File.

Bailey, L.R. 1977. Wood from 'Mount Ararat': Noah's Ark? *Biblical Archaeology* 40: 137–46.

Barnes, G. (ed.). 1995. Buddhist Archaeology. *World Archaeology* 27(2).

Bartlett, J.R. 1990. *The Bible. Faith and Evidence*. London: British Museum.

Bartlett, J.R. (ed.). 1997a. *Archaeology and Biblical Interpretation*. London: Routledge.

Bartlett, J.R. 1997b. What has Archaeology to do with the Bible? In Bartlett, J.R. (ed.), *Archaeology and Biblical Interpretation*. London: Routledge. pp. 1–19.

Blair, J. and Pyrah, C. (eds). 1996. *Church Archaeology. Research Directions for the Future*. York: Council for British Archaeology.

Bortin, V. 1980. Science and the Shroud of Turin. *Biblical Archaeologist* (Spring): 109–17.

Bowie, F. 2000. *The Anthropology of Religion*. Oxford: Blackwell.

Burl, A. 1981. *Rites of the Gods*. London: Dent.

Byrne, P. 1988. Religion and the Religions. In Clarke, P. and Sutherland, S. (eds), *The Study of Religion, Traditional and New Religions*. London: Routledge. pp. 1–28.

Carmichael, D., Hubert, J., Reeves, B. and Schanche, A. (eds). 1994. *Sacred Sites, Sacred Places*. London: Routledge.

Chakrabarti, S. 1999. The Mahabharata. Archaeological and Literary Evidence. In Insoll, T. (ed.), *Case Studies in Archaeology and World Religion*. BAR S755. Oxford: Archaeopress. pp. 166–74.

Clarke, D. 1968. *Analytical Archaeology*. London: Methuen.

Clarke, P. and Burne, P. 1993. *Religion Defined and Explained*. Basingstoke: Macmillan.

Cohn, N. 1996. *Noah's Flood. The Genesis Story in Western Thought*. London: Yale University Press.

Coningham, R. and Young, R. 1999. The Archaeological Visibility of Caste. An Introduction. In Insoll, T. (ed.), *Case Studies in Archaeology and World Religion*. BAR S755. Oxford: Archaeopress. pp. 84–93.

Crone, P. 1987. *Meccan Trade and the Rise of Islam*. Princeton: Princeton University Press.

Crone, P. and Cook, M. 1977. *Hagarism: The Making of the Islamic World*. Cambridge: Cambridge University Press.

Dauphin, C. 1997. On The Pilgrim's Way to the Holy City of Jerusalem. The Basilica of Dor in Israel. In Bartlett, J.R. (ed.), *Archaeology and Biblical Interpretation*. London: Routledge. pp. 145–65.

Demarest, A.A. 1987. Archaeology and Religion. In Eliade, M. (ed.), *The Encyclopedia of Religion*. London: Macmillan.

Dennell, R. 1983. *European Economic Prehistory. A New Approach*. London: Academic Press.

De Vries, J. 1967. *The Study of the Religious*. New York: Harcourt Brace.

Durkheim, E. 1976. *The Elementary Forms of the Religious Life*. London: Allen and Unwin.

Durrans, B. 2000. (Not) Religion in Museums. In Paine, C. (ed.), *Godly Things. Museums, Objects and Religion*. London: Leicester University Press. pp. 57–79.

Eaton, R.M. 1993. *The Rise of Islam and the Bengal Frontier, 1204–1760*. Berkeley: University of California Press.

Eliade, M. 1969. *The Quest. History and Meaning in Religion*. Chicago: University of Chicago Press.

Evans-Pritchard, E.E. 1965. *Theories of Primitive Religion*. Oxford: Oxford University Press.

Faulkner, S. 1998. Burial Site Digs Divide Jews. *Times Higher Education Supplement* (11 Sept.).

Finegan, J. 1952. *The Archaeology of World Religion*. Princeton: Princeton University Press.

Frazer, J.G. 1890. *The Golden Bough*. London: Macmillan.

Frend, W.H.C. 1996. *The Archaeology of Early Christianity*. London: Geoffrey Chapman.

Frend, W.H.C. 1999. Archaeology and Library Work in the Study of Early Christianity. In Insoll, T. (ed.), *Case Studies in Archaeology and World Religion*. BAR S755. Oxford: Archaeopress. pp. 182–7.

Fuller, M. and Fuller, N. 1994. A Medieval Church in Mesopotamia. *Biblical Archaeologist* 57: 38–45.

Garwood, P., Jennings, D., Skeates, R. and Toms, J. (eds). 1991. *Sacred and Profane*. Oxford: Oxbow Books.

Gibson, A. and Simpson, D. 1998. *Prehistoric Ritual and Religion*. Stroud: Sutton Publishing.

Gibson, S. and Taylor, J. 1994. *Beneath the Church of the Holy Sepulchre, Jerusalem*. London: Palestine Exploration Fund.

Gilchrist, R. 1994. *Gender and Material Culture: The Archaeology of Religious Women*. London: Routledge.

Gimbutas, M. 1989. *The Language of the Goddess*. London: Thames and Hudson.

Graham-Campbell, J. (ed.). 1994. The Archaeology of Pilgrimage. *World Archaeology* 26(1).

Grant, A. 1991. Economic or Symbolic? Animals and Ritual Behaviour. In Garwood, P., Jenning, D., Skeates, R. and Toms, J. (eds), *Sacred and Profane*. Oxford: Oxford Commitee for Archaeology. pp. 109–14.

Green, M.J. 1991. *The Sun-Gods of Ancient Europe*. London: Batsford.

Gumbel, A. 1998. Ten Years on, the Debunked Turin Shroud gets a Second Coming. *Independent on Sunday* (1 Feb.).

Hammond, N. 1994. Sand Dunes Yield Saudi Arabia's Early Churches. *The Times* (26 Sept.).

Harrer, H. 1955. *Seven Years in Tibet*. London: Reprint Society.

Hinnells, J.R. (ed.). 1995. *The Penguin Dictionary of Religions*. London: Penguin.

Hoare, R. 1994. *The Turin Shroud is Genuine. The Irrefutable Evidence*. London: Souvenir Press.

Hopkirk, P. 1986. *Foreign Devils on the Silk Road*. Oxford: Oxford University Press.

Hubert, J. 1994. Sacred Beliefs and Beliefs of Sacredness. In Carmichael, D. *et al.* (eds), *Sacred Sites, Sacred Places*. London: Routledge. pp. 9–19.

Insoll, T. 1999a. *The Archaeology of Islam*. Oxford: Blackwell.

Insoll, T. 1999b. *Case Studies in Archaeology and World Religion*. BAR S755. Oxford: Archaeopress.

Insoll, T. Forthcoming. *Archaeology and Religion*. London: Routledge.

Ijzereef, F.G. 1989. Social Differentiation from Animal Bone Studies. In Serjeantson, D. and Waldron, T. (eds), *Diet and Crafts in Towns. The Evidence of Animal Remains from the Roman to the Post-Medieval Periods*. BAR Brit. Ser. 199. Oxford: British Archaeological Reports.

Keller, W. 1965. *The Bible as History. Archaeology Confirms the Book of Books*. London: Hodder and Stoughton.

Kenyon, K.M. 1978. *The Bible and Recent Archaeology*. London: British Museum.

Klimkeit, H.-J. 1982. *Manichaean Art and Calligraphy*. Leiden: E.J. Brill.

Lad, G. 1983. *Mahabharata and Archaeological Evidence*. Poona: Deccan College Postgraduate and Research Institute.

Lahriri, N. 1999. Bodh-Gaya: An Ancient Buddhist Shrine and its Modern History (1891–1904). In Insoll, T. (ed.), *Case Studies in Archaeology and World Religion*. Oxford: Archaeopress. pp. 33–41.

Lewis-Williams, J.D. and Dowson, T. 1988. Signs of all Times: Entoptic Phenomena in Upper Palaeolithic Art. *Current Anthropology* 29: 201–46.

Lieu, S.N.C. 1984. *Manichaeism in the Later Roman Empire and Medieval China: A Historical Survey*. Manchester: Manchester University Press.

Lilley, J.M., Stroud, G., Brothwell, D.R. and Williamson, M.H. 1994. *The Jewish Burial Ground at Jewbury*. York: Council for British Archaeology.

Meyers, M. 1996. Ancient Synagogues. An Archaeological Introduction. In Fines, S. (ed.), *Sacred Realm. The Emergence of the Synagogue in the Ancient World*. Oxford: Oxford University Press. pp. 3–20.

Morris, B. 1987. *Anthropological Studies of Religion*. Cambridge: Cambridge University Press.

Munro-Hay, S. 1991. *Aksum. An African Civilisation of Late Antiquity*. Edinburgh: Edinburgh University Press.

Otto, R. 1950. *The Idea of the Holy*. Oxford: Oxford University Press.

Ovsyannikov, O.V. and Terebikhin, N.M. 1994. Sacred Space in the Culture of the Arctic Regions. In Carmichael, D., Hubert, J., Reeves, B. and Schanche, A. (eds), *Sacred Sites, Sacred Places*. London: Routledge. pp. 44–81.

Parker Pearson, M. 1999. *The Archaeology of Death and Burial*. Stroud: Sutton Publishing.

Phillipson, D. 1998. *Ancient Ethiopia*. London: British Museum.

Picknett, L. and Prince, C. 1994. *Turin Shroud. In Whose Image? The Shocking Truth Unveiled*. London: Bloomsbury Publishers.

Platt, C. (ed.). 1987. Archaeology of the Christian Church. *World Archaeology* 18(3).

Poole, T. 1998. Last Days for China's Forgotten Jews. *Independent on Sunday* (8 Nov.).

Potter, T.W. and Johns, C. 1992. *Roman Britain*. London: British Museum Press.

Rahtz, P. 1991. *Invitation to Archaeology*. Oxford: Blackwell.

Rao, N. 1999. Ayodhya and the Ethics of Archaeology. In Insoll, T. (ed.), *Case Studies in Archaeology and World Religion*. Oxford: Archaeopress. pp. 44–7.

Renfrew, C. 1994. The Archaeology of Religion. In Renfrew, C. and Zubrow, E. (eds), *The Ancient Mind*. Cambridge: Cambridge University Press. pp. 47–54.

Renfrew, C. and Zubrow, E. 1994. *The Ancient Mind*. Cambridge: Cambridge University Press.

Rodwell, W. 1989. *The Archaeology of Religious Places. Churches and Cemeteries in Britain*. Philadelphia: University of Pennsylvania Press.

Rodwell, W. 1993. The Role of the Church in the Development of Roman and Early Anglo-Saxon London. In Carver, M. (ed.), *In Search of Cult*. Woodbridge: Boydell Press. pp. 91–9.

Rosander, E.E. 1998. Introduction. The Islamizing of 'Tradition' and 'Modernity'. In Rosander, E.E. and Westerlund, D. (eds), *African Islam and Islam in Africa*. London: Hurst. pp. 1–27.

Ryan, K. and Crabtree, P.J. 1995. *The Symbolic Role of Animals in Archaeology*. MASCA Research Papers in Science and Archaeology 12. Philadelphia: University of Pennsylvania.

Saliba, J.A. 1976. *'Homo Religiosus' in Mircea Eliade. An Anthropological Evaluation*. Leiden: E.J. Brill.

Semple, S. 1998. A Fear of the Past: The Place of the Prehistoric Burial Mound in the Ideology of Middle and Later Anglo-Saxon England. *World Archaeology* 30: 90–108.

Sharpe, E.J. 1986. *Comparative Religion. A History*. London: Duckworth.

Shaw, R. and Stewart, C. 1994. Introduction: Problematizing Syncretism. In Stewart, C. and Shaw, S. (eds), *Syncretism/Anti Syncretism. The Politics of Religious Synthesis*. London: Routledge. pp. 1–26.

Silberman, N.A. 1998. Whose Game is it Anyway? The Political and Social Transformations of American Biblical Archaeology. In Meskell, L. (ed.), *Archaeology Under Fire*. London: Routledge. pp. 175–88.

Simoons, F. 1994. *Eat Not This Flesh*. Madison: University of Wisconsin Press.

Sims-Williams, N. 1990. Sogdian and Turkish Christians in the Turfan and Tun-Huang Manuscripts. In Cadonna, A. (ed.), *Turfan and Tun-Huang. The Texts*. Firenze: Leo S. Olschki. pp. 43–61.

Sopher, D.E. 1967. *Geography of Religions*. Englewood Cliffs: Prentice Hall.

Spencer, H. 1876. *The Principles of Sociology*. London: Williams & Norgate.

Stein, Sir A. 1903. *Sand-Buried Ruins of Khotan*. London: Fisher Unwin.

Stein, Sir A. 1912. *Ruins of Desert Cathay* (2 vols). London: Macmillan.

Stewart, C. and Shaw, S. (eds). 1994. *Syncretism/Anti Syncretism. The Politics of Religious Synthesis*. London: Routledge.

Talbot Rice, T. 1965. *Ancient Arts of Central Asia*. London: Thames and Hudson.

Teague, K. 1989. Heresy and its Traces. In Hodder, I. (ed.), *The Meanings of Things*. London: Routledge. pp. 130–6.

Tilley, C. 1994. *A Phenomenology of Landscape*. Oxford: Berg.

Trinkhaus, E. 1983. *The Shanidar Neanderthals*. New York: Academic Press.

Tylor, E.B. 1871. *Primitive Culture. Researches into the Development of Mythology, Philosophy, Religion, Art, and Custom*. London: John Murray.

Unger, M.F. 1962a. *Archaeology and the New Testament*. Grand Rapids: Zondervan.

Unger, M.F. 1962b. *Archaeology and the Old Testament*. Grand Rapids: Zondervan.

Van der Veer, P. 1994. Syncretism, Multiculturalism and the Discourse of Tolerance. In Stewart, C. and Shaw, S. (eds), *Syncretism/Anti Syncretism. The Politics of Religious Synthesis*. London: Routledge. pp. 196–211.

Von le Coq, A. 1928 (repr. 1985). *Buried Treasures of Chinese Turkestan*. Oxford: Oxford University Press.

Walker, C. 1996. Palestinians Open New Battleground at Temple Mount. *The Times* (11 Oct.). p. 15.

Wansbrough, J. 1977. *Quranic Studies: Sources and Methods of Scriptural Interpretation*. Oxford: Oxford University Press.

Weber, M. 1963. *The Sociology of Religion*. Boston: Beacon Press.

Whitelam, K.W. 1996. *The Invention of Ancient Israel*. London: Routledge.

Williams, H. 1998. Monuments and the Past in Early Anglo-Saxon England. *World Archaeology* 30: 109–26.

Wilson, I. 1998. *The Blood and the Shroud*. London: Weidenfeld.

Winton Thomas, D. (ed.). 1967. *Archaeology and Old Testament Study*. Oxford: Clarendon Press.

Yadin, Y. 1966. *Masada*. London: Weidenfeld & Nicolson.

Yamauchi, E.M. 1972. *The Stones and the Scriptures*. New York: Holman.

Yeoman, P. and James, H. 1999. The Isle of May: St Ethernan Revealed. *Current Archaeology* 161: 192–7.

Zerubavel, Y. 1995. *Recovered Roots: Collective Memory and the Making of Israeli National Tradition*. Chicago: University of Chicago Press.

Chapter 2

The archaeology of Hinduism

Dilip Chakrabarti

Introduction. A difference in perception: the West vis-à-vis the practising Hindu

Early in the twentieth century, T.H. Holdich commented on Hinduism in his classic work on Indian geography. Unhindered by contemporary dictates of political correctness, he wrote that modern Hinduism might be described 'as the most contemptible religion in existence' (Holdich 1904: 207). He cited in his support Alfred Lyall's wry but accurate description of Hindu ritual behaviour.

> We can scarcely comprehend an ancient religion, still alive and powerful, which is merely a troubled sea, without shore or visible horizon, driven to and fro by the boundless credulity and grotesque invention . . .
>
> The average middle-class Hindu might be brought by one part or another of his everyday religious practice, within any or many of these classes, namely:
>
> 1 The worship of mere stocks and stones and of local configurations, which are unusual or grotesque in size, shape, or position.
> 2 The worship of things inanimate, which are gifted with mysterious motion.
> 3 The worship of animals which are feared.
> 4 The worship of visible things animate or inanimate which are directly or indirectly useful and profitable, or which possess any incomprehensible function or property.
> 5 The worship of a *Deo*, or spirit, a thing without form and void – the vague impersonation of the uncanny sensation that comes over at certain places.
> 6 The worship of dead relatives and other deceased persons known in their lifetime to the worshipper.
> 7 The worship of persons who had a great reputation during life, or who died in some strange or notorious way – at shrines.

  8 The worship, in temples, of the persons belonging to the fore-going class, as demigods or subordinate deities.

  9 The worship of manifold local incarnations of the elder deities, and of their symbols.

10 The worship of departmental deities.

11 The worship of the supreme gods of Hinduism, and of their ancient incarnations and personifications, handed down by the Brahmanic scriptures.

... And with regard to the varieties of worship in the catalogue just finished, they are of course deeply tinged throughout by the strong skylight reflection of over-arching Brahmanism; whence the topmost classes now pretend to derive their meaning immediately.

(Lyall 1882: 3–8)

However, even this notion of 'over-arching Brahmanism' is denied by some Indologists of the West, of whom only one will be cited. Writing in 1995 H. von Stietencron, a professor of Indology at Tubingen, denies any concept of Hindu religious unity before the nineteenth century. According to him this concept was mistakenly built up by the British and later on, this was necessary to build up an Indian national identity.

This, indeed, is a case where nationalist politics in a democratic setting succeeded in propagating Hindu religious unity in order to obtain an impressive statistical majority when compared with other religious communities. It is a manipulated majority which would certainly appear much less dominating, if the two largest religious communities in present-day India, the Vaishnavas and the Saivas, would be recognized as having distinctly separate, though culturally cognate, religious origins.

(Von Stietencron 1995: 52)

Holdich, basically a military surveyor, was apparently impatient with something which passed for a religion but was nothing like the religions he could comprehend. A civilian like Lyall could only outline the situation as he found it: an over-arching framework of Brahmanism, grading into an infinitude of ritual behaviour at grassroots level. There is nothing static about this ritual behaviour which may vary within limits from area to area. To a practising Hindu, there is no contradiction involved in the worship of many gods and the performance of many rituals; he or she believes that everything in the world, both animate and inanimate, contains within it the reflection of the Great Being of the universe. This belief certainly goes back to the body of the texts known as *Upanishads*, which by any reckoning dates from before 600 BCE.

Von Stietencron's emphasis on the mutual exclusivity of the worshippers of Siva and Vishnu and his impatience with their being put together under the rubric of Hinduism has nothing to do with how these cultic divisions are actually accepted by Hindus, who have no difficulty in bowing both to Siva and Vishnu. To its adherents, Hinduism is a way of life – *Sanatana Dharma* or a traditional mode of life which holds together the Hindu social and moral fabric.

The problem of delimiting an archaeological approach

The textual roots of Hindu religious tradition go back to the four Vedas; the *Rigveda, Yajurveda, Samaveda,* and *Atharvaveda* which are conventionally dated to between 1500 and 1000 BCE. More reflective of reality is the belief that these are composite texts containing diverse traditions of diverse periods and cannot represent any specific period in the Indian historic sequence. There is no Vedic Age. Similarly, there is no Vedic Archaeology. The same may be said about the textual corpus associated with the main bodies of the Vedas, such as the *Upanishads*. What is clear from the point of view of the present chapter is that the first textual phase of Indian philosophical and religious tradition has to remain undated and that archaeology has to be kept out of it.

In such a situation archaeology can do only one thing: try to trace different ritual behaviours which Hindus traditionally associate with Hinduism. It is not a question of beginning with a checklist of rituals and looking for their archaeological manifestations. Rather, it is a question of looking at the early archaeological record as a whole and pointing out the categories of evidence which make sense from the point of view of later, well-documented Hinduism.

The first part of the present chapter will be concerned with this question. In the second part a broader assessment will be attempted considering the following question. How does the assortment of archaeological data bearing on Hindu rituals or the attributes of Hindu deities fit in the general framework of India's archaeological development? Third, the issue of the configuration of major and minor Hindu sacred spaces and the general aspects of their continuity will be considered through archaeological evidence.

Archaeological evidence for rituals, symbols, and deities known to modern Hinduism

Attention has been drawn from time to time to different aspects of ritual behaviour recalling Hinduism in Indian archaeological data, one of the first attempts being John Marshall's interpretation of the religion of the

Harappan civilisation in the light of Hindu beliefs (Marshall 1931). Subsequently, scholars have tried to trace several aspects of Hindu religious beliefs in Indian protohistoric data of the second and first millennia BCE, whilst the emergence of iconographic attributes and images of Hindu gods and goddesses in archaeological data of the historic period (late centuries BCE and after) has been well-studied. However, the totality of the archaeological situation has so far escaped attention, something which will be considered here.

Prehistory

From the earlier prehistoric period there exists only one piece of evidence from a late upper palaeolithic context (*c.* 9000–8000 BCE) at Baghor I in the upper Son valley (Figure 2.1). In the centre of a roughly circular rubble-built platform (*c.* 85 cm in diameter), a triangular piece of natural stone, 15 cm high, 6.6 cm wide and *c.* 6.5 cm thick was found (Figures 2.2–2.4). There is no doubt about the association between this stone and the platform; nor is there any dispute about the Upper Palaeolithic date of the complex. The stone displays yellowish brown to reddish brown ellipsoidal or triangular laminations, the arrangement of which is similar to a vulva. This is of interest as exactly the same kind of stone which occurs on the top of a hill near the modern village of Baghor is still collected, put on the top of a rubble platform under a tree and worshipped by villagers as the female principle or *Shakti* in the name of one *Mai* (mother) or another (Kenoyer *et al.* 1983) (Figure 2.4). This practice would appear to have continued, almost in an unchanged physical form, apparently from the final stage of the Upper Palaeolithic.

The Harappan civilisation and its antecedents

The next body of evidence possibly indicative of Hindu ritual practice dates from the Harappan period and immediately before. The Harappan civilisation which had assumed its mature form *before* 2600 BCE and covered a vast area of the subcontinent to the west of the Aravallis, inclusive of the upper part of the Ganga-Yamuna Doab or interfluve and the whole of Gujarat, was the product of village growth over its distribution area from *c.* 4000 BCE. The still earlier process of village development has been traced in Baluchistan and the adjacent areas of the Gomal valley and Bannu. The earliest chronological point for this process is *c.* 7000 BCE at Mehrgarh, south of the Bolan pass in roughly, central Baluchistan. Throughout the sixth and fifth millennia BCE, village life based on domesticated wheat, barley, and cattle, sheep and goat proliferated in different ecological niches to the west of the Indus alluvium, till around 4000 BCE, we see this proliferation spreading to this and adjacent river plains. The

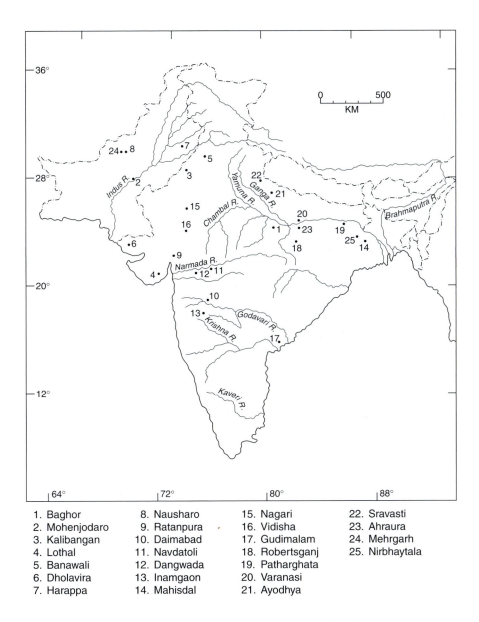

Figure 2.1 Map indicating general location of sites mentioned in the text

1. Baghor	8. Nausharo	15. Nagari	22. Sravasti
2. Mohenjodaro	9. Ratanpura	16. Vidisha	23. Ahraura
3. Kalibangan	10. Daimabad	17. Gudimalam	24. Mehrgarh
4. Lothal	11. Navdatoli	18. Robertsganj	25. Nirbhaytala
5. Banawali	12. Dangwada	19. Patharghata	
6. Dholavira	13. Inamgaon	20. Varanasi	
7. Harappa	14. Mahisdal	21. Ayodhya	

Figure 2.2 Baghor stone: obverse (courtesy, Department of Ancient History and
Archaeology, Allahabad University)

details of this archaeological development are not of concern here, but
the ubiquity of small terracotta female and cattle figurines at various
Harappan sites reflects, at least partly, a ritual concern with mother goddesses and cattle, both Hindu concerns.

There is no specific ritual place or context associated with these figures,
but their ubiquity and abundance cannot be easily discarded; they are
unlikely to be merely children's toys. The ritual use of such terracottas
varies in modern India; a common context is to place them under a tree
as offerings to a wish-fulfilling deity. The small female figurines may also
be fashioned for use in various household folk rituals by women. The black
painted stripes that one occasionally finds on the bodies of cattle figurines
may also recall the custom of worshipping cattle on certain occasions by
bathing them and putting auspicious stripes of turmeric, etc. on them. The
concept of a horned male deity, which one finds prominently in the mature

Figure 2.3 Baghor stone: reverse (courtesy, Department of Ancient History and Archaeology, Allahabad University)

Harappan context, had also developed during this phase, at least during the 'early Harappan' (the second half of the fourth millennium BCE and later) phase of the plains. Such a horned face appears on the painted pottery of this period. Similarly, this period also witnessed emphasis on leaves of the *Pipal* (*Ficus religiosa*) tree as a painted design on pottery. Considering the sanctity of this tree in modern India, it is not unlikely that the repeated use of its leaf as a decorative motif suggests an idea of sanctity attached to this tree at this early date (Figure 2.5).

The Harappan civilisation appears to have entered its late phase by 2000 BCE, but continued until *c.* 1400–1300 BCE. In this late phase settlement was concentrated in the upper Ganga-Yamuna Doab, and in Gujarat, and expansion is evident in the direction of Maharashtra and possibly central India. The starting point of any discussion on the religion of the Harappan civilisation is John Marshall's discussion of the problem in the

Figure 2.4 A modern shrine at Baghor containing similar stones (courtesy, Department of Ancient History and Archaeology, Allahabad University)

first Mohenjodaro report. Whilst some additional details have been provided by data from later excavations at the sites of Kalibangan, Lothal, and Banawali (Lal 1979, Rao 1979, Bisht 1987).

The pride of place in the reconstruction of the Harappan religion is given to the famous *Siva-Pasupati* ('Siva, the lord of animals') seal of Mohenjodaro, for, as Marshall writes, the male god depicted on this seal 'is recognizable at once as a prototype of the historic Siva' and is described thus:

> The God, who is three-faced, is seated on a low Indian throne in a typical attitude of *Yoga*, with legs bent double beneath him, heel to heel, and toes turned downwards. His arms are outstretched, his hands, with thumbs to front, resting on his knees. From wrist to shoulder the arms are covered with bangles, eight smaller and three larger; over his breast is a triangular pectoral or perhaps a series of necklaces or torques, . . . and round his waist a double band. The lower limbs are bare and the phallus seemingly exposed, but it is possible that what appears to be the phallus is in reality the end of the waistband. Crowning his head is a pair of horns meeting in a tall head-dress. To either side of the god are four animals, an elephant and tiger on his

Figure 2.5 Direct worship of a tree, Barabanki, Uttar Pradesh. It symbolises a celestial tree of Hinduism (photo D.K. Chakrabarti)

proper right, a rhinoceros and buffalo on his left. Beneath the throne are two deer standing with heads regardant and horns turned to the centre. At the top of the seal is an inscription of seven letters, the last of which, for lack of room at the right-hand top corner, has been placed between the elephant and the tiger.

(Marshall 1931: 52)

Marshall pointed out a number of distinct features of this seated deity which he associated with Siva of later periods. The first feature is the three-faced representation of its head, which occurs quite commonly in later images of Siva himself or in the images of *Trimurti*, the representation of Brahma and Vishnu along with Siva. The second feature is the *Yogic* posture; the way the figure is shown seated is a common *Asana* or seating posture of a *Yogi* or Hindu mendicant. The third feature is its ithyphallic character. The phallic association of Siva is well known, and the fact that he is shown seated like a *Yogi* in an ithyphallic state does indeed strike a familiar note to anybody conversant with the relevant Hindu traditions. The fourth feature is the figure evident as the lord of the beasts, flanked as it is on both sides by rhino and buffalo, and elephant and tiger. The fifth is the presence of curved horns in the head-dress, which possibly took the form of Siva's trident in later periods. Equally importantly, one cannot ignore the presence of deer below the throne. The presence of animals in a similar position is one of the most common features of medi-aeval Indian images, including those of Jainism and Buddhism. The very concept of *Vahana* or an animal mount is a common one in Hindu iconog-raphy. Alternative interpretations have been suggested, one scholar going so far as to see a female figure instead of the male one and ascribing to it the status of a Roman Vestal Virgin or goddess of the hearth (Atre 1987). Another proposed the figure represented was 'a divine buffalo-man', whatever that may mean (Srinivasan 1983). However, it is only Marshall's explanation which makes sense in the light of Hinduism.

The phallic association of Siva has already been mentioned and is a well-known attribute of Hinduism. Some of the stones found at Mohen-jodaro are unmistakably phallic stones, although whether they were associated with vulva-like stones as might be expected, is unclear. Although the ring-stones illustrated by Marshall (1931: Pl. XIV, 6) are not identical with the components of the stone columns in the Harappan levels of the site of Dholavira in Gujarat, they are not distinctly ring-stones either. What is intriguing is the find of two 'nicely cut and polished monolithic pillars' (*Indian Archaeology – a Review, 1990–91*, p. 11 and Pl. VI B) at Dholavira. One of these two specimens is complete, 1.75 m high, and has a phallic top. Perhaps this was used as a phallic column of worship. Interestingly, a small terracotta representation of what would undoubtedly be consid-ered the replica of a modern *Sivalinga* has been reported by Madhu Bala (1997) from a Harappan context at Kalibangan.

Terracottas were also common at Mohenjodaro. A. Ardeleanu-Jansen (1992) has calculated that of 3,335 terracottas excavated at Mohenjodaro between 1924 and 1938, only 475 could be identified as female images, and these were unevenly distributed. She doubts their use as mother goddesses. However, the uneven distribution of such images need not cause any surprise because they would be expected to be used in household rituals and thus randomly scattered. The fact that the Harappans were quite familiar with female deities is amply shown by a figure represented on a seal from Harappa itself (Marshall 1931: Pl. XII, 12). From between its thighs a plant is clearly shown to be emerging; later scholars have traced the genesis of the idea of a Tantric goddess of the early mediaeval period to this figure (Chattopadhyay 1959).

Marshall (1931) also draws attention to the possible prevalence of tree-worship in the Harappan civilisation, just as it features in modern Hinduism. A seal from Mohenjodaro shows in its top right corner a schema-tised figure with a long pigtail and horned head-dress. It stands in between the trunks of a tree and is fronted to the left by a kneeling supplicant who is followed by an animal, possibly a unicorn. The lower panel shows a row of seven standing figures identical to the figure standing inside the

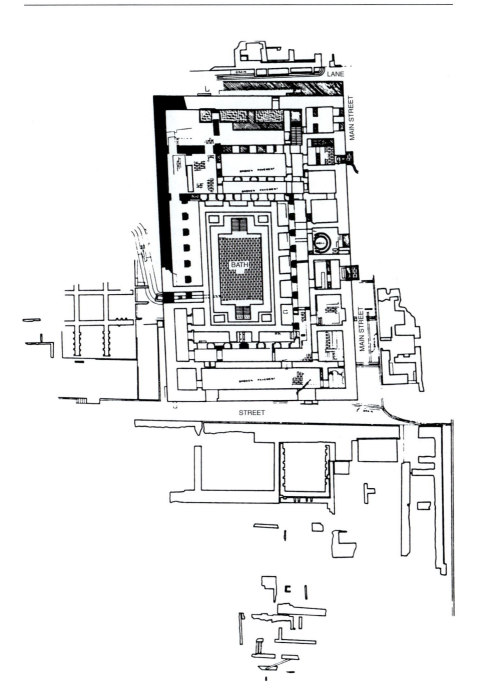

Figure 2.6 Mohenjodaro Great Bath (adapted from Marshall 1931)

trunks of the tree. Some kind of personification of a tree deity can certainly be envisaged in this case. Furthermore, the row of seven deities suggests the concept of *Saptamatrikas* or 'seven mothers' known to Hinduism, and thus the tree deity itself is likely to be a female deity.

Two other general aspects of Harappan religion deserve notice in relation to its links with Hinduism. First, the significance of the Great Bath of Mohenjodaro has been frequently discussed (Figure 2.6). Measuring approximately 23 m by 14 m by 2.43 m, the complex was carefully made water-tight, and although it had a corbelled drain at its south-eastern corner to drain away the water, it had to be filled with water by hand from a well in one of the enclosing rooms. That it was a complex of great significance is also suggested by the fact that it was the only free-standing structure at Mohenjodaro which was surrounded by streets up to 5 m wide on all sides and could thus be completely walked around (Jansen 1989). The association of similar ritual tanks with Hindu temples is well known. Similarly, a series of reservoirs (partly dug into hard rock) has been identified in the Harappan context at Dholavira along the inner side of its perimeter wall. These reservoirs are also similar to Hindu tanks.

The second connected aspect are the fire-altars which have been excavated at Kalibangan and Lothal. These may occur at other sites as well (cf. the Harappan levels at Banawali in Haryana) but the evidence is only clear at these two sites. At Kalibangan fire-altars occur on top of an artificially constructed high platform in the public portion of its citadel complex (Figure 2.7). The top of this platform was accessed by a series of steps cut into it. In fact, there are a number of such platforms in this sector of the site, but the structures on top were destroyed except in this one case. In this respect it is useful to cite the original excavation report:

> . . . atop one of the platforms there lay a series of seven 'fire-altars' in a row. Behind these altars ran a wall in a north-south direction, which shows that people had to face the east while performing rituals at these altars. The altars were oblong in plan, sunk into the ground and lined with clay. They contained ash and charcoal, besides a cylindrical and faceted clay (burnt or unburned) stele standing up near the centre. Though in the series under discussion only fragments of what are called 'terracotta cakes' were obtained, elsewhere these were found in sufficient numbers showing that they formed some kind of an 'offering'. To the west of these fire-altars lay embedded the lower half of a jar. It contained ash and charcoal and was evidently connected with the use of fire-altars. Within a few metres of these altars were a well and a few bath-pavements suggesting ablutions before the performance of a ritual – a tradition still in vogue in India amongst the Hindus.

(Lal 1979: 77–8)

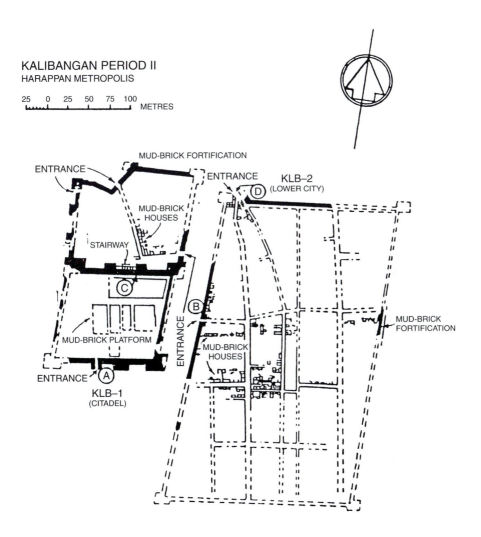

KALIBANGAN PERIOD II
HARAPPAN METROPOLIS

25   0   25   50   75   100
└───┴───┴───┴───┴───┘ METRES

MUD-BRICK FORTIFICATION

ENTRANCE

ENTRANCE

KLB–2
(LOWER CITY)

Ⓓ

MUD-BRICK
HOUSES

STAIRWAY

Ⓒ

Ⓑ

MUD-BRICK
FORTIFICATION

MUD-BRICK PLATFORM

ENTRANCE

MUD-BRICK
HOUSES

ENTRANCE Ⓐ

KLB–1
(CITADEL)

Figure 2.7 Kalibangan site plan (after Lal 1979)

The Kalibangan fire-altars measured roughly 75 cm by 55 cm. At Lothal a similar fire-altar (77.5 cm by 1.05 cm) built of mud-bricks was found inside a house (Rao 1979: 93, fig. 13). The inside of this fire-altar yielded, along with three painted sherds, a carnelian bead, a gold pendant, and the charred mandible of a bovine. Incidentally, the tradition of making offerings including gold, precious stones and the like is still current in Hinduism. It should be noted that these fire-altars do not necessarily denote the custom of fire-worship, as some scholars have proposed

(Dhavalikar 1997: 60). A more convincing explanation is that they performed the function of *Yajnas* for sacrificial rituals of various types connected with Hinduism. In an overwhelming number of cases in modern Hinduism, such *Yajnas* are performed by householders.

Both animal sacrifice and human sacrifice in some form have also been inferred for the Harappan civilisation. A scene on a seal from Harappa shows a man trying to kill a buffalo, and in the same scene there is a seated figure suggesting the presence of a deity. A seal from Kalibangan shows a human figure being struck down before a deity. Animal sacrifice is common in modern Hinduism, and human sacrifice was not entirely unknown in ancient India. Kenoyer (1998: 119) also refers to possible ritual vessels from Mohenjodaro and Harappa including a libation vessel made of conchshell, which would fit in any orthodox Hindu household of today. There are also instances of combined animals, as with that combining the trunk of an elephant, horn of a buffalo, and possible face of a feline in a terracotta from Nausharo, a Harappan site near the Bolan Pass in Baluchistan. It is possible, as Kenoyer (ibid.) argues, that the seals and figurines with combined representations of animals 'reflect the synthesis of many local powers under a single set of deities'.

Evidence for sacrificial pits has been found elsewhere. At the late Harappan site of Ratanpura in Mehsana in north Gujarat the excavators found three circular pits (2.7 m in diameter and 90 cm deep) 'with an earthen lamp and a post-hole at the bottom and filled in with ash, charcoal, charred and uncharred bone pieces, pottery, fragments of three varieties of terracotta sealings and literally hundreds of terracotta lumps of many shapes' (*Indian Archaeology – a Review, 1984–85*, p. 18). Some of these terracotta lumps bore thread-marks, possibly as the result of sacred threads being pressed against them when wet. The use of sacred threads in Hindu rituals is common.

Various intriguing pieces of evidence from a late Harappan context have also emerged from the site of Daimabad (Sali 1986). Several metal objects include a bull chariot driven by a man at the end of a long yoking pole (45 cm by 16 cm); an elephant standing on a platform with holes for wheels (the platform measuring 27 cm by 14 cm, the total height of the object being 25 cm); a rhinoceros (25 cm by 19 cm) standing on two horizontal bars laid on two sets of solid wheels, and a buffalo standing on a level platform laid on four wheels. These are solid objects, containing about 60 kg of metal in total and are not utilitarian objects, especially in view of the wide occurrence of rhinoceros, bull, buffalo and elephant on Harappan seals. All of them are on wheels, and could be pulled. The ceremonial pulling of ritual objects is found in later Hinduism, the most famous example being that of the chariot of Jagannatha of Puri in Orissa.

The Neolithic-Chalcolithic and later protohistoric cultures of non-Harappan India

This section is concerned, approximately, with the third, second and early first millennia BCE in the vast mass of India which lay outside the distribution area of the Harappan civilisation, the main areas being the northern mountains (the area between Swat and Chitral, Kashmir, Ladakh and the Uttar Pradesh Himalayas up to Almorah in the east), south-east Rajasthan, Malwa in central India, Maharashtra, Karnataka, Tamil Nadu, Andhra, Orissa, West Bengal, Bihar and Uttar Pradesh. Chronologically, the earliest point is *c.* 3000 BCE marking the beginning of agriculture in south India and possibly in other areas. From the middle of the second millennium BCE onwards one detects the presence of iron in a number of profiles, and by *c.* 700/600 BCE the early historic period begins in the Ganga plains. The cultural details and complexity of this large time-span are of no concern in the present context, but it is worth remembering that archaeological fieldwork has not been extensive in most of this area, and thus traces of ritual behaviour are by and large sporadic.

A further general observation which can be made is that terracotta cattle figurines are ubiquitous from south-east Rajasthan to south India, though in lesser quantities elsewhere. Terracotta female figurines have also been found but not in large numbers. To some extent this differs from the Harappan evidence but not seriously, because female figurines are rare outside Mohenjodaro and Harappa. It can thus be surmised that a general belief in the sanctity of cattle and female divinities may be assumed for protohistoric non-Harappan India as well.

More specific evidence indicating similarities with Hindu practice seems to be limited to the Malwa (*c.* 1900 – *c.* 1400 BCE) and Nasik-Jorwe cultures of central India and Maharashtra, with data coming from the extensively excavated sites of Navdatoli and Dangwada in Malwa and Daimabad and Inamgaon in Maharashtra (see Sankalia *et al.* 1971, Wakankar 1982, Sali 1986, Dhavalikar *et al.* 1988). Ash and burnt logs of wood were found in a squarish pit of the Malwa culture at Navdatoli, and in view of its context, its interpretation as a sacrificial pit is acceptable. The pit (2.3 m by 1.95 m by 15 cm), mud-plastered on the sides and the floor, had charred wooden posts in the four corners, which could support a canopy. Inside the pit were found burnt wooden splinters arranged north–south, with a log of wood placed east–west over them. Two high-necked pots were also found inside the pit. All Hindu sacrificial pits would carry wooden logs which are arranged inside them by priests.

A further piece of evidence indicating ritual practices at Navdatoli was provided by a large storage jar bearing in appliqué decoration a scene which has been taken to denote the worship of a mother goddess in a temple. A figure is flanked on the right by a female and on the left by a crocodile which has by its side three or four concentric arches. However, the most striking evidence for mother goddess worship has emerged from the Nasik-Jorwe culture level at Inamgaon in Maharashtra. Found carefully buried in a house-floor of *c*. 1400 BCE, an oval and lidded case of unbaked clay was found which had on its top figurines of a female and a bull, also of clay, and with a further female figurine inside. There was also a clay ring below the oval box. The figurine found inside the box has a pinched head, curved arms and heavy breasts. The female figurine found on the top of the box is similar but without a head. This figurine has instead a hole above the abdomen whilst the stylised figure of the bull found associated with it has a hole in its back. If one puts a stick in the hole on the bull's back and tries to put its upper end in the hole below the female figure's abdomen, one gets a good fit, and together they show the female figurine perched above the back of the bull. This is a startling find in the sense that the concept of a goddess riding her mount is a very common theme in the Hindu pantheon. In fact, a specific name – *Visira* or 'a headless female' – has been given to this figurine in the light of a later Hindu goddess bearing this name. Other miscellaneous categories of evidence have also been found in these areas. The report on the excavations at the Malwa culture site of Dangwada is not detailed but there are repeated references to fire-altars with 'well-arranged patterns of burnt wood', the wood in this case being *Butea frondosa*, an essential ritual item of later Hinduism.

The first phase at Daimabad in Maharashtra has also yielded a realistic representation of a phallus in agate. The object was found in a pit (1.6 m in diameter) filled with ash and containing a few potsherds and a small stone. A terracotta representation of a phallus was also obtained from the east Indian Chalcolithic site of Mahishdal in West Bengal. Similarly, there is a distinctly *Sivalinga* type of stone – marked by the outline of a face on one side, according to the excavator (Sali 1987) – in the Malwa culture phase of Daimabad. The specimen is 17.3 cm high, and although one would hesitate to characterise it as a specific, textually mentioned type of *Sivalinga*, it is identical with the modern phallic stone denoting Siva whilst a male figurine of clay (stump head, curved arms, large torso, and short stump legs) from the Nasik-Jorwe culture level of Inamgaon is interesting because of its close similarity with a specimen from the late Harappan context at Lothal.

Early historic India, c. 600–c. 200 BCE

The third and second centuries BCE may be considered an archaeological baseline, from when one begins to find increasing evidence for the Brahmanical cults of Siva, Vishnu and many other major and minor divinities. For example between *c*. 600 BCE and *c*. 300 BCE various symbols traditionally associated with such deities are found on two indigenous coin-types of India – punch-marked coins (mostly silver, but some copper as well) and cast copper coins, which have distributions throughout the subcontinent. There is no confusion about their dating; they appear as early as the beginning of the diagnostic early historic pottery of northern India, Northern Black Polished Ware (NBP), which is dated to c. 600 BCE. The earliest series is known as the *Janapada* (territories/principalities) coins, named after the principalities into which the subcontinent was divided during the sixth century BCE, the time of the Buddha. The symbols occurring on these coins have been studied and certain specific symbols or groups of symbols have been ascribed to individual principalities such as Magadha, Kasi, Kosala, etc. Five Saivite symbols can easily be located on such coins: the bull, footmark of a bull or *Nandipada*, trident, half-moon, and the *Lingam* or phallic emblem itself. The solar motif in the form of a disc is common and may denote a sun-god or *Surya*. Similarly, the representation of spoked wheels sometimes found may suggest the discus of Vishnu, a peacock may stand for the god *Karttikeya*, a female figure standing on, or associated with, a lotus may be *Sri* or *Lakshmi*, the goddess of wealth. These symbols unmistakably indicate that a number of major Hindu cults had assumed their distinct identities during this period (for the coin symbols, see Allan 1936).

The first Vishnu temples are found in the third century BCE. The evidence is limited but conclusive. At Nagari, the ancient city of *Madhyamika* in eastern Rajasthan, an inscription dating from the first century BCE suggests that at this place an extant stone-built enclosure was already associated with the worship of Narayana or Vishnu. Evidence for this earlier structure has been found archaeologically at 60 cm below the first-century BCE ground level of this enclosure where excavation revealed a structure comprising two ellipses, the inner one being 10 m long and 3.5 m broad and separated from the outer one by a 1.8 m-wide circumambulatory path. The outer ellipse was 14 m long. The overall structure was built of mud and timber with a rammed floor of broken bricks and lime. This was the original Vishnu temple mentioned by the inscription and can be securely dated to the third century BCE (Bhandarkar 1920).

A similar piece of evidence comes from Vidisha in Madhya Pradesh where an inscribed pillar dating from the late second century BCE was found. According to the inscription, this pillar was caused to be erected by the Vishnu-worshipping Greek, Heliodorus, who came to the court of a particular king at this place as the emissary of the Indo-Greek king Antialcidas of Taxila in the north-western part of the subcontinent. It is interesting to note that the Greeks who settled in that area were turning to the worship of Vishnu by the second century BCE. Excavations demonstrated that the pillar erected by Heliodorus belonged to the second phase of a Vishnu temple at the site. The first phase of this structure, marked

Figure 2.8 Reconstruction of Vishnu temple, Vidisha (after Khare 1967)

by an inner ellipse (8.10 m long by 3 m broad) and separated by a gap of 2.5 m from an outer ellipse which had a rectangular projection (7 m by 4.85 m) to the east, has been dated towards the end of the third century BCE (Khare 1967) (Figure 2.8). There were two elliptical constructions of about the same period at Dangwada, one with a plinth of boulders and another built only of mud. The structure with the boulder plinth revealed an inscribed clay seal showing this to be a Siva temple. The other structure was only 100 m away and yielded an inscribed clay seal declaring it to be a Vishnu temple.

In the third–second century BCE there is also clear evidence of the worship of minor deities such as *Yakshas* and *Yakshinis*. There are a few *Yaksha* figures in stone, massive, pot-bellied, *dhoti*-clad and wearing a sacred thread from this period. In the third century BCE, i.e. the Mauryan period, the most famous *Yakshini* figure is *Didarganj Yakshini*, but the free-standing female figure from Besnagar is also included in this date-bracket (A.K. Coomaraswamy 1924: 47). The amount of evidence increases dramatically at the beginning of the common era. The sun-god appears in stone in a sculptured relief at Bhaja (second century BCE) in western India. Dating from the first century BCE a 1.5 m high and 30 cm thick

Sivalinga at Gudimallam in Andhra bears on it, in high relief, a two-armed image of Siva standing on a crouching figure representing darkness. Mother goddesses in various forms also appear in the third century BCE and by the first century BCE the figure of *Lakshmi,* standing on a lotus and being lustated by an elephant on either side, is a common motif on terracotta plaques.

The implications of the archaeological evidence

The foregoing provides a brief account of the archaeological evidence for rituals related to modern Hinduism, largely dating from before 200 BCE. The archaeological data relevant to the study of the early history of Hinduism can be seen to be limited, but suggests, even in the present situation, a few points about the evolution of the religion, none of which is apparent from the discussions based on texts. There is no lack of such textual discussions on the historical growth of various Hindu deities. One may consider, for instance, J.N. Banerjea's *The Development of Hindu Iconography* (1956), one of the most famous books on this topic. With regard to every Hindu deity, he first discusses, with commendable scholarship, the textual evolution of the idea of the deity in the series of texts beginning with the *Vedas* and then examines the iconographical literature relevant to the explanation of extant images of that particular deity. The establishment of the theoretical basis for the emergence of a deity and its iconographical types are his main interest; he is not particularly concerned with their historical dimensions. However, Banerjea remains aware of the paucity of data.

Although the iconographic features of many early and late mediaeval Brahmanical images can be fully corroborated by iconographic texts, there are also many examples where the extant iconographical literature is not of much help. On the other hand, there may be detailed iconographic descriptions of a particular type of image, but that image may not occur at all among the known specimens. Banerjea (ibid.) thus infers that only a part of the original iconographical literature and images has survived. The images were destroyed by iconoclasts and people who have vandalised ancient sites over time. Again, textual data suggests that innumerable images were made of wood, as some indeed still are, and it is necessary to note that wooden specimens would have had only a very low survival rate in the Indian climate.

These limitations, however, do not explain the most important feature of the archaeological sequence, that the data becomes quite specific and focused only from the early historic period onwards. But at the beginning of this period that is between *c.* 600 and *c.* 300 BCE our knowledge is still somewhat shadowy and does not yet contain much beyond various relevant symbols on coins. The Mauryan period, the third century BCE,

Figure 2.9 A Mauryan lotus capital (third century BCE) serving as the female base
of a Siva stone in the Nageswarnath Siva temple in Ayodhya
(photo D.K. Chakrabarti)

seems to be the dividing line between what is concrete and what is shadowy
in the archaeology of Hinduism (Figure 2.9). Considering the fact that it
is only under the Mauryan dynastic rule that all parts of the subcontinent
emerged into the clear light of history, the consolidation of a pan-
subcontinental Hinduism during this period makes sense.

What went on before is certainly largely unclear. The discovery of an
Upper Palaeolithic counterpart of a modern ritual item used in mother
goddess worship in the village of Baghor does not suggest anything more
than the fact that the folk-level of Hinduism is rooted in prehistory. An
emphasis on the ritual importance of cattle and female figurines was also
a recurrent emphasis of ritual behaviour in Indian protohistory right from
the point of its beginning in Baluchistan. The religion of the Indus civilisation is better understood if we interpret it in the light of later Hindu
rituals and concepts, but there is also nothing in the Harappan context

which would permit the inference of an organised Brahmanical frame-work in it. Similarly, rituals familiar to modern Hindus keep on occurring in the protohistoric context of non-Harappan India, but again there is no well-defined framework. It seems that we have to put off the emergence of this framework till *c.* 300 BCE i.e. the Mauryan period. This is a point which has been missed by various scholars of Hinduism, but the situation may not be as surprising as it first appears. Even Buddhism which, unlike Hinduism, is a proselytising religion established by a single historical person, could assume a pan-Indian character only during this period. There seems to be a definite correlation between the consolidation of early historic growth in India and the consolidation of her religious configurations – including Hinduism which in turn stretches its roots back to prehistory.

Sacred space and continuity. The dimensions of sacred space in the Indian countryside

The issues of definition, configuration and continuity of Indian sacred places and landscapes are so closely enmeshed in both living tradition and the ancient past – the latter mostly in the form of a vast mass of tradi-tional texts – that their archaeological dimensions are not always immediately apparent. Even the smallest Indian village is likely to have multiple sacred places within its confines: a piece of red cloth tied to a big tree; small heaps of stone as a reminder of the presence of one deity or another; a rarely complete old image waiting to be worshipped by people after they bathe in the nearby pond; or a small whitewashed modern temple with Siva's phallic stone inside, drawing crowds on auspicious dates for Siva but otherwise looking underused. In some cases the village temple may stand on the top of a mound, and even though the temple itself may be modern or not more than a couple of centuries old, the inner sanctum may lie considerably below the contemporary ground level and contain an image dating from over a thousand years and suggesting a clear case of archaeological continuity of the sacredness of the site from the day the original temple was built and the image installed (Figure 2.10). Whilst at other places one may be aware of a cluster of ancient sites in the vicinity of a modern place of worship, and although these peripheral ancient sites may not always be marked only by Hindu deities, one realises that the modern cult centre is in the midst of a landscape which has been consid-ered sacred for a long time.

At a still higher level, there will be regional centres of pilgrimage, some of which may be connected with the wider network of Hindu pilgrimage sites. The great, scripturally praised centres of pilgrimage lie scattered in different parts of the country, and among them a few, such as Varanasi, Gaya, Prayag, Puri, Tirupati, etc., will be universally known and have a pan-Indian clientele of pilgrims. Within a major pan-Indian pilgrim centre,

Figure 2.10 A mud replica of a high phallic stone personifying the resident deity of an archaeological mound near Banaras (photo D.K. Chakrabarti)

again, there may be different geographic layers of sanctity, which will range from the outermost perimeter of the sacred territory in question to the innermost circuit around the place of the deity (Singh 1993).

Two further general points may be made about Indian sacred sites which have implications for archaeologists. First, a sacred landscape need not contain features of Hinduism alone; it may well contain Buddhist and Jaina deities and sacred sites. Even after the coming of Islam in the twelfth century there have been places where both Hindus and Muslims have prayed and made offerings side by side. Before the impact of modern politics and politicised religion, sacredness of a landscape was not always confined to a single religious group. To take only one example, the number of early mediaeval Hindu gods and goddesses recovered from Bodh Gaya is considerable, and indicative of how this very holy space of Buddhism was subsequently integrated into the network of Hindu sacred spaces as well (Lahiri 1999, Trevithick 1999). In part this is explainable by the fact that Bodh Gaya developed in the vicinity of Gaya, one of the holiest areas of Hinduism. Second, in many cases sacredness has been associated with impressive natural features of local landscapes; for example, in the midst of the ridges of the Aravalli range near Delhi a forested ravine leads to a natural year-round accumulation of water at its base. This spot has a sacred status in local tradition; wandering mendicants take shelter in its grottoes, living on the offerings given by villagers who come from far and wide to take a dip in the pool. The ravine as a whole is thought to represent the old hermitage of the ancient sage Parasara who is mentioned in the epic, Mahabharata, and who serves as the ancestor of a lineage of Brahmins (among whom the writer of the present article is one!) all over India. Thus, an epic tradition has been incorporated in this section of the Aravalli landscape near Delhi. Yet there is no archaeological evidence here; it is simply a case of ascribing holiness to an impressive piece of natural scenery and linking it to the epic tradition. There are many such non-archaeological examples of sacred places in India.

Sacred space and archaeology

However, there are many archaeological examples as well. This is evident in looking around the Indian countryside; an extraordinary variety of religious behaviour is manifest in the archaeological record in various ways. Yet the linkages are not always immediately apparent, in many cases they are merely intuitive. An instance of this is provided by considering the 'Kalkaji temple' in modern Delhi which is one of the innumerable mother goddess cult sites dotted around the subcontinent where there is no archaeological sense of the past, but if one looks around, one realises that this modern temple is on the top of an Aravalli ridge and that this ridge has been frequented by people since late Acheulian times. It is still possible to pick up microlithic flakes at the foot of this particular ridge and it is evident that within a short distance another section carries a third-century BCE inscription on it. The linkages are certainly not immediately apparent: modern cult spots, the remains of prehistoric occupation in the area and the message of the third-century BCE Mauryan king Asoka engraved on a stone nearby. On the other hand, the possibility of a linkage cannot be entirely ruled out, because it is unlikely that an Asokan edict would have been engraved in this area unless it had been the meeting point of some kind for people. If so, there has been a continuity of sacredness in this particular part of the Aravallis in Delhi. To take the archaeology of Hinduism beyond the study of iconography, excavated ruins, standing temples and the like it is necessary to focus on the identification of sacred spaces and establish their different categories and, equally importantly, their changing historical dimensions. Two further examples illustrate the utility of this approach, drawn from the author's own fieldwork.

It is a long way from Delhi to the fringe of the Vindhyas at Robertsganj near Mirzapur in Uttar Pradesh. A route from Banaras goes to Surguja in Madhya Pradesh and beyond, with Robertsganj on the way. The immediate target of this route was the upper Son valley, which is reached at Chopan. In the outskirts of Robertsganj towards Chopan there is a low range of hog-backed hills overlooking a narrow valley of paddy-fields. In the northern section of the hills a small peak overlooks the road going to Chopan and it is the sacredness of this peak over a very long period of time that is the concern here. First, in at least two rock shelters there are paintings of deer and cattle in red ochre on the rock surface. Also of significance was the fact somebody had also placed some stones in one of these shelters, and considering that *Bel* leaves (*Bel* is a tree sacred to Siva) and sprinklings of water had also been recently scattered on these stones it would appear that these rock shelters had been converted into a place where Siva is currently worshipped. A local holy man has, in fact, built a small white-washed temple in the immediate vicinity. More remarkable is the presence of an ancient temple on the peak. Sculptural and architectural fragments abound, and include both fourth–fifth century Gupta period remains along with much later tenth–twelfth century CE objects. There is also an inscription in *Sankhalipi* (an esoteric script current during the Gupta period) on the slope of the ridge nearby. If one notes the juxtaposition of these various elements at this spot overlooking one of the major lines of movement between the Ganga valley and central India – 'Mesolithic' rock-paintings, temple remains from the fourth–fifth to the tenth–twelfth centuries, an inscription of the Gupta period – it is obvious that the complex as a whole is related to an old route.

Much further to the east, the Ganga flows past an old ferry crossing at Patharghata near Kahalgaon in Bihar. The Rajmahal hills throw an outlier at this point in the form of a long ridge. Again the following features are noteworthy on the ridge in the vicinity of the ferry point: a panel of presumably Vaishnavite sculptures of *c.* seventh-century CE date on the midpoint of the ridge, with possibly a destroyed temple on its top; large numbers of tenth–twelfth century CE sculptures and sculptural fragments in a modern temple built alongside the ridge; a large rectangular cave also of tenth–twelfth century date dug into the rock at the base of the ridge, and a few grottoes inhabited by modern mendicants. Descending from the boat at Patharghata and climbing the cliff, it is possible to see all these features, make a gesture of obeisance in that direction and move on to the modern village about a kilometre behind the ridge. The modern village of Oriup lies on top of occupation levels dating from the second millennium BCE, and not far, in the direction of Kahalgaon is the famous eighth-century CE Buddhist monastery of Vikramasila. At some distance, the main massif of the Rajmahal hills provides the backdrop and overlooks the main ancient line of communication between the middle and lower Ganga plains. In this case too there is no apparent linkage between these archaeological features of the landscape, but various religious features of different periods are juxtaposed in a limited area on the main overland route from Bihar to the Bengal delta.

Beyond such identifications of sacred spaces, it is also useful to be aware of the local dimensions of each. In the case of the Pachmukhi hill near Robertsganj its location by the side of a major ancient route cannot be ignored; in the case of Patharghata it is the ferry-crossing which merits attention. Whilst it is not possible to comment on the specificity of the Kalkaji example in Delhi, the space around it possibly carries sanctity imbibed from a remote hunting-gathering past.

The variables behind the growth and continuity of a major pilgrim centre: ancient Varanasi

Having referred to the local dimensions of sacred spaces such as those at Pachmukhi hill, Patharghata and Kalkaji, it remains to take up the case of a sacred centre of pan-Indian significance and underline the major historical variables behind the growth and continuity of its sacred tradition. A useful example is provided by modern Banaras (ancient Varanasi), one of the holiest places of Hinduism. The archaeology and history of the place are well known (Chandra 1985, Singh 1985), with occupation continuous from before *c.* 600 BCE and it is a site mentioned in a vast corpus of early Buddhist and other literature as the centre of a kingdom and a major urban centre of the early historic and later periods.

It is only when one tries to understand the location of Banaras with reference to some of the major ancient trade/communication routes that the significance of the place is properly understood. Banaras was possibly the most important Ganga valley terminal point of the routes going towards the Deccan through central India. Further, through Banaras these routes were connected with other urban centres of the central Ganga plain, centres such as Ayodhya and Sravasti. From Banaras there was also a straight route to the area of Gaya/Bodh Gaya, and as the early Buddhist literature indicates, it was a major river-port linked mainly with areas downstream to the east. The route from the central Ganga plain to the Deccan is one of the historic arterial routes of India. From Banaras one first goes to Ahraura across the river either to catch the route going from Ahraura in the direction of Gaya via Chakia or to travel in the direction of Robertsganj to enter the central Indian hills. For central India one may also travel upstream from Banaras to Chunar where one may cross the river to join the route going towards Hanumana and Rewa in central India via Lalganj and Halia. As far as the links with places like Sravasti and Ayodhya are concerned, there is a straight route to these places from Banaras via Jaunpur, and there is also an ancient route to go to the area of Azamgarh and Gorakhpur where there are many ancient sites. All these routes carry distinct archaeological markers along them, and when one visualises ancient Banaras in the light of all these routes it is easy to see why it has had such a continuous historical significance. The fact that Banaras is one of the most important locations of Siva in India is no doubt partly due to the sanctity attached to it in the textual sacred tradition, but one doubts if Banaras would have been as significant a centre of pilgrimage as it is today without its geographical importance as well.

Conclusions

It has been argued here that the emergence of an organised Brahmanical framework only occurred during the early historic period (*c.* 600 BCE – *c.* 200 BCE), although some individual components of Hindu ritual behaviour extend back to prehistory and protohistory. Second, something of the possible types of Hindu sacred spaces and aspects of their continuity over time has been outlined. Finally, it has been shown, with reference to Banaras, how the variables behind the growth and continued significance of major Hindu pilgrim centres may incorporate economic factors such as being located at important crossroads of communication.

It is unlikely that Hinduism was ever a static religion. Even in recent memory it has witnessed the growth of two cults, both of which are adaptations of old forms: *Santoshi Ma* (a mother goddess) and *Hare Krishna* (a form of Krishna worship). Further, in the wake of a heightened sense of Hindu identity after the demolition of a mosque at Ayodhya in 1992, the custom of worshipping *Durga*, a ten-armed and demon-slaying mother goddess, which had hitherto been confined only to the Bengali community, has rapidly spread all over the Ganga plain. As far as such changes are explicit in new iconic forms and new types of temple structures, archaeologists of the future will have no difficulty in tracing the advent of new cults or the extended geographical spread of an old cult, but the ritual behaviour of the Hindus will, *hopefully*, continue to be as chaotic as it is today, and it is unlikely that at the grassroots level of rituals Hinduism will be more easily amenable to archaeological analysis in future.

Archaeology has a very important role to play in defining sacred space and its continuity throughout the subcontinent. The possibilities are immense and go far beyond the limited number of examples cited in this paper. For instance, one recalls a mound – Nirbhaytala in Birbhum district, West Bengal – which is Chalcolithic–Iron Age in origin but carries on the top of its grass-covered slopes an apparently modern temple of *Kali*. The associated sculptures and architectural fragments, however, show that the place has been a centre of the *Kali/Shakti* cult since about the eleventh century CE. It is cult centres of this kind which impart a distinct character to the Indian sacred landscape, and it is towards the understanding of the growth and location of such centres that archaeology can make a substantial contribution in future.

References

Allan, J. 1936. *Catalogue of Coins in the British Museum, Ancient India*. London: British Museum.

Ardeleanu-Jansen, A. 1992. New Evidence on the Distribution of Artifacts: an Approach towards a Qualitative-Quantitative Assessment of the Terracotta Figurines of Mohenjodaro. In Jarrige, C. (ed.), *South Asian Archaeology 1985*. Madison: Wisconsin University Press. pp. 5–14.

Atre, S. 1987. *The Archetypal Mother*. Pune: Ravish Publications.

Bala, M. 1997. Some Unique Antiquities and Pottery from Kalibangan. In Joshi, J.P. *et al.* (eds), *Facets of Indian Civilization – Recent Perspectives*. Delhi: Aryan Books International. pp. 103–6.

Banerjea, J.N. 1956. *The Development of Hindu Iconography*. Calcutta: Calcutta University Press.

Bhandarkar, D.R. 1920. *The Archaeological Remains and Excavations at Nagari*. Calcutta: Archaeological Survey of India.

Bisht, R.S. 1987. Further Excavation at Banawali: 1983–84. In Chattopadhyay, B.D. and Pande, B.M. (eds), *Archaeology and History*, Vol. I. Delhi: Agam Kala. pp. 135–56.

Chakrabarti, Dilip K. 1999. *India – an Archaeological History*. Delhi: Oxford University Press.

Chandra, M. 1985. *Kasi – ka Prachin Itihas*. Varanasi: Visvavidyalaya Prakashan (in Hindi).

Chattopadhyay, D.P. 1959. *Lokayata*. Delhi: People's Publishing House.

Coomaraswamy, A.K. 1924. *The Dance of Siva*. New York: The Sunrise Turn Inc.

Dhavalikar, M.K. 1997. *Indian Protohistory*. Delhi: Books and Books.

Dhavalikar, M.K., Sankalia, H. and Ansari, Z. 1988. *Excavations at Inamgaon*. Pune: Deccan College.

Holdich, T.H. 1904. *India*. London: Henry Frowde.

Jansen, M. 1989. Water Supply and Sewage Disposal at Mohenjodaro. *World Archaeology* 21: 177–92.

Kenoyer, J.M. 1998. *Ancient Cities of the Indus Valley Civilization*. Karachi: Oxford University Press.

Kenoyer, J.M., Clark, J.D., Pal, J.N. and Sharma, G.R. 1983. An Upper Palaeolithic Shrine in India? *Antiquity* 57: 88–94.

Khare, M. 1967. Discovery of a Vishnu Temple near the Heliodorus Pillar, Besnagar, District Vidisha (MP). *Lalitkala* 13: 21–7.

Lahiri, N. 1999. Bodh-Gaya: An Ancient Buddhist Shrine and its Modern History 1891–1901. In Insoll, T. (ed.), *Case Studies in Archaeology and World Religion. The Proceedings of the Cambridge Conference*. BAR S755. Oxford: Archaeopress. pp. 33–43.

Lal, B.B. 1979. Kalibangan and the Indus Civilization. In Agrawal, D.P. and Chakrabarti, D.K. (eds), *Essays in Indian Protohistory*. Delhi: D.K. Publishers' Distributors. pp. 65–97.

Lyall, A.C. 1882. *Asiatic Studies*. London: John Murray.

Marshall, J. (ed.). 1931. *Mohenjodaro and the Indus Civilization*, Vol. I. London: Arthur Probsthein.

Rao, S.R. 1979. *Lothal, a Port Town*, Vol. II. Delhi: Archaeological Survey of India.

Sali, S. 1986. *Daimabad*. Delhi: Archaeological Survey of India.

Sankalia, H., Deo, S. and Ansari, Z. 1971. *Chalcolithic Navdatoli*. Pune: Deccan College.

Singh, B.P. 1985. *Life in Ancient Varanasi: an Account Based on Archaeological Evidence*. Delhi: Sundeep Prakashan.

Singh, R.P.B. (ed.). 1993. *Banaras: Cosmic Order, Sacred City, Hindu Tradition*. Varanasi: Tara Book Agency.

Srinivasan, D. 1983. Unhinging Siva from the Indus Civilization. *Journal of the Royal Asiatic Society* (unnumbered vol.): 77–89.

Stietencron, H. von. 1995. Religious Configurations in Pre-Muslim India and the Modern Concept of Hinduism. In Dalmia, V. and Stietencron, H. von. (eds), *Representing Hinduism*. Delhi: Sage Publications. pp. 51–81.

Trevithick, A. 1999. British Archaeologists, Hindu Abbots, and Burmese Buddhists: the Mahabodhi Temple at Bodh Gaya, 1811–1877. *Modern Asian Studies* 33: 635–56.

Wakankar, V.S. 1982. Chalcolithic Malwa. In Sharma, R.K. (ed.), *Indian Archaeology, New Perspectives*. Delhi: Agam Kala. pp. 224–44.

Chapter 3

The archaeology of Buddhism

Robin Coningham

Introduction

During the first half of the first millennium BCE a number of heterodoxical teachers emerged from the mainstream Hindu belief system within
the northern part of the Indian subcontinent, partly as a response to the
creation of state and urban forms. One of the most successful and influential of these teachers was the individual known as Siddhartha Gautama,
although more widely recognised by his title of *Buddha* or 'one who has
attained enlightenment' (Figure 3.1). Once an extremely influential force
in Asia, there are now only 6.6 million Buddhists within India, the only
majority Buddhist communities lying within Sri Lanka and south-east Asia.
Traditionally knowledge of the history and nature of Buddhism has come
from a combination of two sources, ancient texts and modern devotional
practices. Archaeology has seldom been utilised in this process, apart
from the largely unscientific clearing of 'Buddhist' monuments. Indeed,
the role of archaeology may be summarised in de Jong's words: 'Buddhist
art, inscriptions and coins . . . cannot be understood without the support
given by the texts' (1975: 15). These views are so widely held that when
such clearing has revealed material evidence which conflicts with these
two sources, it is commonly interpreted as a local aberration or degener-
ative practice (Coningham 1998: 121). However, an increasing number of
scholars (Coningham 1995a, 1998, Coningham and Edwards 1998,
Schopen 1997, Trainor 1997) have begun to question this premise, suggesting that it is possible to use archaeology to test the antiquity of such
practices, and thus demonstrate a pervasive tradition which is at odds with
the traditionally held modes of 'Buddhist' behaviour. In fact, when examined in detail, archaeologically based knowledge of Buddhism, and of the
Buddha himself, is extremely slight. For example, the date of his birth and
death and even the location of his childhood home, Kapilavastu, are still
unknown.

The aim of this chapter is to question many of the traditionally accepted
generalisations of Buddhist archaeology and to provide a basis from which

Figure 3.1 Pilgrims and monks in 1992 passing in front of a twelfth-century CE *Buddha* image at the Gal *Vihara*, Polonnaruva, Sri Lanka (photo R. Coningham)

a new typology of Buddhist archaeology may be created. It is divided into three main sections. The first will present the textual narrative of the life of the *Buddha* before critically reviewing his life from an archaeological perspective; the second will introduce the accepted typology of Buddhist monuments – *stupa*, *griha* and *vihara* – and question both its integrity and 'Buddhist' nature; whilst the third will provide a series of case studies illustrating the extremely complex and variable nature of Buddhist practice through space and time. These case studies will include an examination of the variability of three contemporary Buddhist monuments, reflecting the spatial dynamics of patronage; an exposition of differing patterns of the power, function, and definition of Buddhist relics; and finally, the archaeological visibility of Buddhist sectarianism and the extent to which it may be possible to distinguish between Buddhism's two major traditions, the *Hinayana* and *Mahayana*. The chapter will conclude with an examination of the question of the archaeological visibility of Buddhism and will attempt to identify specific elements of material culture which may be termed or interpreted as 'Buddhist' with reference to diet, the role of women and artefacts recovered from Buddhist monasteries or *viharas*. This chapter will not provide an encyclopedic survey of Buddhist monuments, artefacts, thought and practice, but will begin to confront a number of the generalisations which have been made about Buddhism and its archaeology.

These generalisations have been in part created by the extreme focus on textual readings (Coningham 1995a), that is the sayings of the *Buddha* or those of his followers, to the detriment of archaeology. An attempt will be made to demonstrate that these generalisations, concerning past patterns of Buddhist thought and action, are deeply flawed without reference to archaeology. Many of these flaws are derived from nineteenth-century European studies of Buddhism, when scholars were of the opinion that modern Buddhism presented a degenerate and variable pattern of devotion (Cunningham 1854: 3, Coningham 1998: 121). It is the intention of this chapter to refute such concepts and to demonstrate that from the earliest extant evidence, Buddhism has reflected the needs and desires of many and, as such, has always been adaptable – therefore abrogating the presence of a canonic typology of Buddhist practice or material culture. Before commencing, it should be noted that inscriptions and chronicles have been studied in translation, that the use of Sanskrit and Pali terms have followed the conventions used by Debala Mitra (1971) and that all diacritics have been dispensed with following the convention used by Robinson (1989).

The life of the *Buddha*: a textual narrative

Much of the *Buddha*'s narrative is provided by the writings of two Chinese pilgrims, Fa-hsien and Hsuan-tsang, who travelled to the sacred places of Buddhism in the fifth and the seventh centuries CE (Dutt 1962: 25). Their records provided an important resource, as noted, after their translation into European languages: 'It is not a little surprising that we should have to acknowledge the fact that the voyages of two Chinese travellers . . . have done more to elucidate the history and geography of Buddhism in India, than all . . . the Sanskrit and Pali books of India' (Beal 1869: vi). Their own sources included the *Buddha*'s *sutra-pitaka* or 'sermons' and the *vinaya-pitaka* or 'monastic rules' (Dutt 1962). Compiled after his death, they were transmitted verbally until at least the third century BCE. As Buddhism spread, schisms increased resulting in the re-adaptations of both and the creation of differing philosophical rationalisations of the *sutras* – the *Abhidharma* (Losty 1985: 40). According to these traditions, Gautama Siddhartha was born during the first half of the first millennium BCE to Suddhodana, *raja* or 'ruler' of the Sakyas – a clan of *Kshatriyas* or 'warriors' close to the Himalayas. Despite his rank, Siddhartha was born in the Lumbini garden as his mother, Maya Devi, travelled from her husband's capital, Kapilavastu, to Devadaha where her parents resided (Beal 1869: 85–8). Following prophecies concerning Siddhartha's future as a renounceant, his parents diverted him with worldly pleasures but, at the age of 29, he encountered four sights which revealed the transience of existence. These consisted of an old man, an ill man, a dead man and an ascetic. He abandoned his wife, child and family and set out to seek enlightenment and free himself from the cycle of rebirth. Leaving the city, he shaved his head, donned the dress of an ascetic and sent his horse and groom back with his regalia – symbols of his *Mahabhinishkramana* or 'Great Departure'. He studied under two teachers, Arada Kalama and Rudraka Ramaputra, but left them, dissatisfied, and travelled to Bodh Gaya where he was reduced to a skeletal state through meditation and austerities (ibid.: 120–3). Having failed to achieve enlightenment through harsh practices, Siddhartha ate but was left by his disciples in disgust. Shortly afterwards he sat under a pipal tree and committed himself to death or enlightenment. Here, at the age of 33, resisting the attempts of Mara, the god of desire, and his seductive daughters to distract him, Siddhartha became the *Buddha* or 'enlightened one'. The *Buddha* then travelled to Muchilinda and preached his new *Dharma* or 'doctrine/law' to two merchants who had offered him refreshment and they became his first *Upasaka* or 'lay followers'. He then visited the deer park of Sarnath and offered his former disciples his *Dharma*, stating that all beings were linked to the cycle of rebirth through suffering and that, as suffering was linked to unsatisfied desires, the only way to detach oneself was to remove the causes of suffering (Mitra 1971: 3).

This knowledge, the Four Noble Truths, consisted of suffering, the cause of suffering, the removal of the cause and the way leading to the removal of the cause. Advocating a middle path between self-gratification and self-mortification, both of which result in further suffering, the *Buddha* advised the following of the Eightfold Path to remove the acquisition of further suffering and to cancel suffering gained in previous lives. The Eightfold Path consisted of right views, thoughts, speech, actions, means of livelihood, exertion, mindfulness and meditation (Mitra 1971: 3). This exposition is known as the *dharma-chakra-pravartana* or 'setting the wheel of the law in motion' and thus converting his former disciples, the *Sangha* or 'order' was formed. Spending each rainy season on retreat, the *Buddha* travelled through northern India for the next 45 years preaching the *Dharma* and converting lay followers, monks and nuns. As the *Sangha* expanded, the *Vinaya* was delivered to ensure that its rigorous nature was retained (Dutt 1962: 75). During this period he visited many of the major kingdoms and urban centres and his converts and followers ranged from the most powerful rulers, through the emergent mercantile classes, to the lower castes (ibid.: 104).

The broad range of followers which the *Buddha* gained, highlights the appealing message of the *Dharma* – universal equality and charity, delivered in local vernacular dialects by a disciplined and ordered body of renounceants in a period of heterodoxical expansion (Mitra 1971: 3). Such was the appeal that even Brahmans were attracted to the *Sangha*, as with two of his most important disciples, Sariputra and Maudgalyayana (Beal 1869: 57). Indeed, the *Buddha* successfully competed with some of the other heterodoxical leaders of the age, for example Purana Kasyapa, Maskari Gosaliputra of Ajivikas and Mahavira of Jains and Sanjayi Vairatiputra at Sravasti. At the age of 79, the *Buddha* suffered from dysentery and, travelling to Kusinagara, underwent his *mahaparinirvana* or 'great passing away' thus achieving *nirvana* or 'the release from the cycle of rebirth' (ibid.: 94). His body was cremated and his ashes divided into eight portions and distributed to Ajatasatru of Magadha, the Lichchhavis of Vaisali, the Sakyas of Kapilavastu, the Bulis of Allakappa, the Koliyas of Ramagrama, a Brahmin of Vethadipa and the Mallas of Pava. The cremation urn was retained by the Brahmin who had divided the portions and the fire's embers were given to the Moriyas of Pipphalivana; ten *stupas* or 'mounds' were then erected over these relics.

The life of the *Buddha*: an archaeological narrative

As was noted above, much of the *Buddha*'s narrative is derived from textual sources compiled centuries after the events described whilst archaeology has been largely neglected. Indeed, the statement that 'Buddhist research is dominated by textually-based scholars, or by historians of art or architecture, relegating archaeologists to a solitary role of primary producer, not venturing further than the description of excavated remains' (Coningham 1998: 122) adequately summarises the current position. This position owes much to the early history of archaeology in south Asia when, in the eighteenth and nineteenth century, European officials began to order the monumental remains of civilisations that they had encountered in Asia and attempt to link them with Western chronologies. Whilst some of this ordering, such as the hypothesis that the Buddhist monuments of Sanchi were linked with Stonehenge (Cunningham 1854: v), had questionable results, many began to identify monuments and sites with information contained within the available textual sources; Prinsep, for example, identified the Mauryan ruler Asoka from the Sri Lankan *Mahavamsa*, a historical chronicle complied in the fourth century CE (Bechert 1978: 3), with the Priyadarsi named in the series of rock edicts (Cunningham 1854: 101) dating to the third century BCE whilst General Cunningham used it to correlate between the names of a number of the *Buddha*'s disciples and inscribed relic caskets in stupa 2 at Sanchi in Central India (ibid.: 119).

This methodology continued to be used into the late nineteenth century, as illustrated by the fieldwork of Dr A. Fuhrer in the Nepali Terai between 1895 and 1898. In 1895 Fuhrer, of the Archaeological Survey of India, had been deputed to study Asokan edicts in the Nepali Terai and arranged to meet the region's Governor at the latter's camp beside a small shrine of Rummindei (Fuhrer 1897: 23). Beside the shrine they cleared the base of a pillar and exposed an Asokan inscription identifying the site with Lumbini, the birthplace of the *Buddha* (Rana 1999). Having confirmed the site's topography with the descriptions of the Chinese pilgrims, Fuhrer then proceeded to identify a series of other sites associated with the life of the *Buddha*, leading him to state that 'all the sacred Buddhist sites in the western portion of the Nepali Terai, mentioned by the Chinese pilgrims, have been satisfactorily identified' (Fuhrer 1897: 47). Indeed, although the locations of many of the sites of Buddhist pilgrimage were lost during the mediaeval period, most of them had been rediscovered by the beginning of the twentieth century – causing one scholar to herald Cunningham as the 'hero of the Buddhist Renaissance' (Ahir 1989: 2) (Figure 3.2). The latter, a late nineteenth- and early twentieth-century CE phenomenon, was largely inspired by a reaffirmation in Buddhism by the westernised Sri Lankan, Burmese and Thai elites in reaction to increasingly active Christian missions and a growing demand for self-determination. The Renaissance itself was one of the responsible catalysts for the study of the Buddhist past, and saw the resanctification of sites under the auspices of individuals and organisations ranging from the Burmese king to the Maha Bodhi Society (ibid.: 12) and even the Viceroy (Lahiri 1999: 40).

It is useful to review the archaeological evidence from four of these sites, Lumbini, Bodh Gaya, Sarnath and Kusinagara as they had all been identified for pilgrimage by the *Buddha* prior to his death (Beal 1869: 126). As noted above, the birthplace of the *Buddha*, Lumbini, owes its identification to the presence of an inscription which records that the emperor Asoka visited the site in person (Fuhrer 1897: 17). Despite a century of excavations at the site, most recently in 1996 (Rijjal 1996: 5), nothing earlier than the third century BCE has been recovered from the sacred precincts (Figure 3.3). Similarly, the earliest evidence of a Buddhist construction at Bodh Gaya is limited to the middle of the third century BCE if the identification of a polished sandstone throne as Mauryan is correct (Hartel 1995: 144, Mitra 1971: 61). The same is true of Sarnath, where the earliest monuments date to the Mauryan period and, in particular, to the reign of the emperor Asoka (Hartel 1995: 145, Mitra 1971: 67, Allchin 1995a: 244). Sarnath's identification as the setting of the First Sermon is supported by the fact that Asoka's pillar was crowned with four lions carrying a wheel representing the *dharma-chakra-pravartana* – a symbol selected for the crest of the Republic of India (Agrawala 1964). A similarly late phenomenon is found at Kusinagara where not even remains of the Mauryan

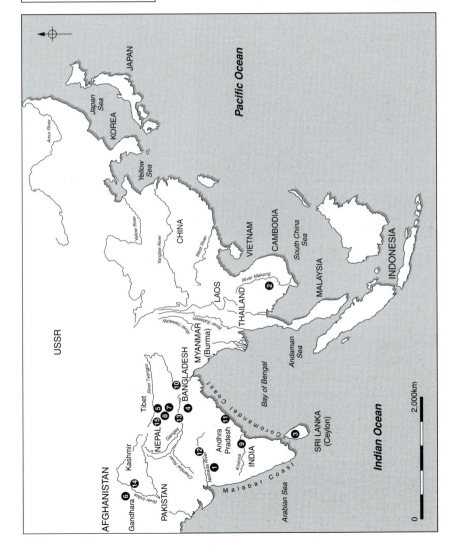

Key to sites

1 Ajanta
2 Angkor
3 Anuradhapura
4 Bodh Gaya
5 Bodnath
6 Butkara
7 Kusingara
8 Lumbini
9 Nagarjunakonda
10 Pahapur
11 Salihundam
12 Sanchi
13 Sarnath
14 Taxila
15 Tilaurakot

Figure 3.2
Map showing the location of
Buddhist sites in southern Asia
as mentioned in the text
(prepared by Steve Cheshire)

Figure 3.3 View of the third-century BCE Asokan pillar at Lumbini (Nepal) – the birth place of the *Buddha* (photo R. Coningham)

period are found (Hartel 1996: 143, Mitra 1971: 70). Indeed, the sole example of a possibly pre-Asokan stupa was excavated at Vaisali, the site of one of the *nirvana* stupas (Allchin 1995a: 243). This clay stupa, with diameter of 7.8 m and height of 3.3 m, has been referred to as 'pre-Mauryan' (Mitra 1971: 75) and possibly sixth-century BCE by its excavator (Allchin 1995a: 243). The absence of any radiocarbon sequence at the site, however, weakens this claim.

Sculptural evidence corroborating the narrative's details are even later, with one of the greatest sources being the genre of Gandharan art. Named after the ancient region which stretched from the Kabul to the Indus, it developed between the first and sixth centuries CE (Harle 1992, Pugachenkova 1994, Zwalf 1996). Mass-produced, devotional and instructive (Wheeler 1968: 150), it 'absorbed the earlier Graeco-Bactrian traditions current in the area and was also receptive to ideas and trends of the contemporary West through international trade and commerce' (Pugachenkova 1994: 371). As Mitra (1971: 255–60) has demonstrated, its panels depict scenes from the *Buddha*'s life such as the Great Renunciation, the *Buddha*'s emaciated state at Bodh Gaya, Mara's onslaughts, the First Sermon and the *Mahaparanivana*. These sculptural narratives can be paralleled by earlier examples from central India, where scenes from the *Lalitavistara* or 'life of the historical *Buddha*' are depicted on structural features dating to the first century BCE at both Sanchi and Bharut (ibid.: 97).

It is clear, therefore, that whilst most of the sites and details associated with the *Buddha* have been identified archaeologically, all the evidence postdates him by at least two centuries. Whilst there are clear dangers of using textual sources compiled centuries after the actual event (Coningham 1995a: 232), this is not to question the existence of this influential teacher in the middle of the third millennium BCE, but to highlight the inadequacies of Buddhist archaeology in identifying and dating Buddhism's earliest phases. In retrospect one can attribute the latter to the methodologies followed by the archaeological pioneers who vigorously cleared and conserved. Whilst they reflected accepted early archaeological practice, they stripped most of the *in situ* deposits which might later have been excavated in order to phase and date these key sites. This factor, in association with the dependence on texts, has led to a state of affairs where even 'The date of the Buddha's passing away, at age eighty, varies wildly between dates of 2420 and 290 BCE' (Coningham 1998: 122). Whilst covering the extremes, the debate fluctuates between a long, uncorrected 'southern Buddhist' chronology of 544/3 BCE or a long corrected 'southern Buddhist' chronology of 480 BCE and a short one of 368, 383, 384, 386, 390 or 340 BCE (Bechert 1995: 12–16). In Bechert's words, following a major conference on the date 'There is no information on the dates of the historical Buddha, the founder of the Buddhist religion, which has been unanimously handed down by all major Buddhist traditions and universally accepted by scholars, nor have scholars been in a position to arrive at a general agreement concerning this question.' (1995: 12).

Further debate surrounds the identification of Kapilavastu, the childhood home of the *Buddha*, and appears to be fuelled by a national controversy (Coningham 1998: 122). In 1899, following Fuhrer's suggestions, P.C. Mukherji identified it at Tilaurakot, some 28 km west of Lumbini (Mukherji 1901: 3–4). There, he surveyed a fortified city covering an area of 500 m by 400 m with a rich hinterland of Buddhist monuments. Using a combination of the records of the Chinese pilgrims and the site's close proximity to Asokan pillars at Gotihawa and Niglihawa, Mukherji stated that 'no other ancient site has so much claim ... as being situated in the right position and fulfilling all other conditions' (ibid.: 50). Investigations were not renewed until 1962 when a team from the Archaeological Survey of

India cut a section across the rampart. Mukherji's identification was challenged by the team's director, who reported that it could not be Kapilavastu as its earliest occupation began centuries after the *Buddha*'s death – 'it is certainly not earlier than the third century BCE and is most probably not later than the second century BCE' (Mitra 1972: 18). These conclusions were then contested by the results of excavations, conducted by Nepali archaeologists between 1967 and 1972, which suggested that the site's sequence began in the first half of the first millennium BCE (Mishra 1978).

The result of this contradiction, in combination with Srivastava's advocacy of Piprahwa as Kapilavastu (Srivastava 1986), has led to the division of archaeologists into those who identify the Indian site of Piprahwa as Kapilavastu (Chakrabarti 1995: 187, Srivastava 1986) and those who support the Nepali site of Tilaurakot (Hartel 1995: 151). More recently, further survey and excavation has been undertaken (Coningham and Schmidt 1997) and whilst the survey revealed that during the first half of the first millennium CE the city had a grid-iron plan, the excavation attempted to solve the chronological debate. The trench was excavated to virgin soil at a depth of 3.5 m in order to collect carbon samples for the first absolute chronometric dates of the site. The measurements of the dates are still awaited, but it is clear that the lowest contexts contain sherds of the ceramic type, Painted Grey Ware (PGW). PGW is allocated to the Iron Age of the Gangetic plain and is dated to between the beginning of the first millennium BCE and the sixth or seventh century BCE (Erdosy 1995: 80–1). In conclusion, it is possible to state that there are no other major Early Historic city sites in the vicinity of Lumbini (Allchin 1995b) and that the relative sequence at Tilaurakot appears to confirm that the site's earliest occupation is contemporary with the *Buddha*.

A review of the typology of Buddhist monuments

This section will introduce the three monuments, *stupa* or 'mound', *griha* or 'sanctuary' and *vihara* or 'monastery', commonly used to designate an archaeological site as Buddhist, before questioning their integrity as a typology of 'Buddhist' structures. Whilst some scholars have identified as many as 20 Buddhist structural sub-units (Bandaranayake 1974a: 27–8), most accept Mitra's broad tripartite division of *stupa*, *chaitya-griha* or 'stupa sanctuary' and *vihara* (Mitra 1972, Allchin 1995a, Chakrabarti 1995, Nagaraju 1981), notwithstanding, an expansion of the second category to include the *bodhi-griha* or 'Bodhi-tree sanctuary' (Sarkar 1966, Bandaranayake 1974a, Zwalf 1985: 26) and *Buddha-griha* or 'Buddha image sanctuary' (Subrahmanyam 1964). Although the individual elements of this simple typology have altered through time and space, their presence or absence represents the major technique for identifying Buddhist sites:

Figure 3.4 The *Bhikkhuni* or nun Dharmasila in front of her home at the sacred city of Anuradhapura (Sri Lanka) in 1998 (photo R. Coningham)

'Architecturally, one or all of the following elements should be present at a "Buddhist" site: the *stupa*, the *chaitya* worship hall containing a *stupa*, and the *vihara* or the monastery' (Chakrabarti 1995: 192). Before introducing the three monuments, a number of general points should be made as to the integrity of this tripartite division. First, it should be acknowledged that whilst such monuments are frequently identified during excavations, they represent only a fragment of Buddhist practice. The remainder of which is archaeologically invisible as typified by the home of the *Bhikkhuni* or 'nun' Dharmasila (Bartholomeusz 1994: 191–2), who lives in the Sri Lankan city of Anuradhapura. The archaeological identification of her flimsy shelter would be nothing short of miraculous (Figure 3.4). Second, it should be noted that there is overlap between our categories as illustrated by the presence of small *stupas* within *vihara* cells; erected in memory, in Marshall's view, of 'men of specially holy reputation' (Marshall 1951: 246). Finally, it should also be noted that structures encountered during excavations are often too fragmentary to identify or do not conform to the categories, as illustrated by the brick platforms exposed during the excavations at the Buddhist complex at Salihundam. Their excavator stated that the 'exact purpose for which they were built is not quite intelligible but they may also be votive in character' (Subrahmanyam 1964: 32), further stressing the extremely complex nature of Buddhist material culture.

The stupa

The *stupa* is the most resilient of the three monuments as well as being the oldest having been built over the *Buddha*'s remains following his *Mahaparinirvana* (Beal 1869: 94). It comprises a solid mound of soil, brick, or earth and, although the earliest known example of a Buddhist *stupa* may only date back to pre-Mauryan times (Allchin 1995a: 243), is thought to have been a pre-Buddhist monument (Mitra 1971: 21). Indeed, some scholars have suggested that it developed directly from the megalithic tombs of the south Indian Iron Age (Longhurst 1936: 12), although its frequent co-occurrence with Gandharan Iron Age megalithic sites suggests a northern influence to others (Tucci 1977: 10). Four categories of *stupa* were commonly made, those containing corporeal relics of the *Buddha*, his disciples and saints; those containing objects of use such as the *Buddha*'s begging bowl; those commemorating incidents from the *Buddha*'s life or places visited by him; and finally, those votive *stupas*, built by pilgrims, *Bhikkhus* or 'monks' and *Bhikkhunis* for 'obtaining religious merit' (Mitra 1971: 21–2). Although the earliest examples were simple and small constructions, for example the Vaisali *stupa* was only 8 m in diameter (Allchin 1995a: 243), they soon became enormous and elaborate as at Sanchi (Marshall, Foucher and Majumdar 1940) or the twelfth-century CE Damila Thupa at Polonnaruva with a diameter of 182 m. Their relic chambers were also transformed, changing from simple slab boxes (Cunningham 1854: 285) to representations of the Buddhist universe (Paranavitana 1946: 24). *Stupas* were frequently remodelled but seldom levelled as the sanctity of the monument was so great that earlier forms were merely placed within an outer shell. The great *stupa* at Butkara I in Gandhara illustrates this process no fewer than five times over a period of a millennium (Faccenna 1980) (Figure 3.5). *Stupas* were often opened in the past, and such activities were traditionally ascribed to 'treasure-hunters' (Longhurst 1936: 14); however, they would be better termed 'relic-hunters' who wish to redistribute and venerate valuable and histori-cal relics (Byrne 1995: 276). *Stupas* are one of the most widely spread Buddhist monuments, being found from Pakistan in the west to Japan in the east (Barnes 1995: 177–8, Dallapiccola and Lallemant 1980).

Due to its enduring construction, the *stupa* is one of the most recognis-able Buddhist monuments, although the identification of votive *stupas* is more difficult as many were built of sand or earth (Byrne 1995: 271). Often, the *stupa*'s presence as an eroded mound is the only sign of a Buddhist complex, as illustrated by the subsequent discovery of a *vihara* beside the Andandheri *stupa* mound in north-west Pakistan (Dani 1971: 34). That the identification of *stupas* can be applied to archaeological features is confirmed at the Buddhist complex at Salihundam in India's state of Andhra Pradesh (Subrahmanyam 1964: i). Covering 2 ha, it was

Figure 3.5 The great *stupa* of Butkara I in the Swat Valley (Pakistan) showing five phases of construction between the third century BCE and the fifth century CE (photo R. Coningham)

occupied between the second or third century BCE and the seventh century CE. Circular brick structures with a diameter of between 2.5 and 13 m were interpreted as *stupas*, with a subdivision of *stupas* and votive *stupas*, according to size. Further significance was placed on a row of three votive *stupas*, which were interpreted by the excavator as representing the Buddhist *triratna* or 'three jewels' – the *Buddha, Sangha* and *Dharma* (ibid.: 28–32). Whilst these identifications confirm our typology, the division of *stupas* into votive or non-votive on size is unrealistic as its actual relic content will control this division.

That the identification of the Buddhist *stupas* is often highly problematic can be illustrated in archaeological contexts with reference to three specific examples. The first is provided by Fuhrer's study of sacred Buddhist sites in the Terai and, in particular, his identification of 17 square brick *stupas* at Sagarhawa as the scene of Vidudabha's massacre of the *Buddha's* clansmen – the Sakyas (Mukherji 1901: 28). The *stupas* measured between 1–6 m² and up to 2.5 m high and contained carved bricks in their lowest foundations as well as relic caskets. As the carvings depicted assorted lotuses, *svastikas*, daggers, arrows, *trisulas* or 'tridents', Fuhrer interpreted them as symbols of the slaughtered Buddhist warriors (ibid.: 26–8). These claims were later rejected by Mitra who suggested that they were not *stupas:* as the caskets 'did not contain ashes or bones, there will be little justification for identifying these structures with Buddhist stupas' (Mitra 1972: 233). Moreover, she reinterpreted the carvings as Hindu motifs and the foundations as those of Hindu temples as the site 'did not produce any antiquity specifically Buddhist and there are textual prescriptions for the deposit of precious things in the foundations of temples' (ibid.: 235–47). It should be noted, however, that the symbol of the *svastika* was also used in the base of three of the Buddhist *stupas* excavated at Nagarjunakonda (Sarkar 1962: 78), suggesting that such symbolism did also occur within Buddhist monuments.

The second example is centred on one of the earliest references to the rebuilding or enlarging of a *stupa*, as recorded in the Asokan pillar edict at Nigali Sagar in the Terai (Trainor 1997, Coningham 1998). This edict, written in the early Brahmi script, recorded that during the third century BCE, Asoka: 'increased the stupa of Buddha Konakamana to double [its former size]' (Thapar 1963: 261). This is not just the earliest reference to a *stupa* or its veneration, but also the earliest reference to one of Gautama *Buddha*'s predecessors, Konakamana, the twenty-second of the line of twenty-four *Buddhas* which preceded him (Trainor 1997: 43). That such individuals were part of early Buddhist tradition is supported by the presence of the names of the last seven, Vipasyin, Sikhin, Visabhu, Krakuchchhanda, Konagamana, Kasyapa and Sakyamuni, on a railing dating to the second half of the second century BCE at Bharhut (Mitra 1971: 95). However, if Konakamuni's name had not been mentioned by Asoka on his edict, it would have been assumed that the monument referred to commemorated the Gautama or historical *Buddha*, as stated elsewhere 'how then, with the absence of an inscription, is one to identify which structures are dedicated to the Gautama Buddha and which to the other twenty-four?' (Coningham 1998: 123).

The third example which has been chosen illustrates the difficulties involved in distinguishing between Jain and Buddhist *stupas*, as both hetero-doxical movements used this monument. Nowhere is this ability more problematic than at the Early Historic city of Sirkap in the Punjab (Coningham 1998: 123). Sirkap's excavator, Marshall, excavated a locality, Block 1A, in the lower city which was interpreted as a Jain complex rather than a Buddhist one. It consisted of a quadrangle of cells facing on to a large central *stupa* measuring 10 m^2 (Marshall 1951: 142–5). In addition to the presence of three smaller *stupas* and three votive *stupas*, two small terracotta tanks containing model shrines, mother goddess figurines, birds, snakes, and snails were recovered from the courtyard. The presence of these tanks, combined with an absence of Buddhist sculptures, led Marshall to identify 1A as Jain stating that 'We know . . . that Taxila was an impor-tant centre of Jainism, with numerous monuments of that faith in and around the city, and it can hardly be doubted that some, at any rate, of the stupas unearthed at Sirkap and the neighbourhood belong to the Jains, though which particular ones is necessarily conjectural, since no inscriptions or anything else of a definitely Jain character have been found in any of them.' (Ibid.: 145). In conclusion, we may reiterate our earlier comments that it is often difficult to differentiate which early Buddhist *stupas* 'were dedicated to Buddhists, as opposed to Jains, let alone which *Buddha*' (Coningham 1998: 123). Complexities are thus evident in identifying this monument form.

The griha

The sanctuary or *griha* has also been identified as one of the fundamental Buddhist monuments (Allchin 1995a, Sarkar 1966, Mitra 1971, Chakrabarti 1995). Varying in shape between apsidal, circular and quadrilateral, it consists of a 'hall with the object of worship' (Charkrabarti 1995: 195), although the classic rock-cut examples from western India are highly ornate with elaborate facades, central doorways with large *chaitya* or horse-shaped windows above, central chambers with vaulted ceilings and apsidal ends with *stupas*, surrounded by pillars from circumabulatory side-aisles (Brown 1956: 22). Whilst many of the earliest examples have the *stupa* as the ritual focus, as at the Mauryan example of Bairat (Mitra 1971: 42), later examples were often provided with a *Buddha* image as focus, as at Nagarjunakonda (Sarkar 1962: 73) and Salihundam (Subrahmanyam 1964: 28). Archaeologically, these structures are distinct as shown by their multiple discovery at Salihundam and Taxila (Marshall 1951: 150). It is interesting to note that although Mitra distinguishes between the Buddhist *griha* and temple (Mitra 1971: 52), her convention is not followed by other scholars (Allchin 1995a, Sarkar 1966, Chakrabarti 1995). Perhaps Mitra herself disavows this division stating that 'there is no difference in the treatment of Buddhist, Jaina and Brahmanical temples produced in a particular zone at a given period' (Mitra 1971: 52), whilst Rowlands and Brown have suggested that later developments of Hindu temple styles are derived from the earlier Buddhist *chaitya-griha* (Rowlands 1953: 166, Brown 1956: 63).

The Buddhist sanctuary reached colossal proportions in eastern India in the eighth century CE with the construction of a quadrangular *vihara* and courtyard centred on a 22 m high sanctuary at Paharpur (Dikshit 1938: 18). The latter was built on a cruciform plan with recessed projecting corners and an elevation raised on three solid superimposed terraces (ibid.). This was surrounded by circumambulatory galleries and four image halls, from which staircases led to the upper level; however, the summit is too eroded to allow a reconstruction of the uppermost sanctuary. The stepped, or terraced, sanctuary at the centre of a square enclosure was to reach its fluorescence in Cambodia with the construction of Angkor Thom by

Jayavarman VII (r. 1181–1201 CE). Consisting of an enclosure measuring 13 km², its centre is marked by a 45 m high step-terrace sanctuary known as the Bayon (Dumarcay 1973). The Bayon's central cell contained a *Buddha* image and its 50 towers and the enclosure's four entrance gates are surmounted by images of the *Buddha*'s face gazing in four directions. As with the other step-terrace sanctuaries of Angkor, the complex appears to have functioned as Jayavarman's ceremonial capital as well as housing, in the Bayon, his personal cult temple and mausoleum (Moron 1978: 65). The simple form of the *stupa-griha*, however, survived in Sri Lanka late in the mediaeval period, when the *Vatadage* or 'circular relic-house' was built by Parakramabahu I (r. 1153–1186 CE) at his capital, Polonnaruva (Paranavitana 1946: 80).

It is very notable that one category of *griha*, the *bodhi-griha* or 'bodhi-tree sanctuary', is absent from the excavation reports of Buddhist sites. Indeed, this absence is more puzzling considering the presence of depictions of such sanctuaries at the early *stupas* of Bharhut, Sanchi, Mathura and Amaravati, which range in plan from square and circular to polygonal and apsidal (Sarkar 1966: 6) and suggest a popularity due to the fact that the Bodhi-tree was an aniconic symbol of the *Buddha* as well as commemorating his enlightenment. That such sanctuaries existed is supported by an inscription dating to the third century CE, recording the donation of a *bodhi-griha* at Nagarjunakonda in India's Deccan Plateau (Sarkar 1966: 6) and their longevity is illustrated by their presence in all modern Sri Lankan Buddhist complexes. One of the few archaeological examples of a *bodhi-griha* to be identified was excavated at the site of Sigiriya in Sri Lanka (Bandaranayake 1984: 49) (Figure 3.6). This structure dates to between the seventh and tenth centuries CE and consisted of a low elliptical wall of semi-dressed gneiss blocks and rubble with a diameter of 10 m centred on a 2 m-high dressed stone platform measuring 4.2 m². At the centre of the platform was a stone-lined pit, measuring 2.5 m deep and 0.90 m², filled with a dark, organic soil. The absence of comparable structures can be explained by their frequent misidentification as other forms of sanctuary, indeed, Bandaranayake has provided a list of 25 such examples (ibid.: 155). Perhaps a re-examination of the monuments adjacent to the *bodhi-griha* inscription at Nagarjunakonda might further enable Bandaranayake's hypothesis to be tested.

There has, however, been a tendency by scholars to assume that most fragmentary apsidal foundations can be identified as Buddhist, as Sarkar has for the structure exposed at Brahmagiri (Sarkar 1966: 109). Indeed, Hartel's identification of a Kushan period free-standing apsidal structure at Sonkh, complete with colonnade, stone railing and gate, as the sanctuary of a naga cult belies such suggestions (Hartel 1974: 110). This complexity also surrounds the identification of rock-cut sanctuaries as Buddhist, rather than Jain, Hindu, Zoroastrian or even Christian (Ball

Figure 3.6 The seventh- to tenth-century CE *bodhi-griha* at Sigiriya (Sri Lanka)
(photo R. Coningham)

1986: 105). Whilst there is little doubt that *chaitya-griha* 19 at Ajanta in western India was dedicated to the *Buddha*, the attribution of Buddhism to many other rock-cut and natural caves in the region is in doubt as indicated by von Mitterwallner's research in south-west India (1981). In Goa he surveyed a series of caves, devoid of evidence, and found it difficult to interpret one as either a Hindu swami's cell for yogic exercises or as a Buddhist monument and debated whether another was 'the initiative of the Saivas, Jainas or Buddhists?' (ibid.: 474). A similar question mark must be held over the Buddhist attribution to the Homay Qal'a caves in Afghanistan (Verardi 1979: 125), the rock-cut caves of south-western Iran (Ball 1986: 105) and the Gondrani caves of western Pakistan (Fairservis 1971: 413).

The vihara

The final category to be considered here, the monastery, is identified as a discrete type of monument by the majority of scholars (Chakrabarti 1995, Allchin 1995a, Mitra 1971). Although the classic *vihara* plan dates to the Kushan period, it is, as Allchin has stressed, by no means the only plan nor the earliest (Allchin 1995a: 246) (Figure 3.7). Whilst the first members of the *Sangha* were renounceant wanderers, the early Buddhist texts also describe an increasing number of donations of dwellings set within *aramas* or 'parks' (Sarkar 1966: 8). Brown has suggested that 'as these wandering ascetics were resolved into groups . . . so their huts were grouped around an open space to make the first monasteries . . . From such elementary beginnings was evolved the conventional arrangement of a hostel consisting of a series of cells enclosing three sides of a square courtyard, the remaining side being left open for the entrance.' (Brown 1956: 16). As the earliest *viharas* were built of perishable materials, many of these have vanished, however 'the well-preserved rock-cut caves of the Deccan furnish a continuous evolution of the rock-cut monastery from the third–second century BCE onwards' (Mitra 1971: 32). Using this evidence, it can be suggested that the earliest examples consisted of single cells or irregular groups of cells but that by the second century BCE a more consistent plan was reached, that of a congregational hall opening out into the cliff face and surrounded on three sides by cells (ibid.: 33). The earlier *viharas* were simple and plain but later forms were more ornate with decorated pillared verandahs but it is noticeable that in most cases there were no kitchens provided as the *Sangha* were expected to beg for their food. Although such *viharas* were still in use in the fifth century CE, the free-standing quadrangle was by then more numerous. This pattern of development, however, is mirrored in the free-standing remains at Taxila's Dharmarajika complex, where early units comprised a short range of buildings fronted by a verandah but later ones comprised the quadrangle (Marshall 1951: 246). Marshall has suggested that this development illustrated the changing relationship between lay-folk and *Sangha*.

The validity of this category of monument can be confirmed by its application to the Early Historic landscape of Taxila in Pakistan. Indeed, Taxila's excavator stated that 'all the religious foundations which have so far been excavated outside the cities belong to the Buddhist faith and present us with a graphic picture, or perhaps I should rather say film, of the development of Buddhism' (Marshall 1951: xvii). The *viharas* of Taxila have frequently been cited by scholars as the type site of this category (Mitra 1971, Chakrabarti 1995), and that at Mohra Moradu is highly representative. Located on the Hathial ridge some 3.5 km from Sirkap, it consists of a stupa court in the east and a *vihara* in the west. Measuring 48 m by 30 m (Marshall 1951, pl. 93), the latter is formed of two parts,

Figure 3.7 The fourth- to fifth-century CE *vihara* at Mohra Moradu (Taxila, Pakistan) (photo R. Coningham)

a square courtyard, some 30 m², and a rectangular area of larger rooms (ibid.). The courtyard was reached by an northern gateway and was bounded by 27 cells, each of which opened on to a verandah – Cell 15 also led to a first floor, whilst 7 led to the western rooms. The cells, some 3.6 m high, varied between 6–15 m² in area and were provided with small alcoves and, in some cases, high ventilation slits (ibid.: 360). Although largely empty, some cells contained store-jars and water-vessels and one had been converted into a sanctuary complete with 3.6 m high votive *stupa*. Alcoves and plinths in the portico and the courtyard were also provided with small clay figures of the *Buddha, Bodhisattvas*, attendants, the god Indra and donors. The functions of the eastern rooms were identified by the excavator as an assembly hall, a kitchen, a refectory and a bath (ibid.: 362). This quadrangular model reached its zenith with the construction of Paharpur, the largest *vihara* enclosure in south Asia. It comprised a courtyard of 22 ha centring on a 22 m-high temple and filled with shrines, votive *stupas*, kitchens and wells surrounded by 177 cells (Dikshit 1938). The Buddhist complexes at Anuradhapura were on an even larger scale, covering 20 km², and included an array of *stupas*, shrines and sanctuaries, ecclesiastical buildings, residential buildings, refectories, bath-houses and hospitals (Bandaranayake 1974b: 27–8).

There are, however, also difficulties associated with the identification of all courtyard or quadrangular structures as Buddhist *viharas*. Complex 1A at Sirkap, as we have already seen, was identified as Jain but its plan conforms to that of a quadrangular Buddhist monastery (Marshall 1951: 142). The acropolis of Sirkap, to the south of the lower city, also provides an interesting discussion as to the identification of such *viharas* amongst its three monumental complexes, the Kunala, the Gahi and the Mahal. The first two conform to the classic model of the quadrangular *vihara* beside *stupa* court, whilst the Mahal consists of a slightly irregular series of courtyards surrounded by single cells covering an exposed area of 73 by 94 m. Despite its similarity with the *quadrangular* plan and the recovery of a ladle recording that it had been donated to the *Uttararama* or 'northern monastery', Marshall rejected a monastic identification stating that 'one thing that is certain [is] that the Mahal building . . . was not the "Northern sangharama" referred to in this inscription' (ibid.: 215), suggesting instead that it was a palace. Dani has refuted Marshall's findings suggesting that the plan conforms to patterns of a religious and educational context and that 'There is no reason, therefore, to think that these buildings were not part of *Uttararama*' (Dani 1986: 109).

This differentiation between palace and *vihara* is a problem also encountered in Nepal and Sri Lanka. In the former, a complex of brick cells faced by verandahs and courtyards was recorded at Tilaurakot which has been identified by some scholars as a palace (Rijal 1996: 30) but by others as a *vihara*, causing the site managers to erect signs noting an 'ancient structural complex'. Bandaranayake has reinterpreted the complex known as the *Daladage* or 'Temple of the Tooth' at Anuradhapura as a royal palace (Bandaranayake 1974a: 383). If Bandaranayake's hypothesis is correct, it suggests that the structures of the Buddhist elite, whether lay or *Sangha*, may have used similar plans and materials, and will frequently be impossible to differentiate from fragmentary foundations. Finally, it should be noted that in inscriptions 'the term *vihara* generally indicates a Buddhist monastery, though it is sometimes used for the Jaina or Hindu monasteries also' (Mitterwallner 1981: 499).

The case studies

Having thus critically reviewed the archaeological evidence of the *Buddha*'s life and the integrity of the tripartite typology of Buddhist monuments, three selected case studies of Buddhist practice will be considered to examine the variability of Buddhist material culture. These studies differ both in date and geographical area but all are linked by the questioning of traditionally accepted generalisations concerning Buddhist archaeology.

Patterns of Buddhist patronage

A crucial tenet of Buddhist teaching is the need for patronage (Dutt 1962: 36) and the aim of this case study is to demonstrate that changing patterns of patronage are visible within the developmental history of a number of Buddhist sites. As noted above, many of the earliest *stupas* are dated to the Mauryan period, suggesting that the core of these monuments were imperial foundations, part of the expansion of Mauryan hegemony (Marshall, Foucher and Majumdar 1940, Faccenna 1980). This integration of disparate communities, regions and religions is certainly attested by the variety of languages in which Asoka's edicts and inscriptions are found (Allchin and Norman 1985). However, following the break-up of the Mauryan empire, patronage shifted from the ruler to the individual, making monuments 'the concrete expression of the piety and prosperity of the private citizens who sponsored its building and decoration' (Fynes 1995: 48). This pattern is not uniform as the development of Sanchi indicates a communal effort directed at a single development, whilst those of Gandhara show an individually based development with numerous foci (Faccenna 1980, Marshall 1951) and those of Sri Lanka are royal throughout (Paranavitana 1946). The details of these three contemporary examples illustrate the complexities of differing patterns of patronage in south Asia.

The first example examines the development of the Buddhist site of Sanchi in India. Although never visited by the *Buddha*, Sanchi became an important pilgrimage centre and flourished between the third century BCE and the twelfth century CE (Marshall, Foucher and Majumdar 1940: 18). Whilst the complex consists of *stupas*, sanctuaries, pillars and monasteries, the dynamics of Buddhist patronage can be best demonstrated at the great *stupa*. The first phase consisted of the construction of a brick *stupa* measuring some 18 m in diameter and 8 m in height (Cunningham 1854: 269). Marshall attributed its construction to the middle of the third century BCE and thus to the personality of Asoka (Marshall, Foucher and Majumdar 1940: 20). It was doubled in size and provided with a 3.2 m high stone railing in the second century BCE and, a hundred years later, four 8.5 m-high gateways were added. Although the second phase was probably completed during the life of the Sunga ruler, Agnimitra (*c.* 148 BCE), and the gates during the reign of Satakarni II, the Satavahana ruler (r. BCE 50–25), neither individual was responsible for these alterations (ibid.: 18–38). In contrast to its Asokan foundation, it was completed by hundreds of donors, lay-folk and *Sangha*, whose identities can be recognised from inscriptions incised on the elements that they dedicated. Summarised as 'multitudes of good Buddhists anxious to help on the work – lay-worshippers and other townsfolk from Vidisa, monks and nuns from Sanchi and the neighbouring monasteries of Akara, pilgrims from further afield' (ibid.: 34), this pattern confirms the passing of patronage from the state to the community.

A parallel example is found at Sirkap's Dharmarajika *stupa* in Taxila (Marshall 1951: 231–5). The earliest phase consisted of a foundation of limestone masonry, which Marshall attributed to the patronage of the Mauryan Emperor Asoka. The drum and dome was remodelled, enlarged and surrounded by a ring of 12 small *stupas*, no more than 2 m high, in the middle of the first century BCE. These *stupas* were then levelled and used as a foundation for a ring of 25 small image sanctuaries in the middle of the first century CE (ibid.: 249). This pattern suggests a similar beginning to that of Sanchi with an imperial foundation, but whilst the former monument was embellished collectively by numerous donors, at the Dharmarajika *stupa* individual donors created their own votive monuments rather than working in a single communal effort!

These patterns are, however, different again to those of contemporary Buddhist *stupas* at Anuradhapura in Sri Lanka. As discussed elsewhere (Coningham 1995a), the *Mahavamsa* records that the monk Mahinda, a son of Asoka, was deputed by the Buddhist elders to take the message of the *Buddha* to the island of Sri Lanka (ibid.: 226). Having converted the king, Devanampiya Tissa (r. 250–210 BCE), and the inhabitants of his capital Anuradhapura, Mahinda was presented by the king with a small *stupa*, the Thuparama *stupa*, built over the *Buddha*'s right collarbone. Unlike the examples of the Dharmarajika and Sanchi *stupas*, Devanampiya's *stupa* was never enlarged. Conversely, successive kings appeared to favour the construction of their own ever larger *stupas* between 161 BCE and 301 CE (Coningham 1999). These three examples suggest that there was a mosaic pattern of patronage even within a specific time span, and that regions demonstrated different patterns of patronage, resulting in different developmental patterns for the same Buddhist monument.

The power of Buddhist relics

Similar complexity is evident when considering the role of relics – a key category of Buddhist practice as their importance had been stressed the moment the *Buddha*'s remains were cremated (Trainor 1997: 35). Indeed, as already noted, ten relics were distributed at Kusinagara, being the eight portions of ashes, the cremation urn which had held those ashes and even the embers of the cremation fire (Mitra 1971: 7). All were encased in a *stupa* and became objects of veneration. These relics, each sealed in a particular locality, strengthened the fixed nature of northern India's ritual landscape. Trainor believes, however, that this trend changed in the third century BCE with Asoka's widespread collection and redistribution of relics (Trainor 1997: 40) thus meeting the expanding demand for authentic relics as well as enabling regions which had never been visited by the *Buddha* during his lifetime to be sanctified and unified by the presence of his relics. Buddhist relics are commonly divided into three groups within the Theravada tradition, corporeal relics, relics of use and relics of commemoration (Mitra 1971: 20, Trainor 1997: 30). Trainor has further explained that the value of 'Buddhist relics, as material objects around which particular ritualized activities are centred, draw their meaning and authority from their alleged connection with powerful religious figures from the past' (ibid.: 27).

As previously noted (Coningham 1998: 125), attempts to actually apply such categories to archaeological examples of relic deposition are extremely complex, if not puzzling. The enormous variety of relics can be illustrated by describing those recovered from the relic caskets of *stupas* at a single complex, the Dharmarajika at Taxila. These included bone, ash, carnelian chips, metal pins, coins, precious and semi-precious stone beads, silver leaf, coral, clay and even nothing at all (Marshall 1951: 167–241). It is thus clear that if many of these otherwise utilitarian objects had not been recovered from the caskets of Buddhist *stupas*, their ritual value would have been archaeologically invisible. A number of attempts have even been made to ascribe an economic value to relics, as illustrated by the excavators of a hoard of 44 badly worn and debased coins deposited in the great *stupa* of Butkara I who stated that this votive deposit reflected 'the poorness not only of the donor(s), but generally of the locality' (Faccenna, Gobl and Khan 1993: 106) or by Zwalf's suggestion that 'where offerings are modest, intention must have justified the deposit' (Zwalf 1985: 26). Surely such attempts to attribute economic or even relative values to relics are most inappropriate as illustrated by the following example from Nepal. During the 1999 excavations at Tilaurakot a group of Tibetan monks visited the trench and requested sieved soil from the spoil heaps. On being asked why, they responded that they wanted to take the soil back to their monastery to enshrine and venerate it as it came from the lowest levels of the site – levels upon which the *Buddha* himself might have walked as a child.

A very particular form of relic devotion developed in Sri Lanka and south-east Asia in the mediaeval period and still persists today. Whilst the antiquity of relic veneration in Sri Lanka has been supported by the *Mahavamsa*'s references to the enshrining of the collarbone of the *Buddha* in the Thuparama *stupa* in the third century BCE (Coningham 1995a: 228), the full impact of the relic cult occurs only in the fourth century CE with the arrival of the Tooth Relic from eastern India (Hocart 1931: 1–4). The importance of this Relic was soon confirmed with its installation within a *Daladage* or 'Tooth Relic Temple' close to the royal palace (Coningham and Lewer 1999: 863). With the loss of Anuradhapura, in 1017 CE to south Indian expeditions, power shifted southwards to Polonnaruva where the Relic was housed during much of this time (Coningham 1995b: 134).

Following the collapse of Polonnaruva, the Relic shifted from the cities of Dambadeniya and Yapahuwa to Kurunagala in the fourteenth century CE but moved south again in the fifteenth century, before being enshrined in the last independent capital, Kandy (ibid.: 145–54). It is clear from this complex history that during this unsettled time the Relic, housed in *Daladages* in successive capitals, became the symbol of sovereignty, something that continued during the period of colonial rule, with the British Governor performing the ceremonial role of the Sinhalese king in its ritual veneration, until this was halted by missionaries in 1846 (Hocart 1931: 4).

The power of the Tooth is still revered today, as illustrated by the suicide bombing of its *Daladage* by the Tamil Tigers in 1998, in the words of Tamil groups 'the targeting of the temple, a symbol of Buddhist chauvinism is the unfortunate consequence of militant Buddhism' (Coningham and Lewer 1999: 864). A parallel example is found with the Emerald Buddha of Thailand which holds a similar position to the Tooth Relic, lodged as it is within the grounds of the capital's royal palace. It too underwent a complex series of travels, indicating its importance, before being installed hundreds of years later in Bangkok as 'the patron and guardian, at one and the same time, of the Cakkri dynasty and the country over which it rules' (Tambiah 1984: 214–15). Although the power of relics was only really realised in the extremes of the Buddhist world, it illustrates the flexibility and mobility of Buddhist devotion. Unlike the static landscape of the historical *Buddha*, the mobility of portable relics allowed both kingship and the royal patronage of Buddhism a continuum, despite the highly transient nature of the centralised and urbanised power.

The archaeology of Buddhist sectarianism

Sectarianism appears to have been present within the *Sangha* from its earliest times, indeed, the process of schism was authorised within the *Vinayapitaka* (Dutt 1962: 84). The Buddhist traditions record that during the First Buddhist Council, held immediately following the *Buddha*'s *Mahaparanivana*, a unified corpus of his sermons and monastic regulations was agreed by his disciples, but that less than one hundred years later, a Second Council had to be held to suppress heretical teachings (ibid.: 114, 172). The *Mahavamsa* records that a Third Council was held in the third century BCE at which additional members were expelled (Thapar 1963: 42), and whilst no other supporting evidence for such a council exists, Asoka's edicts at Kausambi, Bairat and Sanchi warn against schism within the *Sangha* and the latter even advocates that schismists, whether nun or monk, should be expelled from the order's residences and forbidden its garments (Sarkar 1966: 98).

These early schisms were followed by the 'Great Schism' or *Mahabheda* – the emergence of the major schools of the orthodox and the *Mahasanghikas*

(Sarkar 1966: 97, Bechert 1973: 9). This schism would eventually lead, in the early centuries CE, to the differentiation of the numerous sects and schools into the orthodox *Hinayan* or 'lesser vehicle' and the *Mahayana* or 'greater vehicle'. The former has been characterised as analysing the Buddhist rules and doctrines whilst focusing on the historical individual of the *Buddha* (Dutt 1962: 261) and holding that salvation can only be individual (Mitra 1971: 13, Bechert 1973: 11) as once reaching nirvana, the individual reaches extinction and, unable to perform good or evil, is powerless to assist others (Gombrich 1971: 17). The latter has been characterised as being more philosophical and less puritanical and aiming towards the salvation of all beings (Bechert 1973: 11, Gombrich 1971: 13). By allowing all to reach Buddhahood through the acquisition of virtue, it also allowed the emergence of the *Bodhisattva*, an individual who, in Gombrich's words (ibid.: 17) 'first attains every moral perfection over a vast series of lives and preaches his wisdom to others to save them. Out of his infinite compassion he denies himself the supreme bliss, but works in the world to bring others towards it'. Though simplified into southern and northern spheres of influence (Conze 1959) or chronological developments, the relationship between the two is extremely complex: 'Hinayanist and Mahayanist monk-scholars worked, each in his own tradition of scholarship, side by side in the monasteries of India' (Dutt 1962: 248), and Bechert has suggested that the differences between the two were not even that great (Bechert 1973: 14) and that there were even sections from *Hinayana* schools who actually accepted *Mahayana* doctrine.

It is necessary both to consider the evidence for such traditions within the archaeological record, and to attempt to investigate the archaeology of sectarianism. It is certainly clear that major changes in devotional practices and doctrine are visible, as illustrated by the spread of the *Buddha* image. During the first half of the first millennium BCE, the *Buddha* was not depicted in human form, rather by a number of pre-Buddhist symbols such as an empty throne, a *Bodhi*-tree, a *stupa*, the wheel, the umbrella, and the footprint (Mitra 1971: 11, Harle 1992: 44). During the first centuries CE, accompanying the development of *Mahayana*, the first images were produced, more or less simultaneously, in the regions of Gandhara and Mathura (Mitra 1971: 13, van Lohuizen de Leeuw 1981: 400, Allchin 1992: 47). This physical shift can be illustrated from a number of archaeological sites but nowhere is this clearer than in the rock-cut monuments of Ajanta (Mitra 1968). The caves, consisting of 5 *chaitya-grihas* and 25 *viharas*, were dated to two main periods, the first between the first and second centuries BCE and the second between the fifth and sixth centuries CE (ibid.: 5). As already noted, the *chaitya-grihas* consisted of an apsidal hall with *stupa* surrounded by an circumambulatory passage whilst the *viharas* generally consisted of a central hall flanked by ranges of cells. Whilst the earlier phases made no provision for the *Buddha* image, the later phase included the image in both sets of monuments. The changes are paralleled by those at Taxila, although somewhat earlier in the first century CE, when the ring of votive *stupas* surrounding the Dharmarajika *stupa* were replaced by a ring of image shrines (Marshall 1951: 248).

Whilst such major changes are frequently recognisable, the archaeological visibility of minor sects is more difficult as illustrated at Nagarjunakonda, where rescue excavations prior to the flooding of the valley by the Krishna dam have provided the plans of 27 Buddhist complexes, all dating to the third and fourth centuries CE (Sarkar 1960, 1966, Sarkar and Misra 1966). Of these, inscriptions at six attest to the presence of four different sects, the *Mahasasaka*, the *Bahusrutiya*, the *Mahavihara-vasin* and the *Apara-mahavina-seliya*. Whilst the first two were sub-sects of the *Mahasanghikas*, the latter two represented the orthodox mainstream – the *Mahavihara-vasins* were even a Sri Lankan sect. Sarkar has contended that each sect is recognisable from the ground plans of the buildings, arguing that 'ideo-

Figure 3.8 Urinal, dating to between the eighth and tenth century CE, depicting a wealthy *vihara*, western monasteries, Anuradhapura (Sri Lanka) (photo R. Coningham)

logical differences manifested themselves in monastic architecture' (Sarkar 1966: 78). Monasteries belonging to Sri Lankan sects, for example, were provided with *stupas* built on a solid foundation, whilst *stupas* belonging to the *Apara-mahavina-seliya* and *Mahasasaka* sects had wheel-shaped foundations. Despite these sectarian differences, many of the establishments exhibited the *Buddha* image in later phases such as at the orthodox monastery 43, leading Sarkar to note that 'many sects started their careers in the valley without the Buddha-image, but most of them succumbed to the idea after a period of Resistance . . . This change was effected within a maximum period of a century.' (Ibid.: 78–9). It should be noted, however, that no image was found at the *Apara-mahavina-seliya* monastery 9, suggesting that even within sects there were further sub-sects. Sectarianism is also apparent at Anuradhapura (Coningham 1999), with the archaeological identification of the western monasteries as the *Tapovana* or 'grove of penitents' (Hocart 1924: 43, Geiger 1960: 203). This area, belonging to a sect known as the *Pamsukulins* or 'those clothed in rags from dustheaps', is notable as it has none of the three classic categories of Buddhist monuments (Coningham 1995a: 235). This forest-dwelling sect, activating their own reformation, allowed only a single form of ornamentation: surprisingly, their urinals were carved with images of wealthy *viharas* (Figure 3.8).

Conclusion: towards an archaeology of Buddhism

At the outset of this chapter, it was stated that the main aim was to question many of the traditionally accepted generalisations and typologies of Buddhist archaeology and to provide a basis from which a new typology of Buddhist might be created. It has been demonstrated that there is no contemporary evidence of the individual known as the *Buddha*, and that even his image has no historical relevance as the first examples were produced centuries after his death. The dates of his birth and death are still the cause of debate as is even the identification of his childhood home. It has also been demonstrated that confusion even surrounds the typology of Buddhist monuments as they are largely shared with other contemporary traditions. The variability and flexibility of Buddhism has been demonstrated through the three case studies considered and it has been noted that many of the early Buddhist symbols are indistinguishable from those of other traditions. This is not, of course, to deny the presence of an archaeology of Buddhism, merely to suggest that its manifestations are complex and that our current typologies and generalisations are too simplistic.

Indeed, whilst the statement that 'the state of Buddhism in different regions and localities happens to be so scattered and discontinuous that a whole or integrated picture of any given period of Buddhist history hardly evolves' (Dutt 1962: 28) may be acceptable, the view that there was no Buddhist period of Indian history should be robustly resisted. Undoubtedly, Chakrabarti is correct in suggesting that 'Buddhism provided only a segment . . . of the composite religious culture of India' (1995: 201), however, even after its disappearance in northern India, powerful elements of its nature, 'crypto-Buddhism' (Dutt 1962: 20), still play 'a vital functioning part of our cultural heritage' (ibid.), perhaps explaining the ease with which hundreds of thousands of low-caste Hindus converted to Buddhism in order to escape their untouchable status in the 1950s (Ahir 1989: 149). It must be acknowledged, however, that only a fragment of the spatial and temporal nature of Buddhist archaeology has been examined thus far within this study. Indeed, a number of issues have not yet been discussed such as the definition of a Buddhist diet, the role of women in Buddhism or even the archaeology of Buddhist artefacts. These will now be considered, again with reference to examples from both archaeology and contemporary practice in an attempt to further define an archaeology of Buddhism.

The role of a Buddhist diet, for example, has not been examined, although whether such a diet existed within the early *Sangha* is unclear as monks and nuns would beg in villages and towns (Coningham 1995a: 233). However, the provision of refectories and kitchens in *viharas* by the middle of the first millennium CE suggests a more corporate footing. Unfortunately, any study of diet is limited as there are few excavation reports which have acknowledged the presence of faunal remains at Buddhist sites. Indeed, there are cases where bones have been thrown away due to their apparently baffling presence, monks being forbidden from taking the life of animals. It is unfortunate, therefore, that despite the thousands of metres of soil excavated at the seven sites of the Sri Lankan Unesco Cultural Triangle since the programme began in 1980 (Coningham and Lewer 1999: 865) faunal remains have only been recorded from two, the Abhayagiri *vihara* at Anuradhapura (Wikramagamage 1984: 87) and the Sigiriya *vihara* (Bandaranayake 1984: 61, 1988: 17, 1989: 21), and these have never been identified. Until a full environmental archaeology programme is conducted at a Buddhist site, Buddhist diet will have to be reconstructed from unreliable textual sources or contemporary practice (Tambiah 1969), or restricted to comments on the dietary habits of the lay population (Coningham and Young 1999).

Similarly, the presence of women within the archaeology of Buddhism has seldom been examined in detail, and the present study is no exception (see also MacLean this volume). Although one might be tempted to suggest that this invisibility is due to the fact that Buddhist ascetics are visually sexless, it is more likely to have come about because the south Asian orders of *Bhikkhunis* or 'nuns' ceased in the twelfth century CE (Bartholomeusz 1994: 21). Despite the disappearance of the female order, the textual record suggests that women renounceants and donors played a major role; the *Mahavamsa*, for example, records that Asoka's daughter, Sanghamitta, became a *Bhikkhuni* and introduced both a sapling from the Bodhi-tree and her own order to Sri Lanka in the third century BCE (Coningham 1995a: 228). Inscriptions at Sanchi record the donations of both nuns and lay-women (Marshall, Foucher and Majumdar 1940), and many of the *viharas* at Nagarjunakonda record the munificence of women from the ruling Brahmanical elite (Dutt 1962: 129). It is also surprising that amongst the thousands of Buddhist complexes that have been excavated there is only one tentative identification of a convent, and this was generated by the presence of restricted accessibility and private bathrooms alone (Sarkar and Misra 1966: 39, Dutt 1962: 134).

The final theme needing consideration is that of the archaeology of specifically Buddhist artefacts, as often the identification of Buddhist sites has come about through a combination of architectural and artefactual evidence (Marshall 1951: 225). The majority of such studies have been restricted to the archaeology of formal Buddhist sites, that is sites with one or more of the three Buddhist monuments, and are therefore limited in their interpretations of Buddhist material culture. As previously suggested, much Buddhist archaeology has been oriented towards the smallest group within the Buddhist community, the *Sangha* (Coningham 1998: 123), although the beginnings of a study of an urban lay-community have been reported elsewhere (Coningham 1998, Coningham and Edwards 1998). Indeed, whilst the creation of a new typology of lay Buddhist archaeology awaits a more detailed study of the complexities of contemporary lay practice (Gellner 1992, Tambiah 1969) (Figure 3.9), the beginnings of a formal Buddhist archaeology may start with reference to 'Buddhist' artefacts, although it has been stressed that *Bhikkhus* and *Bhikkhunis* were allowed few personal possessions (Marshall 1951: 240).

Yet examples exist and excavations at the Jaulian *vihara* at Taxila recovered a number of artefacts which can be classified as 'Buddhist' including bells, *dharmachakra* pendants, *Bodhisattvas* images, birchbark manuscripts and votive *stupas*. However, the site's spearheads, adzes, spades, gold pendants, finger rings and beads are not (ibid.: 385–7). In parallel, the bangles, mirrors, terracotta horses, hooks, earrings, antimony-rods, chisels, knives and arrowheads from the *vihara* at Saidu Sharif I are surprising, whilst its *dharmachakra*, *Bodhi*-leaf and *svastika* pendants all conform to categories of Buddhist symbols (Callieri 1989: 183). Similarly, the gaming pieces, ear ornaments, arrowheads, terracotta goddesses and horses at Salihundam do not conform, whilst the stone lotus medallions, terracotta *Buddha* and *stupa* plaques, inscribed conch shells and moulded bricks and sherds with *trisulas*, *nandipadas* and *svastikas* again conform to Buddhist typologies (Subrahmanyam 1964: 48). Indeed, if the inclusive nature of categories of Buddhist relics is considered, it may have to be admitted that the artefactual

Figure 3.9 Pilgrims and monks in 1999 circumambulating the *stupa* of Bodhnath
(c. sixth to fourteenth century CE), Kathmandu (Nepal)
(photo R. Coningham)

taxonomies conceived by Buddhists, whether lay or *Sangha*, male or female, will never be fully understood.

There is also, underlying much research concerning the archaeology of Buddhism, the concept that those who venerated the *Buddha* or offered donations were Buddhists (Paranavitana 1970: lxviii). However, the differentiation between Buddhism and other contemporary orthodox and heterodox traditions was not always distinct. Perhaps the need to allocate discrete categories of religious jurisdiction owes more to the concepts of a British census rather than responding to actual practice. That such discrete divisions cannot be applied to the past is illustrated by the twelfth-century CE inscription at Polonnaruva's Rankot *vihara* recording the donation of cows to 'the Lord *Buddha*' by a Tamil, and presumably Hindu, mercantile corporation (Veluppillai 1982: 218); the donation of many Sri Lankan Buddhist caves by *Brahmans* (Coningham 1995a: 231); and the donations of the ladies of the Brahmanical elite at Nagarjunakonda to the valley's Buddhist *viharas* – the donatrix Camti-Siri even repairing the great *stupa* so that her Brahmanical son-in-law, King Virapurisa-data might enjoy a long life and victory (Dutt 1962: 129). The Government of British India even presented relics from Taxila to the Buddhists of Sri Lanka in 1917 (Marshall 1951: 242), a precedent followed by the Government of the Islamic Republic of Pakistan in the 1950s. Even today in Sri Lanka, the present conflict has not halted the veneration of sites such as Adam's Peak (Paranavitana 1958) by Christians, Hindus, Muslims and Buddhists. The relationship between traditions was, and is, extremely complex; undoubtedly, the *Sangha* attracted the lay community with its harsh ascetic practices; miraculous powers; desire to be in the wilderness; strong organisation; and authority of distant knowledge (Coningham 1995a: 239). It is too simplistic to attribute the spread of early Buddhism in Asia to royal patronage (ibid., Dutt 1962: 27, Fynes 1995); it is due rather to its ability to mobilise popular support as demonstrated by Tambiah's study of Buddhist millennial movements (Tambiah 1984).

Perhaps, when analysing the spread of Buddhism one should not attempt to identify prime movers but rather adopt the features of Robb's simulation model for the random diffusion of language based on the premise that often 'random, directionless processes can add up to directed results' (1991: 287). His model demonstrates that communities, whether they be religious or linguistic, 'grow, dwindle, fuse, merge or go extinct for reasons as varied as intermarriage, demographic change, ecological shift, internecine conflict, economic stress, external political pressure, opportunism, or the assimilation of refugees' (ibid.). Certainly such a model would support Dutt's statement with regard to India that 'The . . . developments of Buddhism in different parts of the country were neither uniform nor centrally regulated. Buddhism was never a "church"' (Dutt 1962: 28). Thus in the light of the above complexities concerning traditionally accepted generalisations of Buddhist monuments, artefacts and practices it can be reiterated that 'the rematerialisation of Buddhist archaeology has barely begun' (Coningham 1998: 126).

References

Agrawala, V.S. 1964. *The Wheel Flag of India Chakra-Dhvaja*. Varanasi: Prithivi Prakashan.

Ahir, D.C. 1989. *The Pioneers of the Buddhist Revival in India*. Delhi: Sri Satguru Publications.

Allchin, F.R. 1992. The Emergence of the Buddha Image. In Errington, E. and Cribb, J. (eds), *The Crossroads of Asia: Transformation in Image and Symbol*. Cambridge: Ancient India and Iran Trust. pp. 40–1.

Allchin, F.R. 1995a. Mauryan Architecture and Art. In Allchin, F.R. (ed.), *The Archaeology of Early Historic South Asia*. Cambridge: Cambridge University Press. pp. 222–73.

Allchin, F.R. (ed.). 1995b. *The Archaeology of Early Historic South Asia*. Cambridge: Cambridge University Press.

Allchin, F.R. and Norman, K.R. 1985. Guide to Asokan Inscriptions. *South Asian Studies* 1: 43–50.

Ball, W. 1986. Some Rock-Cut Monuments in Southern Iran. *Iran* 24: 95–116.

Bandaranayake, S.D. 1974a. *Sinhalese Monastic Architecture: the Viharas of Anuradhapura*. Leiden: E.J. Brill.

Bandaranayake, S.D. 1974b. Buddhist Tree-Temples in Sri Lanka. In Van Lohuizen de Leeuw, J.E. and Ubaghs, J.M.M. (eds), *South Asian Archaeology 1973*. Leiden: E.J. Brill. pp. 136–60.

Bandaranayake, S.D. 1984. *Sigiriya Project: First Archaeological Excavation and Research Report 1982*. Colombo: Central Cultural Fund.

Bandaranayake, S.D. 1988. *Sigiriya Project: Second Archaeological Excavation and Research Report 1982*. Colombo: Central Cultural Fund.

Bandaranayake, S.D. 1989. *Sigiriya Project: Third Archaeological Excavation and Research Report 1983*. Colombo: Central Cultural Fund.

Barnes, G.L. 1995. An Introduction to Buddhist Archaeology. *World Archaeology* 27: 165–82.

Bartholomeusz, T.J. 1994. *Women Under the Bo Tree: Buddhist Nuns in Sri Lanka*. Cambridge: Cambridge University Press.

Beal, S. 1869. *Travels of Fah-Hian and Sung-Yun*. London: Trubner & Co.

Bechert, H. 1973. Notes on the Formation of Buddhist Sects and the Origins of Mahayana. In *German Scholars on India*. Varanasi: Chowkhamba Sanskrit Series. pp. 6–18.

Bechert, H. 1978. The Beginnings of Buddhist Historiography: The Mahavamsa and Political Thinking. In Smith, B.L. (ed.), *Religion and the Legitimisation of Power in Sri Lanka*. Chambersburg: Anima & Conococheague Associates. pp. 1–12.

Bechert, H. 1995. Introductory Essay: The Dates of the Historical Buddha – A Controversial Issue. In Bechert, H. (ed.), *When Did the Buddha Live? The Controversy on the Dating of the Historical Buddha*. Delhi: Sri Satguru Publications. pp. 11–36.

Brown, P. 1956. *Indian Architecture: Buddhist and Hindu Periods*. Bombay: D.B. Taraporevala Sons & Co.

Byrne, D. 1995. Buddhist Stupa and Thai Social Practice. *World Archaeology* 27: 266–81.

Callieri, P. 1989. *Saidu Sharif I (Swat, Pakistan): The Buddhist Sacred Area – The Monastery*. Rome: Istituto Italiano per il Medio ed Estremo Oriente.

Chakrabarti, D.K. 1995. Buddhist Sites Across South Asia as Influenced by Political and Economic Forces. *World Archaeology* 27: 185–202.

Coningham, R.A.E. 1995a. Monks, Caves and Kings: A Reassessment of the Nature of Early Buddhism in Sri Lanka (Ceylon). *World Archaeology* 27: 222–42.

Coningham, R.A.E. 1995b. 'Urban Texts: An Interpretation of the Architectural, Textual and Artefactual Records of a Sri Lankan Early Historic City'. Cambridge: University of Cambridge unpublished doctoral dissertation.

Coningham, R.A.E. 1998. Buddhism 'Rematerialized' and the Archaeology of the Gautama Buddha. *Cambridge Archaeological Journal* 8: 121–6

Coningham, R.A.E. 1999. *Anuradhapura, Volume 1: The Site*. Society for South Asian Studies Monograph No. 3. Oxford: Archaeopress.

Coningham, R.A.E. and Edwards, B. 1998. Space and Society at Sirkap, Taxila: A Re-Examination of Urban Form and Meaning. *Ancient Pakistan* 12: 47–76.

Coningham, R.A.E. and Lewer, N. 1999. Paradise Lost: The Bombing of the Temple of the Tooth – A Unesco World Heritage Site in Sri Lanka. *Antiquity* 73: 857–66.

Coningham, R.A.E. and Schmidt, A. 1997. 'Nomination of Tilaurakot and Ramagram: Non-Destructive Archaeological Investigations'. Paris: Unesco unpublished report.

Coningham, R.A.E. and Young, R.L. 1999. The Archaeology of Caste. In Insoll, T. (ed.), *Case Studies in Archaeology and World Religions*. Oxford: Archaeopress. pp. 84–93.

Conze, E. 1959. *Buddhism: Its Essence and Development.* New York: Harper.

Cunningham, A. 1854. *The Bhilsa Topes or Buddhist Monuments of Central India.* London: Smith & Elder.

Dallapiccola, A.L. and Lallemant, S.Z.-A. (eds) 1980. *The Stupa: Its Religious, Historical and Architectural Significance.* Wiesbaden: Franz Steiner.

Dani, A.H., 1971. Excavations at Andandheri. *Ancient Pakistan* 4: 33–64.

Dani, A.H. 1986. *The Historic City of Taxila.* Paris: Unesco.

Davy, J. 1821. *An Account of the Interior of Ceylon.* London: Longman, Hurst, Rees, Orme and Brown.

Dikshit, R.B.K.N. 1938. *Excavations at Paharpur, Bengal.* Calcutta: Archaeological Survey of India.

Dumarcay, J. 1973. *Le Bayon: Histoire Architecturale du Temple.* Paris: Ecole Française d'Extreme-Orient.

Dutt, S. 1962. *Buddhist Monks and Monasteries of India.* London: George Allen & Unwin.

Erdosy, G. 1995. The Prelude to Urbanisation: Ethnicity and the Rise of Late Vedic Chiefdoms. In Allchin, F.R. (ed.), *The Archaeology of Early Historic South Asia: The Emergence of Cities and States.* Cambridge: Cambridge University Press. pp. 73–98.

Faccenna, D. 1980. *Butkara I (Swat, Pakistan) 1956–1962.* Rome: Istituto Italiano per il Medio ed Estremo Oriente.

Faccenna, D., Gobl, R. and Khan, M.A. 1993. A Report on the Recent Discovery of a Deposit of Coins in the Sacred Area of Butkara I (Swat, Pakistan). *East and West* 43: 95–113.

Fairservis, W. 1971. *The Roots of Ancient India.* London: George Allen & Unwin.

Fuhrer, A. 1897. *Monograph on Buddha Sakyamuni's Birthplace in the Nepalese Terai.* Allahabad: Archaeological Survey of India.

Fynes, R.C.C. 1995. The Religious Patronage of the Satavahana Dynasty. *South Asian Studies* 11: 43–55.

Geiger, W. 1960. *Culture of Ceylon in the Mediaeval Times.* Wiesbaden: Otto Harrassowitz.

Gellner, D.N. 1992. *Monk, Householder and Tantric Priest: Newar Buddhism and its Hierachy of Ritual.* Cambridge: Cambridge University Press.

Gombrich, R. 1971. *Practice and Precept: Traditional Buddhism in the Rural Highlands of Ceylon.* Oxford: Clarendon Press.

Harle, J. 1992. The Kushan Art of Gandhara. In Errington, E. and Cribb, J. (eds), *The Crossroads of Asia: Transformation in Image and Symbol.* Cambridge: Ancient India and Iran Trust. pp. 40–1.

Hartel, H. 1974. The Apsidal Temple no. 2 at Sonkh. In Van Lohuizen de Leeuw, J.E. and Ubaghs, J.M.M. (eds)., *South Asian Archaeology 1973.* Leiden: E.J. Brill. pp. 103–10.

Hartel, H. 1995. Archaeological Research on Ancient Buddhist Sites. In Bechert, H. (ed.), *When Did the Buddha Live? The Controversy on the Dating of the Historical Buddha*. Delhi: Sri Satguru Publications. pp. 141–60.

Hocart, A.M. 1924. *Anuradhapura*. Colombo: Archaeological Survey of Ceylon.

Hocart, A.M. 1931. *The Temple of the Tooth in Kandy*. Colombo: Archaeological Survey of Ceylon.

Jong, J.W. de. 1975. The Study of Buddhism: Problems and Perspectives. *Studies in Indo-Pacific Art and Culture* 4: 7–30.

Lahiri, N. 1999. Bodh-Gaya: An Ancient Buddhist Shrine and its Modern History (1891–1904). In Insoll, T. (ed.), *Case Studies in Archaeology and World Religion*. Oxford: Archaeopress. pp. 33–41.

Lohuizen de Leeuw, J.E. van. 1981. New Evidence with Regard to the Origin of the Buddha Image. In Hartel, H. (ed.), *South Asian Studies 1979*. Berlin: Dietrich Reimer. pp. 377–400.

Longhurst, A.H. 1936. *The Story of the Stupa*. Colombo: Ceylon Government Press.

Losty, J.P. 1985. The Scriptures and their Transmission. In Zwalf, V. (ed.), *Buddhism: Art and Faith*. London: British Museum Press. pp. 40–1.

Marshall, J.H. 1951. *Taxila*. Cambridge: Cambridge University Press.

Marshall, J.H., Foucher, A. and Majumdar, N.G. 1940. *The Monuments of Sanchi*. Delhi: Archaeological Survey of India.

Mishra, T.N. 1978. *The Location of Kapilavastu and Archaeological Excavations 1967–1972*. Kathmandu: Lumbini Development Committee.

Mitra, D. 1968. *Ajanta*. Delhi: Archaeological Survey of India.

Mitra, D. 1971. *Buddhist Monuments*. Calcutta: Sahitya Samsad.

Mitra, D. 1972. *Excavations at Tailaura-Kot and Kodan and Explorations in the Nepalese Terai*. Kathmandu: Department of Archaeology.

Mitterwallner, G. von. 1981. 2 Natural Caves and 11 Man-Made Cave Excavations of Goa. In Hartel, H. (ed.), *South Asian Studies 1979*. Berlin: Dietrich Reimer. pp. 469–99.

Moron, E.M. 1978. Angkor: Relationships Between the Pyramid-Temple and the City. *Art and Archaeology Research Papers* 14: 27–39.

Mukherji, P.C. 1901. *A Report on a Tour of Exploration of the Antiquities in the Tarai, Nepal*. Calcutta: Archaeological Survey of India.

Nagaraju, S. 1981. *Buddhist Architecture of Western India*. Delhi: Agam Kala Prakashan.

Paranavitana, S. 1946. *The Stupa in Ceylon*. Colombo: Archaeological Survey of Ceylon.

Paranavitana, S. 1958. *The God of Adam's Peak*. Artibus Asiae Supplementum, 28.

Paranavitana, S. 1970. *Inscriptions of Ceylon*. Colombo: Archaeological Survey of Ceylon.

Pugachenkova, G.A. 1994. Kushan Art. In Harmatta, J. (ed.), *History of Civilisations of Central Asia, volume 2*. Paris: Unesco. pp. 331–96.

Rana, D.S. 1999. The Role of General Khadga Shumsher Rana in the Discovery of Lumbini. *Lumbini* 5: 12–13.

Rijal, B.K. 1996. *100 years of Archaeological Research in Lumbini, Kapilavastu and Devadaha*. Kathmandu: S.K. International Publishing House.

Robb, J. 1991. Random Causes with Directed Effects: The Indo-European Language Spread and the Stochastic Loss of Lineages. *Antiquity* 65: 287–91.

Robinson, F. (ed.). 1989. *The Cambridge Encyclopedia of India, Pakistan, Bangladesh, Sri Lanka, Nepal, Bhutan and the Maldives*. Cambridge: Cambridge University Press.

Rowlands, B. 1953. *The Art and Architecture of India.* Harmondsworth: Penguin.

Sarkar, H. 1962. Some Aspects of the Buddhist Monuments at Nagarjunakonda. *Ancient India* 16: 65–84.

Sarkar, H. 1966. *Studies in Early Buddhist Architecture of India.* Delhi: Munshiram Manoharlal.

Sarkar, H. and Misra, B.N. 1966. *Nagarjunakonda.* Delhi: Archaeological Survey of India.

Schopen, G. 1997. *Bones, Stones and Buddhist Monks.* Honolulu: University of Hawaii.

Srivastava, K.M. 1986. *Buddha's Relics from Kapilavastu.* Delhi: Agam Kala Prakashan.

Subrahmanyam, R. 1964. *Salihundam: A Buddhist Site in Andhra Pradesh.* Hyderabad: Government of Andhra Pradesh.

Tambiah, S.J. 1969. Animals are Good to Think and Good to Prohibit. *Ethnology* 8: 424–59.

Tambiah, S.J. 1984. *The Buddhist Saints of the Forest and the Cult of Amulets.* Cambridge: Cambridge University Press.

Thapar, R. 1961. *Asoka and the Decline of the Mauryas.* Oxford: Oxford University Press.

Trainor, K. 1997. *Relics, Ritual and Representation in Buddhism.* Cambridge: Cambridge University Press.

Tucci, G. 1977. On Swat: The Dards and Connected Problems. *East and West* 27: 9–104.

Veluppillai, A. 1982. Four Fragmentary Inscriptions from Polonnaruva. In Prematilleke, P.L. (ed.), *Alahan Parivena, Polonnaruva: Third Archaeological Excavation Report 1982.* Colombo: Central Cultural Fund. pp. 213–24.

Verardi, G. 1979. The Buddhist Cave Complex of Homay Qal'a. In Van Lohuizen de Leeuw, J.E. (ed.), *South Asian Archaeology 1975.* Leiden: E.J. Brill. pp. 119–26.

Wheeler, R.E.M. 1968. *Flames Over Persepolis.* London: Thames and Hudson.

Wickramagamage, C. 1984. *Abhayagiri Vihara Project: First Archaeological Excavation and Research Report 1982.* Colombo: Central Cultural Fund.

Zwalf, W. (ed.). 1985. *Buddhism: Art and Faith.* London: British Museum Press.

Zwalf, W. 1996. *A catalogue of the Gandhara Sculpture in the British Museum.* London: British Museum Press.

Chapter 4

The archaeology of Judaism

Rachel Hachlili

Introduction

The archaeology of Judaism is the term meaning art, archaeology and
material culture created specifically for the Jewish community. Its form
and content were determined by the desires of all classes. It was executed
in accordance with the spiritual and secular requirements of local congregations and was employed to satisfy both functional and recreational needs.
The archaeology of Judaism, from the Second Temple period to the end
of Late Antiquity (late second century BCE – seventh century CE), the
period under consideration here, reflects a culture which came into being
not in consequence of a nation's isolation but as the result of a necessity
to absorb and assimilate, and to compete with, the culture of others.
Simultaneously with absorbing and assimilating elements from its
Hellenistic, Roman pagan, and later Christian, surroundings, Jewish art
and archaeology retained and clung to its fundamentally spiritual basis,
and to its essential beliefs and customs.

   The worship of objects, whether natural or created by a person, was of
significance in ancient times. With the proliferation of polytheistic beliefs
the necessity for organised symbols was realised. In the case of Judaism,
however, visual art was not an indispensable attribute of worship. On the
contrary, a constant battle raged between the Jewish religion, which was
expressed in abstract values, and pagan worship, where symbols and
tangible objects were used. Although Judaism in principle rejected pagan
symbols, they nevertheless penetrated Jewish art and archaeology as
decorative motifs, devoid of their original meaning. Jewish art and archaeology found expression in various aspects of Jewish life; secular, sacred,
and funerary. It adorned public and private buildings, tombs, sarcophagi,
and ossuaries, some of which, such as the synagogue interiors and exteriors
and the tomb facades in Jerusalem, were vigorously and splendidly
decorated.

   This study examines the available data, both in Israel and where relevant in the Diaspora, and aims for comprehensive aspects of interpretation

by determining the meaning and significance of the material culture presented. It draws attention to what seems truly distinctive in the archaeology of Judaism. The purpose of this chapter is to assess the archaeology of Judaism in respect of these main aspects; the synagogue, Jewish burial customs, Jewish symbols and iconography, inscriptions, dietary remains, and the domestic and community environment.

The synagogue

Two important institutions distinguish Judaism: the Jerusalem Temple and the synagogue. Throughout Jewish history both have been dominant in Jewish religious, social, and cultural life. The Jerusalem Temple was the focal point for the Jewish nation, the centre for worship and the place where political, economic and spiritual affairs of world Jewry could be discussed and determined. The Temple of the Second Temple period was conformed with the temple of biblical Israel in its main religious and architectural features.

During the first century BCE – first century CE, the Temple in Jerusalem was still the centre of worship and ritual of the entire Jewish community in Judea and the Diaspora. Here Jews could participate in ceremonies and in the teaching of the Law conducted in the Temple courtyards, and could settle administrative questions in the Temple courts (Safrai 1987). The destruction of Jerusalem and the Temple was a turning point in the creation of the synagogue, both in architectural terms and in the customs and rituals practised. The response to the catastrophe of 70 CE was the use of Torah reading, study and prayer to supplement the sacrificial cult, so that public worship by study and prayer was now the cult of the synagogue. This new, important, and unique Jewish institution was invented during the Second Temple period (Schürer *et al.* 1979, II: 427–8; Cohen 1984: 151–74; Safrai 1987: 31–51).

The synagogue institution was a revolutionary concept in terms of worship and faith. First, it was a place of new ways of worship, not only for the privileged few, namely the priests, but for a large, participating community fulfilling the need for individual self-expression. Its aim was to supplement or replace the Temple and its sacrificial cult. The main elements of temple worship, offerings and sacrifices, were not transferred to the synagogue, not even symbolically. Second, it provided a structure to house the Torah shrine, the central place of worship built on to the wall oriented to Jerusalem. Finally, it was also used as an assembly house for communal as well as for religious occasions.

The relationship between Temple and synagogue was further strengthened by the use of related iconography and symbols of the Temple in the architecture and decoration of synagogues (Hachlili 1988: Chapters VII–IX, 1998: Chapters II, VII). The Jewish communities in the Land of

Israel and the Diaspora were anxious to preserve and remember the sanctity of the Temple, its sacred vessels, its cult, and its ceremonies, so they used them in the synagogue decoration as well as in the religious services.

Synagogue, *Beth Ha-Knesseth* in Hebrew and *synagoge* in Greek, both mean 'House of Assembly'. The origin of the synagogue is still disputed, and various theories have been promoted concerning these origins, their date, form, function, and location (Levine 1996, Hachlili 1997, 1998: 15–22). As early as the mid-third century BCE, inscriptions mention Egyptian synagogues; Jews in the first century CE believed the synagogue to be a very ancient institution dating back to the time of Moses; Talmudic tradition mentions that there were synagogues during the Babylonian exile. Some scholars assume that the synagogue was established by Diaspora Jews, and maintain that it is likely that the synagogue first developed in Ptolemaic Egypt. Gutmann (1981: 3–4) maintains that the emergence of the synagogue was the result of the Hasmonaean revolution in second- century BCE Judaea, when the synagogue, an institution unique to the Pharisees, became a meeting place where prayers and ceremonies were practised by individual Jews. Safrai (1976: 912–13, 918) sees the synagogue as developing from the public Torah-reading assemblies at the time of Ezra (fifth century BCE).

The archaeological sources for synagogue origins are to be found in the assembly halls of the Second Temple period (Hachlili 1997a). Following the destruction of the Temple they were adapted to function also as places of local worship in addition to their previous function of community centre, becoming symbols of the uniqueness of the Jewish community. Jewish aspirations in the Diaspora for a separate identity and community life resulted in the construction of assembly structures in Egypt and Babylon during the Second Temple period; for example, concurrently at Delos a dwelling house was used for assembly purposes. These local centres probably existed as community assembly halls where services would be conducted on Sabbaths and feast days (Hachlili 1988: 138–40). The Zealot assembly structures at the fortresses of Masada, Herodium and Gamla probably served as local assembly halls during the years of the revolt against Rome, a time when it was extremely difficult for the congregation to travel to Jerusalem to participate in Temple worship.

Two recently uncovered structures at Jericho (Netzer *et al.* 1999) and Kiryat Sefer (Magen *et al.* 1999: 27–30) are also deemed to be synagogues of this period. During the time these structures served as small community centres, worship may have been conducted in them, even though no convincing evidence has yet been found. Such structures may have had a focal point in the centre of the hall, which would explain the function of the benches lining the walls: the congregation would have faced inwards. The excavated structures are assumed by scholars to be synagogues because of the circumstantial evidence of similarity in architectural plan, hence in

function, even though no actual proof has been uncovered. Common architectural features are (a) their construction as oblong halls; (b) the division
of the hall by rows of columns into a central nave and surrounding aisles;
(c) stepped benches erected along all four walls of the hall facing the centre.
The structures also share a similar period for their construction, namely
the first century CE (although those in Gamla and Jericho may have been
erected by the end of the first century BCE). The pre-70 CE structures
conceivably had didactic functions as well as being centres for assembly
and for the community, but they were not places of cult or worship. As
long as the Temple existed in Jerusalem, the Jews were careful to avoid
any competition with it. Epigraphic and literary sources are also infor-
mative, such as the Theodotus inscription from Mount Ophel which
records a synagogue in Jerusalem (Frey 1952: no. 1404). Josephus and the
New Testament (*Against Apion* 2, 175; *Acts* 15:21), also attest to the existence of synagogues in the first century CE which were centres of Scripture
reading and studies.

After the destruction of the Temple, the sages established the 'act' of
compulsory prayer, a new institution in Jewish life, invented for social and
educational reasons (Cohen 1984: 165, Fleisher 1991: 28 and n. 9; on the
sanctity of the synagogue see Fine 1997: 61–79). This imposition of prayer
on the Jewish community as a law was one of the most important in the
history of the nation. It not only mitigated the theological calamity, it also
consolidated the dispersed survivors as a unique national and religious unit
(Fleisher 1991: 34–5). The synagogue building began functioning now as
an assembly hall for the local congregation as well as a spiritual, religious,
and social centre; it was not a substitute for, nor did it replace the Temple,
but it served only local needs.

Synagogues of Late Antiquity operated as a combination of congregational assembly hall and, more importantly, a place for reading the Torah,
for obligatory prayer, and for instituting and teaching religious law, the
halacha. The congregation inside the hall prayed facing the Torah shrine,
that is, facing Jerusalem and the Temple. Thus the distinctive feature of
the later synagogue emerges, the Torah shrine built on the Jerusalem
oriented wall, which determined the synagogue orientation and which
symbolised the sanctity of the place, being a reminder of the Temple.

The focus of synagogal activities, according to literary sources, consisted
of reading the Torah, the Scriptures. This was the primary purpose of the
synagogue for its congregation, who participated both by reading and by
paying attention to other readers. Regular prayer services were held on
the Sabbaths and the feast days. Daily prayers involving a large number
of worshippers were established only after the destruction of the Second
Temple (Safrai 1976: 922–7, 942–3, Fleisher 1991: 28–30). The synagogue
generally belonged to a local community and was governed by three representatives: the *archisynagogus*, the president; the receiver of alms, who was

a civic official, and the minister (*hazzan*). The *archisynagogus* managed religious and financial affairs (Rajak and Noy 1993) and the *hazzan* was the executive officer in charge of the practical details of running the synagogue. He was the master of ceremonies, and a paid employee (Safrai 1976: 933 ff., Schürer *et al.* 1979 II: 427–39). Construction of a synagogue would be decided upon by the heads of the community and financed by private and public donations. Numerous dedicatory Hebrew, Aramaic, and Greek inscriptions found in synagogue excavations indicate that the finance for the erection of the structure and its decoration as well as for repairs, remodelling, or rebuilding came from private and public donors, usually Jewish.

The synagogue building in Late Antiquity functioned as an assembly hall for the local Jewish congregation as well as a spiritual, religious, and social centre. It served the community for fund-raising, charitable collections, congregational affairs, and as a type of court of public interests. Institutions adjoining the synagogue included schools and, in annexes, hostels, guest houses, and residences for synagogue officials. Sometimes ritual baths (*miqvaoth*) were also built on to it or close by. Its use as a community assembly centre determined its architectural plan which took the form of a large hall divided only by supporting columns, and with benches around it. The many different architectural styles uncovered verify that they were not built according to a stereotype, nor were they designed according to an authoritative law; no universal or uniform synagogue plan existed. Opinions vary considerably as to the evolution of synagogue architecture. Several attempts have been made to categorise and explain the different types and the divergence in style of the synagogues scattered throughout many regions (Hachlili 1988: 141–233, 1998: 14–95).

Some features encountered in most of the excavated and surveyed synagogues in the Land of Israel direct attention to an originality and individuality in their plans (Figures 4.1 and 4.2). These features include the Torah shrine, the triple portal, the gallery, as well as various methods of ornamentation of the facade, interior, and floors. The highly ornamented facade exterior, characteristic of the Galilean and Golan synagogues (Figure 4.3), is an additional original feature. Differences in plans among contemporary synagogues are usually due to regional and local traditions and local priorities as well as fashion. Changes in synagogue designs probably came about as a result of changes in theological concepts. Whereas Galilean synagogues indicate a preference for entrances and Torah shrines both on the same Jerusalem-oriented wall, in other localities the Torah shrine is on the Jerusalem-oriented wall and the entrance is on another.

From its inception, the Torah shrine became a permanent fixture in the synagogue building. Built on the Jerusalem-oriented wall, the Torah shrine was the receptacle for the Ark of the Scrolls and took the form or

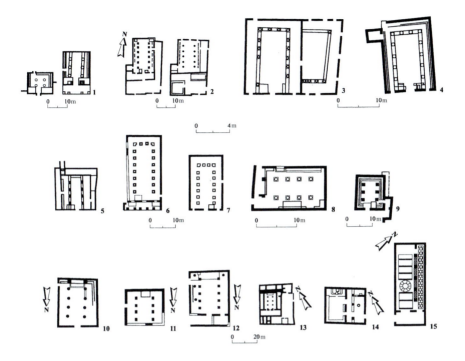

Figure 4.1 Plans of synagogues with aediculae

structure of aedicula, niche, or apse. It was the physical symbol of
the direction of the reading of the Torah and prayer. Chronologically, the
aedicula is the earliest type of Torah shrine, already in existence by
the second century CE, and the most popular type in Galilean and Golan
synagogues (Figure 4.1). Though constructed for use as a permanent structure, it was an appendage built on to the original internal wall only after
the synagogue building had been constructed. In the case of synagogues
which possessed two flanking aediculae, these seem to have had separate
functions (Figure 4.4). One aedicula served to house the Ark of the Scrolls,
and the other may have held the menorah. An important stage in the
evolution of the Torah shrine form is the later development of the apse,
during the later fifth and sixth centuries (Figure 4.2). The apse is a dominant architectural feature in the synagogue, functioning as the container
for the Ark and possibly the menoroth. Typological differences in the
Torah shrines should be attributed to local preferences, the popular vogue,
or historical development.

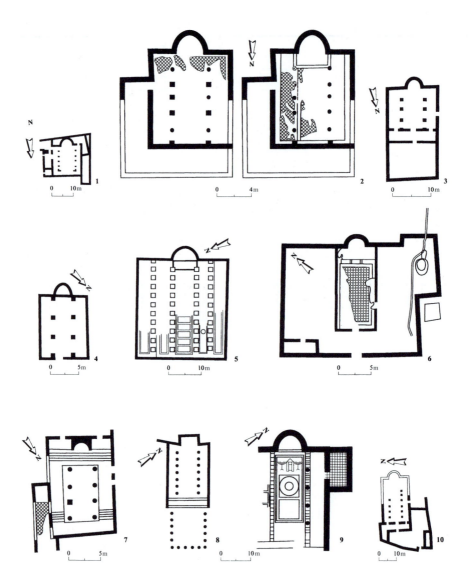

Figure 4.2 Plans of synagogues with apses

Figure 4.3 The facade of the Galilean synagogue of Bar'am

Scholarly opinion differs concerning the origin of the synagogue building plan and its sources of inspiration, such as the Hellenistic basilica, the pagan triclinium, or other public structures. It appears most likely that synagogue structures were a synthesis and accumulation of a variety of plans and architectural features which were themselves influenced by traditional customs as well as by contemporary fashion, together with the Jewish congregation's social and religious needs. The rich ornamentation of the facade, walls, floors, and other areas of the synagogue was influenced by contemporary architectural styles in secular and religious buildings in the Land of Israel and Syria. A combination of all these elements resulted in a house of worship functionally planned and lavishly decorated by the Jewish congregation for itself. Utilising previously constituted tenets within their own tradition, the Jews also adapted various elements of architecture and art from their neighbours. In this way, they succeeded in creating aesthetic and monumental structures which harmonised with the spirit of Judaism in the Land of Israel.

The discovery of Diaspora synagogue buildings which have been surveyed or excavated in Syria, Turkey, Greece, Italy, Yugoslavia, North Africa, Bulgaria, and Spain indicates that they do not have much in common architecturally; in fact, they rarely have similar features among

Figure 4.4 Sardis synagogue, two aediculae on the inner east wall (courtesy, Archaeological Exploration of Sardis)

themselves or to synagogues in the Land of Israel. Most of the Diaspora synagogues had several stages of use, but most of them were either built in the third and fourth centuries or flourished at that time (Rutgers 1998: 97–135, Hachlili 1998: 14–95). The Delos (Greece) and Ostia (Italy) synagogues were probably the earliest Diaspora synagogues, whilst the Dura Europos synagogue is dated to the middle of the third century. The dating of the end of some synagogues is determined by their subsequent conversion into churches, probably in the fifth century.

The plans seem to be local and not part of established types. However, there were two factors that determined the architectural plan of each of the Diaspora synagogues. The first was the local artistic and architectural traditions and fashions. But second, several circumstances peculiar to the Diaspora synagogues seem to have exerted some influences that ultimately determined their plans. For example, the Dura Europos synagogue was a dwelling that was subsequently converted into an assembly hall. Some synagogues were built as part of a public complex in a prominent site in the city, for instance, the Sardis synagogue, which was part of the monumental Roman bath and gymnasium complex. An important fact in the fragmentary architectural survival of some Diaspora synagogues was the intentional converting of the synagogue into a church. An instance of this is provided by the Apamea (Syria) synagogue at the end of the fourth century. Characteristic features of the Diaspora synagogue include a fore-court, a main hall, which was not divided by columns; it was usually a hall with a Torah shrine, elders' seat, and sometimes benches. The main feature and focal point of the Diaspora synagogues was also the Torah shrine which consisted of the same three forms, aedicula, niche, and apse, built on the wall oriented towards Jerusalem.

In summary, it appears that the construction of most of the synagogues in the Land of Israel and in the Diaspora took local topography into consideration; their orientation, however, was determined by the Jerusalem-oriented Torah shrine structure. Consequently, the differences in synagogue orientation depend on local traditions or fashions regarding the location of the Torah shrine. The synagogue was not only a centre of worship and religious life but also a community centre, holding educational, social, and financial activities.

Jewish burial customs

Jewish burial customs in the Second Temple period are known from the finds at the two main excavated cemeteries of Jerusalem and Jericho in the Land of Israel (Hachlili 1988: 89–119, Rahmani 1961, 1994: 53–9). The cemeteries of Jerusalem and Jericho were located outside the city limits. They consist of rock-hewn loculi tombs; whilst a number of monu-mental tombs were discovered in Jerusalem in the Kidron Valley (Figure 4.5) (Avigad 1950–1). The loculi tombs, which are the most common form of tomb in the Second Temple period, consist of a square burial chamber, often with a pit dug into its floor to enable a person to stand upright. One to three arched loculi are hewn into three walls, the entrance wall excepted, and the loculi are sealed with blocking stones (Figure 4.6). The tomb is closed by a blocking stone or by mudbrick and small stones. In some Jerusalem tombs another type of burial is found: the arcosolia which is a bench-like aperture with an arched ceiling hewn into the length of the wall, probably a later type of burial. A few tombs also have a court-yard which apparently served for community meetings probably as a 'mourning place', whilst a *miqveh* (ritual bath) is attached to the courtyard at other tombs.

The Jericho cemetery evidence proves that the loculi tombs were designed first to accommodate primary burial in wooden coffins. The same tomb plan continued to be used for ossuary burials. The Jericho excava-tions indicate (Hachlili and Killebrew 1983, 1999: 166–75) that these loculi tombs can be classified into primary burial in wooden coffins followed by secondary burials of collected bones, placed either in limestone ossuaries or piled in heaps. In Jerusalem, primary burials in wooden coffins did not survive, owing to poor preservation of organic material. The orientation

Figure 4.5 Tomb of Zechariah, Jerusalem

of the burials in the coffins has no special significance as the bodies were placed in all directions; so were the bones in ossuaries. Grave goods were found in both wooden coffins and ossuary tombs. Items that were personal possessions were mostly found with women and children in their wooden coffins, and objects of daily life were usually placed in the tomb itself. In the first century CE a complete change occurred: secondary burial of bones in ossuaries, peculiar to Jewish burial practices, replaced primary burial in wooden coffins or in loculi. The ossuaries were sometimes decorated (Figure 4.7) and inscriptions were incised or written on the front, back, or sides, mentioning the deceased's name and family relations. The Jerusalem and Jericho cemeteries reflect differences between social classes, evident in the monumental family tombs in the Kidron Valley in Jerusalem and other family loculi tombs of various sizes and quality. In Jericho the 'Goliath' tomb with its wall painting and two rooms indicates that it was the tomb of a prominent family in Jericho.

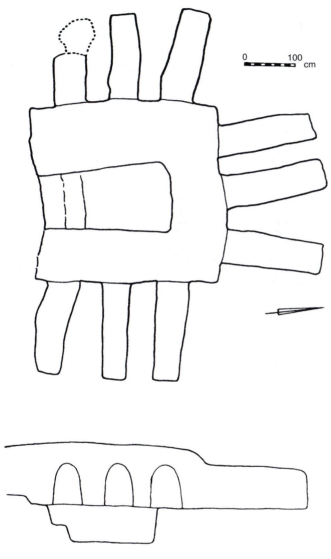

0 ___ 100 cm

Figure 4.6 Loculi tomb plan

Another form of Jewish burial was found at the Qumran and En el-Ghuweir (in the Dead Sea area) cemeteries (Hachlili 1993). All tombs (with few exceptions) are oriented in a north–south axis, seen on the surface at the Qumran cemetery, which was usually also the orientation of the body in the grave. The grave is hewn in the ground, with a pile of stones

Figure 4.7 Decorated ossuary from a Jerusalem tomb (courtesy, Israel Antiquities
Authority)

placed on top, as found at both Qumran and En el-Ghuweir. A similar
form of burial was discovered in a group of tombs at Beth Zafafa in
Jerusalem. The sole form of these burials is an individual interment in the
shaft or in a wooden coffin. The Qumran cemeteries show that the communities used exactly the same individual tomb for all their dead during
the periods of occupation. It is also clear that the individual burials at
Qumran and En el-Ghuweir are not family tombs as they have no inscription, no commemoration whatsoever. These cemeteries possibly served a
Jewish Second Temple sect, the Essenes.

The excavations in the extended Jerusalem necropolis and the Jericho
cemetery reveal that two completely different burial customs, one chronologically, typologically, and stratigraphically following the other, were
practised by Jews of the Second Temple period. The earlier custom, which
first appears among Jews in the first century BCE, was of a primary individual burial in a wooden coffin. This was followed in the first century
CE by secondary burials of collected bones, placed either in limestone
ossuaries or piled in heaps.

Jewish burial practices of the late Second Temple period reveal a corresponding importance accorded to the individual and the family. This is
reflected in the plan of the loculi tomb, which provided for individual
burial of coffins or ossuaries in separate loculi, while at the same time

allowing a family to be buried together in the same tomb. The entire population and not just the upper classes were given individual burials. This practice is probably related to the increasing importance bestowed on the individual in contemporary Hellenistic society, and to the Jewish belief in individual resurrection of the body. This belief is reflected in sources dating as early as the second century BCE (Rahmani 1961: 117–18, n. 6). Similarly, burial in wooden coffins was practised in En-Gedi and in the cemetery of the Qumran sect.

The second type of burial found in Jerusalem and in the Jericho cemetery, previously referred to, which chronologically followed the coffin burials, is that of conscious secondary burial of the bones, placed either in individual ossuaries or in communal burials in loculi. This complete change in burial customs occurred early in the first century CE, simultaneously with a change in the political status of Judaea, which now became a Roman province. No theory has so far been able to account for this drastic change in burial customs; unfortunately, all sources dealing with ossilegium describe only the custom itself without mentioning the reasons for its sudden appearance. To sum up, it is most extraordinary that in the Second Temple period Jewish burial customs usually among the most conservative customs in a society, underwent rapid changes. Loculi tombs appeared with primary coffin burials, and within a century secondary burial in ossuaries in similar loculi tombs had become the prevalent custom, a practice which lacks parallels in any other contemporary neighbouring culture. Still, these customs were short-lived and show little affinity with either the earlier Israelite customs or the later Jewish rituals of Late Antiquity which contain only traces of these Second Temple period customs. Moreover, archaeological investigation has been unable to uncover the causes for these ossuary burial innovations.

In the third and fourth centuries CE another change in Jewish burial customs occurs. It is found in the Jewish necropolis at Beth She'arim, which was the central burial ground for Jews from the Land of Israel and neighbouring areas (Mazar 1973; Avigad 1976). The catacombs in the Beth She'arim cemetery were expanded and occupied during those centuries until their destruction in 352 CE. The Beth She'arim burial place consists of catacombs, with a frontal courtyard and portals constructed of stone doors imitating wooden doors with nails (Mazar 1973: Plan 1–5, Pl. VI; Avigad 1976: figs. 3–5, Pls. 25: 1; 27: 2; 28: 1). Several burial halls spaced out along a corridor were hewn in the rock. The graves were mainly loculi or arcosolia types and it is clear that the burial customs, namely primary inhumation in arcosolia, coffins, and sarcophagi, had little in common with those of the Second Temple period. On the walls were carved, painted, or incised decoration, in a popular art style, many depicting the menorah (see below). Decorated marble or clay sarcophagi contained the primary burials of the Jews from the Land of Israel or the reinterred remains of Diaspora Jews. Not until the third century did Jews begin to practise the custom of reinterment in the Land of Israel (Gafni 1981), and especially abundant evidence for this practice is to be seen in the Beth She'arim cemetery (Schwabe and Lifshitz 1974: 219). By this time burial had become commercialised, a public enterprise, and was directed apparently by the burial society (*Hevrah Kadisha*), which sold burial places to any purchaser (Avigad 1976: 253, 265).

In the Diaspora, Jewish burials are identified either by those found in a recognised Jewish burial context, or that show Jewish symbols or inscriptions (Hachlili 1998: 263–310). The Jews were buried mainly in three types of graves: loculi tombs, hypogea, and in catacombs. Loculi tombs are rock-cut tombs consisting of a shaft with steps leading down to a chamber with loculi hewn into each of the walls. The loculi are usually sealed by stone slabs or stelae, and they are sometimes decorated in relief and painted. Tombs are occasionally decorated, and they sometimes contain inscriptions and lamps decorated with menoroth. Loculi tombs are typical of Egyptian burial customs and have been found in the Jewish cemetery at Leontopolis and Alexandria dating from the second century BCE to the first century CE. These tombs are similar to contemporary tombs in Jerusalem and Jericho. Another type of loculi tomb was found at Gammarath Hill, Carthage (Tunis). These also have a stairway and chamber, but many more loculi, about 15 to 17, surround the chamber. They are dated to a later period, possibly the second to third centuries CE.

The Jewish catacombs in Rome are series of passageways and stairs flanked by several loculi or niche tiers (Noy 1993: XIX, Rutgers 1995). Burial cubicula, loculi, arcosolia, niches, and apses were carved into the catacombs. Stone slabs or terracotta tiles seal the openings, and sometimes the deceased's name and age is painted or carved on them, in Greek or Latin. The loculi are rectangular, carved into the walls at different heights. Arcosolia are cut into the walls a few feet above floor level and contain one or two graves each. This form of burial is found in the cemeteries of Rome, Venosa (Sicily), and Malta. These catacombs may have begun originally as family tombs. As the tomb grew to include more family members, deeper levels had to be dug, passageways were extended, and more cubicula and loculi were added, till the tomb had developed into a communal burial site and become a catacomb. The catacombs of Rome, both Jewish and Christian, were located in a circle around the ancient city outside the walls. The Jewish catacombs in Rome (Rutgers 1995: 96, Hachlili 1998: 266–73, fig. VI-3) were used only by Jews and are: Monteverde on the Via Portuensis (destroyed in 1928), Vigna Randanini, and two catacombs under Villa Torlonia (the garden of Mussolini's villa) on the Via Nomentana. Three smaller catacombs, hypogea, are now lost (Leon 1960); on the Via Lubicana, in Vigna Cimarra, and on the Via Appia Pignatelli.

Jewish catacombs are found at several Roman cemeteries where they are set side by side with Christian and pagan burial sites. It is estimated that the known Jewish catacombs of Rome contained about 100,000 graves, but

Figure 4.8 Jewish sarcophagus found in a catacomb in Rome

there is no indication of how long any of the cemeteries were in use. (Jews are believed to have numbered about 10 per cent of the inhabitants of the Roman Empire.) The catacombs' underground galleries were dug in the tufaceous, volcanic soil, on several levels. The Jewish catacombs seem to have been enlarged as the need arose, as observed in the Monteverde and Vigna Randanini catacombs; the Villa Torlonia catacombs, however, were systematically planned. Three catacombs are accessible today, but only with special permission as they are not open to the public.

The main architectural features are the subterranean passageways or corridors which either lead to cubicula or have walls with loculi, niches, or arcosolia scooped out of them. Vigna Randanini has loculi in tiers, arcosolia, and burial shafts below floor levels. Monteverde mainly has loculi in superimposed tiers cut directly into the passageways. Smaller niches and loculi were cut for children. Wall paintings adorned some rooms, walls, arcosolia ceilings, and doorways; remains survived only at Villa Torlonia and Vigna Randanini. Epitaphs were inscribed on marble slabs set into the exterior stucco sealing, or, in the case of impecunious deceased, painted on or scratched into the seals. Most of the marble inscriptions were removed in antiquity, which prevents us from associating them with specific tombs. The identification of specific catacombs as Jewish is based on Jewish motifs depicted in wall paintings and on sarcophagi (Figure 4.8), and on the approximately six hundred Greek and Latin funerary inscriptions found in them. No Christian or pagan motifs were found. At present there is no proof that Jews in Rome buried their dead in any other way. The general dating for the catacombs is the third–fourth century CE (Rutgers 1998: 45–71).

Iconography and symbolism

Iconography and symbolism provide a further important element within the archaeology of Judaism. The art of Second Temple Judaism was aniconic. Hellenistic influences are shown in the adopted decorative and architectural motifs, but no figurative designs are depicted in this period. However, Jewish symbolic and figurative art is an extensive and essential part of Jewish art in Late Antiquity. A major change occurred at the end of the second century CE, and even more so during the third century CE, when representational art began to flourish. It was at this time that the barriers within which Judaism protected itself against foreign influences were being shattered. During this period the Jews acquired some of the customs and decorative elements from surrounding cultures and began to develop their own figurative and representational art, using pagan motifs, figures, and animals, for both synagogal and funerary art (Hachlili 1988: 234–316).

Conflicting opinions and heated arguments have existed about the phenomenon of representational art, due to the prohibition of the second of the Ten Commandments; 'Thou shalt not make unto thee any graven image, or any likeness of anything that is in the heaven above, or that is in the earth beneath, or that is in the water under the earth: Thou shalt not bow down thyself to them, nor serve them' (*Exod.* 20:4, 5; *Deut.* 5:8, 9). Despite this prohibition figurative art developed from the turn of the second century CE onwards among both the Jewish communities in the Land of Israel and in the Diaspora.

The Jewish attitude to art was basically decorative, to add beauty and ornamentation to their buildings. Even mythological scenes found their way into Jewish buildings, Jews of the Late Antique period were indeed unafraid of idolatry. Judaism was indifferent to pictures and did not ascribe to them any sanctity, so there was no reason to prevent the depiction of representations on pavements which were trodden upon. Furthermore, walking upon mosaic pavements with such depictions insured that no sanctity or sacred quality which would cause their worship could be attached to the scenes. Such a depiction could not be treated as a 'graven image' prohibited by the law. Judaism attached much more importance to the written word, as may be deduced from the iconoclastic destruction of the Na'aran synagogue pavement, in which the letters, however, were preserved, and from the synagogues at Rehov and 'En Gedi (all synagogues in the Land of Israel) where the floors paved with long inscriptions were left untouched.

Symbolic and figurative art became possible for several reasons. First, the attitude of the rabbis became more tolerant. Such changes, reflected in Talmudic literature, were the result of political, economic, and social circumstances (Urbach 1959). Second, the influence of the surrounding cultures, from which certain pagan and mythological motifs were taken, became much stronger. And last, Jewish literature, legends, and Midrashim influenced artistic traditions.

Jewish symbols

The seven-branched candelabrum (the Menorah), the accompanying ritual objects – *lulav, ethrog, shofar,* incense shovel or vase, the Shewbread table, the Torah shrine and the Ark of the Scrolls, are Jewish symbols appearing in both synagogal and funerary art (Hachlili 1988: 234–85, 1998: 311–78). They express profound and significant values distinctly associated with Judaism and were used frequently by Jews throughout late antiquity in both the Land of Israel and the Diaspora. Derived from the accoutrements used in the Temple rites (three sacred vessels stood in the sanctuary of the Second Temple period: the menorah, the Shewbread table, and the incense altar), this limited repertoire holds a prominent place in the vocabulary of Jewish art. These same sacred vessels also stood in the sanctuary of the First Temple, together with the Ark of the Tabernacle, which stood in the Holy of Holies. During the Second Temple period, the menorah and Shewbread table probably signified the priestly offices and their duties. Only after the

Figure 4.9
Menorah on the Jericho
synagogue mosaic
pavement

destruction of the Temple was the menorah's image transformed from a limited official emblem into a well-recognised Jewish symbol.

The importance of the menorah as a symbol can be charted. Following the destruction of the Temple, the menorah developed into the most important Jewish symbol (Figure 4.9). The menorah satisfied the desires of the Jewish people for a symbol which would, by reminding them of the past, represent both their spiritual and national aspirations. Furthermore, these motifs were chosen as symbols by the Jewish people at a time of conflict with the numerically and powerfully growing Christian community (Hachlili 1997b). The menorah, Torah shrine, and ritual objects came to be associated with Judaism and to be developed and recognised as Jewish symbols from the third century CE on. Depictions of a menorah flanked by ritual objects, or of the elaborate Torah shrine flanked by menoroth and ritual objects, came to symbolise participation in the annual pilgrimages, of which the Feast of Tabernacles was the most important, and, by association, the Temple and its eventual rebuilding.

The menorah was an integral part of the Temple ritual and the most important of the Temple vessels. Its later representation served the purpose of reminding the Jews of their previous glory as well as their pride in the Temple, and expressed the longing and hope for the renewal of the Temple services and worship. Furthermore, its unique and impressive design made it an excellent choice for a symbol to signify the meaning of Judaism: instantly recognisable, the menorah symbol would be immediately associated with the Jews, it was the most important identifying symbol of Judaism. Thus it can be seen that the purposes the menorah served were many. As a link with ancient rites and worship, as a symbol of the Jewish faith, and as a visual emblem always recognisable. By this process a national symbol was created which satisfied the Jews' need for self-identity, while living among Christians and pagans.

Biblical themes

The mid-third century Dura-Europos (Syria) synagogue hall is covered by wall paintings consisting of biblical scenes (Kraeling 1979); they are considered some of the most important and unique in the ancient world. It was the visual expression of a community's religious philosophy. Many of these paintings depict narrative scenes that are based not only on the biblical chapters but also include additional details, embellishments and interpretation from *midrashim* and *aggadoth*. By this time, therefore, these stories must have become traditional, popular folk legends, which were then rendered in art. The narrative scenes were probably based on artistic forerunners, albeit sketches only, but allowing for much artistic freedom. Furthermore, the fact that the paintings were narrated within a contemporary iconographic repertoire indicates that this repertoire had traditional, inherited, graphical origins and was not based on the written word. These painted scenes are not illustrations for a written text but are themselves illustrations of stylised folk stories. The scenes were chosen for their connotative force and their ability to illuminate Jewish traditional stories based on well-known biblical themes, enhanced and elaborated with *midrashim* and other legendary details. Artistic depictions of folk tales apparently existed already by the third century. The wall paintings of the Dura synagogue are thus the earliest confirmation that folk tales based on biblical stories with legendary additions found artistic expression in painted narrative scenes. The Dura-Europos synagogue paintings are an original, unique and distinctive work of art, attesting to the importance the Jewish community placed on their national-religious tradition (written, oral and visual).

Biblical scenes on synagogue mosaic pavements were selected from a relatively few biblical stories: The Sacrifice of Isaac, Noah's Ark, Daniel in the lion's den, and King David (Hachlili 1988: 287–300, Weiss and Netzer 1996: 18–25, 30–3). Noteworthy is the recurrence of biblical scenes in more than one synagogue mosaic pavement in the Land of Israel and on mosaics and wall paintings in the Diaspora. Biblical stories would naturally be included as subject matter for the decoration of synagogues, and they were depicted in simple narratives, although some of the scenes as a whole may have had symbolic meanings (Kraeling 1979: 363, 385). The scenes had in common the illustration of the theme of salvation and were associated with prayers offered in time of drought (Avi-Yonah 1975: 53). These subjects were part of the prayers such as 'Remember' and 'He that answereth . . .' (Sukenik 1932: 56 and n. 4). The choice of themes derived from the religio-cultural climate of the period and was meant to be a reminder of, and reference to, traditional historical events. Some scholars conjecture an intention in using these themes for symbolic or didactic purposes (Goodenough [1953, I: 253] connected the symbolism with Eastern mystery religions). However, the style, form, and artistic depiction on each of these floors are completely different, and each scene may be traced to a distinct influence or source. They do not seem to have a common denominator in style or origins. It may reasonably be inferred that pattern books of Jewish motifs and themes existed in antiquity and were used in the Jewish communities by donors, artists, and artisans.

The zodiac panel

A further interesting feature which is found in several synagogues ranging in date from the fourth to the seventh century CE (and discovered so far only in Israel), are mosaics showing the zodiac cycle (Hachlili 1977, 1988: 301–9, Avi-Yonah 1981, Weiss and Netzer 1996: 26–9). This use, over two centuries, of a pagan motif, invites many questions as to its function in the synagogue. The zodiac cycle in all of these synagogues occupies the centre

Figure 4.10 The zodiac design on four synagogue mosaic pavements in the Land of Israel: Hammath Tiberias, Sepphoris, Na'aran, Beth'Alpha

of a three-panel mosaic floor. The design consists of a square framing two concentric circles (Figure 4.10), the innermost containing a portrayal of the sun-god in a chariot. The outer, larger, circle depicts the zodiac divided into twelve radial units, each containing one of the signs and bearing its Hebrew name. Outside the zodiac circle, and in the corners of the square frame, are symbolically represented busts of the four seasons. These are named in Hebrew, after the month with which the season begins.

The recurrence of the zodiac design in a number of synagogue mosaic pavements indicates its relevance to religious thought, and its important place in synagogal art. Scholars have attempted to explain the significance and meaning of the Jewish zodiac panel in various ways. The most logical explanation seems to be that the Jewish zodiac mosaic functioned as a calendar (Hachlili 1977: 72, 76, 1988: 308–9), consisting as it does of three requisite sections: (1) the four seasons which represent the year; (2) the twelve signs of the zodiac, representing the months, and (3) the sun god, symbolising the day, the night being denoted by the background of the crescent moon and stars.

It is characteristic of Jewish art that a pagan subject, in this case the zodiac, should be adapted to express a Jewish idea such as an annual calendar. In the Roman world zodiac signs were of cosmic and astro-nomical significance, whereas in Christian art, as in Roman, the calendar was represented by the labours of the months (Hachlili 1977: fig. 17). Jewish art preferred an abstract and symbolic zodiac, in order to ensure the religious nature of the calendar. The use of the zodiac several times makes it clear that the Jewish community was not interested merely in a strictly decorative design for its floors. Through this balanced illustration of the three elements, sun god (representing day and night), zodiac signs (representing the twelve months) and the four seasons (symbolising the year), a two-fold purpose, of significance and design, could be achieved. Annual religious rituals consequently could be graphically portrayed in the synagogue's interior decoration itself. From this it can be seen that the fundamentally pagan zodiac cycle came to serve the Jewish community as a popular, symbolic calendar, and was employed as a significant frame-work for the annual synagogue rituals.

Inscriptions

Inscriptions have been discovered at synagogue and burial sites throughout the Land of Israel and the Diaspora, sometimes in secondary use. The majority are Aramaic and Hebrew in the Land of Israel, and Greek and Latin in the Diaspora (Frey 1936, 1952 [rev. Lifshitz 1975], Lifshitz 1967, Noy 1993, 1995). The importance of the inscriptions, especially from the Diaspora, lies in their providing a picture of the geographical dispersion of the Jewish communities; sometimes the only data available about a whole community are from an inscription. Inscriptions also provide data for a Jewish onomasticon, as well as helping to delineate subjects such as community organisations, names, titles, professions, traditions, relations with the Land of Israel, and religious ideas. Synagogues in the Land of Israel reveal about 110 Aramaic and Hebrew, and about 50 Greek inscrip-tions dating to the third to seventh centuries CE. Inscriptions are found either carved on stone architectural fragments of synagogues, such as lintels, column bases, and chancel screens, or worked into mosaic pavements. A few are painted on plaster. The inscriptions include dedicatory texts in commemoration of the officials and donors, some of which also mention the artists or builders of the synagogue. Other inscriptions include literary texts, and explanatory inscriptions of names and text, inserted in mosaic pavements, beside the portrayals of biblical scenes and the zodiac.

A few inscriptions include dates of the synagogue's construction or dedication. These play an important and organic part in floor composition in the synagogue, and are often depicted within a wreath or in a *tabula ansata*. Sometimes inscriptions are accompanied by the Hebrew formula *shalom* ('peace' in Hebrew), and the prayer 'Peace upon Israel' (*Psalms* 125:5). This formula appears on several synagogue mosaic pavements in a central medallion enclosing the menorah, with the word *shalom* appearing above. The same *shalom* inscription also appears on funerary objects, on some Diaspora tombstones, on a sarcophagus and on a gold glass from Rome. The 'Peace upon Israel' inscription in Hebrew, under the menorah, appears on the Jericho mosaic pavement (Figure 4.9) and on several tombstones and a stamped tile. Sometimes the word *amen* is added. This formula of the words *shalom* and *amen* on inscriptions found in synagogues and in a funerary context came to fulfil a function in Jewish liturgical practices (Rutgers 1998: 165–6). The majority of inscriptions found in synagogues name private Jewish donors who made gifts of mosaics or various furnishings. These inscriptions, therefore, attest to the financing and construction of the synagogues as well as their restoration by private donations or by the use of community funds. Donations were occasionally given in fulfilment of vows; seldom were they given by women. Other donors mentioned include officials, administrators, and artisans.

Funerary inscriptions of the Second Temple period are composed in Hebrew, Aramaic, and Greek in the Land of Israel. Most are inscribed or written on ossuaries, a few appear on a tomb's facade or inside a tomb. The Aramaic, Hebrew, and Greek inscriptions found in the Beth She'arim catacombs mainly record the names of the tomb owners; sometimes a sentiment is added. Longer inscriptions are written on the walls. Their purpose was to identify the graves of the deceased for visitors (Schwabe and Lifshitz 1974: 219). The inscriptions found at Beth She'arim indicate that the interred were people of importance such as rabbis, public officials, merchants, craftsmen, and scribes.

Jewish funerary inscriptions in the Diaspora were meant to identify the deceased. Greek and Latin appear in the same proportion as in non-Jewish inscriptions. However, certain epitaphs found in the catacombs of Rome were used only by Jews. Furthermore, ideas and ideals appearing in the Jewish inscriptions are not found in the non-Jewish ones. Both the synagogue and the funerary inscriptions indicate the status of the Jewish population in any city where they lived. They also testify to the importance the Jews ascribed to communal work (Rutgers 1995: 198, 201). In addition, they shed light on the organisation of the Jewish community, its leaders, their position and vocation, and even on the position of women as benefactors.

Dietary remains

Although the Jewish diet was prescribed by religious law it seems difficult to find archaeological data to confirm it, due to few remains and a lack of research (but see Insoll this volume). Some indication of a former Jewish diet might be inferred from the menorah, Judaism's most typical and wide-spread symbol in antiquity, which was incised or painted on storage jars and bowls dated to the fourth and fifth centuries. The menorah stamps and incisions on the storage jars and bowls may indicate that the Jewish community marked the food (seal of *kashrut*?) produced only for their own consumption (Arthur 1989: 139). But they might also imply that the potters, or the clients who purchased these storage jars, were Jewish (or Samaritan [Landgraf 1980: 76]), or equally that these menoroth were a sign of the Jewish manufacturer of products for the general public.

The traditional domestic environment

Both the traditional domestic environment and the community environment i.e. the settlement, are dubious categories of archaeological evidence to examine within a Jewish archaeological context. The dwelling house is not invested with a religious significance within Judaism and nothing would set it apart from structures inhabited by people of other faiths. A more pertinent question is if it is feasible archaeologically to recognise a Jewish settlement. The main feature which clearly defines the identity of a Jewish settlement is the existence and location of the synagogue as a religious and community centre. According to Jewish law the synagogue should be located at the centre or highest point of the site, though this is not always the case. Similarly, Jewish burials could also justify determination of a settlement as Jewish.

A settlement's development is understood in terms of the needs of the individual family that occupied each structure. An example is provided by considering the Golan village of Qasrin where the structures were built of roughly hewn stone or basalt blocks with chips inserted between the courses of these blocks. Many houses, entered via a single door, consisted of two, four, or more chambers, sometimes with an upper story that may have served as a sleeping loft (Killebrew and Fine 1991). In the living quarters of the houses, the floors are paved at times with roughly cut, well-laid stone blocks, plaster, or coarser stones and pebbles. A courtyard divided into different activity areas, including a kitchen with ovens, is also common. We do not have enough information about privacy or gender segregation. Houses were gradually enlarged over several generations, according to the needs of the occupants. Some rooms served as storage rooms. Space boundaries varied and were indeterminate. A path paved with gravel and pebbles or alleys separated the houses. However, all these components can hardly be recognised as purely Jewish. They evidently were part of traditional and local domestic architecture, which also represented Christian, pagan, and other dwellings. Hence, Jewish domestic architecture is based on environmental, traditional, and cultural conditions similar to those pertaining to other inhabitants of a site. To actually recognise and prove Jewish domestic or communal existence is thus difficult and the identification of the other elements discussed is thus essential to recognise the former presence of a Jewish community.

Conclusions

This chapter has attempted a brief study of ancient Jewish community life as related by archaeological finds in the Second Temple period and Late Antiquity. Particular features have been presented including the synagogue, Jewish burial customs, inscriptions, dietary remains, the domestic and community environment, and importance placed on Jewish symbols and iconography. This data indicates that many features of the archaeology of Judaism appear at sites throughout the Land of Israel and the Diaspora. Clearly, too, the Jews used local traditions and were subject to local fashions when constructing their religious edifices, or when burying their dead, but with the addition of Jewish symbols or presentation of the art in a way that expressed their religious convictions. Uniform worship did not require a uniform scheme in architectural elements and decorative forms.

Archaeology attests to a general representation of ancient Jewish life. The material culture presented is not an absolute picture, exceptions are found in all areas. Not all Jews were buried by the practices described, not all of them participated in the synagogue services. However, it seems quite possible that most of the communities adhered to the traditions and that religious laws affected all aspects of life.

In the Land of Israel, as in the Diaspora, the synagogue encapsulated not only the religious cult and ceremonies but also community life and organisation as well as a national tradition commemorating the significance of the Temple for Jews. Jewish synagogue and funerary architecture and art, like other contemporary arts, were designed to convey a message. This message contained a fundamental belief in the customs and traditions of the Jewish people and was expressed in the use of specific symbols and iconography. The menorah is the most popular, and whenever only one symbol is present, it will generally be the menorah; it takes on the profound significance of the Temple, thereby preserving the remembrance of the place and its ceremonies. The menorah likewise symbolises Judaism when synagogues and Jewish tombs and catacombs are to be distinguished from Christian or pagan structures, in the Land of Israel and the Diaspora. Thus, despite elements borrowed from neighbouring cultures, Jewish art and archaeology retained the fundamental beliefs, customs, and traditions of the Jewish people.

References

Arthur, P. 1989. Some Observations on the Economy of Bruttium under the Late Roman Empire. *Journal of Roman Archaeology* 2: 133–42.

Avigad, N. 1950-1. The Rock-carved Facades of the Jerusalem Necropolis. *Israel Exploration Journal* 1: 96–109.

Avigad, N. 1976. *Beth She'arim, III.* Jerusalem: Massada Press.

Avi-Yonah, M. 1975. *Ancient Mosaics.* London: Cassell.

Avi-Yonah, M. 1981. Le Symbolisme du Zodiaque dans l'art Judéo-Byzantin. *Art in Ancient Palestine. Selected Studies.* Jerusalem: Magnes Press. pp. 396–7.

Cohen, S.J.D. 1984. The Temple and the Synagogue. In Madsen, T.G. (ed.), *The Temple in Antiquity.* Provo: Brigham Young University Press. pp. 151–74.

Fine, S. 1997. *This Holy Place. On the Sanctity of the Synagogue during the Greco-Roman period.* Notre Dame: University of Notre Dame.

Fleisher, E., 1991. Annual and Triennial Reading of the Bible in the Old Synagogue. *Tarbiz* 61: 28–30 (in Hebrew with English summary).

Frey, J.-B. 1936. *Corpus Inscriptionum Judaicarum, Vol. I.* Roma, Città del Vaticano.

Frey, J.-B. 1952. *Corpus Inscriptionum Judaicarum, Vol. II,* repr. 1975. New York: Ktav Publishing House.

Gafni, I. 1981. Reinterment in the Land of Israel: Notes on the Origin and Development of the Custom. *The Jerusalem Cathedra* 1: 96–104.

Goodenough, E.R. 1953–64. *Jewish Symbols in the Greco-Roman Period. Vols 1–13.* New York: Pantheon Books.

Grabar, A. 1968. *Christian Iconography, A Study of its Origins.* Bollingen Series XXV.10. Princeton: Princeton University Press.

Gutmann, J. 1981. Synagogue Origins: Theories and Facts. In Gutmann, J. (ed.), *Ancient Synagogues – The State of Research.* Chico, California: Scholars Press (Judaics Studies no. 22). pp. 1–6.

Hachlili, R. 1977. The Zodiac in Ancient Jewish Art: Representation and Significance. *Bulletin of the American Schools of Oriental Research* 228: 61–77.

Hachlili, R. 1988. *Ancient Jewish Art and Archaeology in the Land of Israel.* Leiden: E.J. Brill.

Hachlili, R. 1997a. The Origin of the Synagogue, A Re-assessment. *Journal for the Study of Judaism* 28: 34–47.

Hachlili, R. 1997b. Aspects of Similarity and Diversity in the Architecture and Art of Ancient Synagogues and Churches in the Land of Israel. *Zeitschrift des Deutschen Palästina-Vereins* 113: 92–125.

Hachlili, R. 1998. *Ancient Jewish Art and Archaeology in the Diaspora.* Leiden: E.J. Brill.

Hachlili, R. and Killebrew, A. 1983. Jewish Funerary Customs during the Second Temple Period in Light of the Excavations at the Jericho Necropolis. *Palestine Exploration Quarterly* 115: 109–32.

Hachlili, R. and Killebrew, A. 1999. *Jericho, The Jewish Cemetery of the Second Temple Period.* Jerusalem: The Israel Antiquities Authority Reports no. 7.

Killebrew, A. and Fine, S. 1991. Qasrin – Reconstructing Village Life in Talmudic Times. *Biblical Archaeology Review* 17: 44–57.

Kraeling, C.H. 1979. *The Synagogue: The Excavations at Dura Europos, Final Report VIII, Part 1.* Second edition. New Haven, New York: Ktav Publishing House.

Landgraf, J. 1980. Keisan's Byzantine Pottery. In Briend, J. *et al.* (eds), *Tell Keisan.* Fribourg: Editions Universitaires. pp. 51–69.

Leon, H.J. 1960. *The Jews of Ancient Rome*. Philadelphia: Jewish Publication Society of America.

Levine, L.I. 1996. The Nature and Origin of the Palestinian Synagogue Reconsidered. *Journal of Biblical Literature* 115: 425–48.

Lifshitz, B. 1967. *Donateurs et Fondateurs dans les Synagogue Juives*. Cahiers de la Revue Biblique 7. Paris: J. Gabalda.

Magen, Y., Zionit, Y. and Sirkis, E. 1999. Kiryat Sefer – A Jewish Village and Synagogue of the Second Temple Period. *Qadmoniot* 117: 25–32 (in Hebrew).

Mazar, B. 1973. *Beth She'arim, I*. Jerusalem: Massada Press.

Netzer, E., Kalman, Y. and Loris, R. 1999. A Hasmonean Period Synagogue at Jericho. *Qadmoniot* 117: 17–24 (in Hebrew).

Noy, D. 1993. *Jewish Inscriptions of Western Europe, Vol. 1*. Cambridge: Cambridge University Press.

Noy, D. 1995. *Jewish Inscriptions of Western Europe, Vol. 2*. Cambridge: Cambridge University Press.

Rahmani, L.Y. 1961. Jewish Rock-Cut Tombs in Jerusalem. *Atiqot* 3: 93–120.

Rahmani, L.Y. 1994. *A Catalogue of Ossuaries in the Collection of the State of Israel*. Jerusalem: The Israel Antiquities Authority.

Rajak, T. and Noy, D. 1993. Archisynagogoi: Office, Title and Social Status in the Greco-Jewish Synagogue. *Journal of Roman Studies* 83: 75–93.

Rutgers, L.V. 1995. *The Jews in Late Ancient Rome*. Leiden: E.J. Brill.

Rutgers, L.V. 1998. *The Hidden Heritage of Diaspora Judaism*. Leuven: Peeters.

Safrai, S. 1976. The Synagogue. In Safrai, S. and Stern, M. (eds), *The Jewish People in the First Century*. Assen: van Gorcum. pp. 908–50.

Safrai, S., 1987. The Temple and the Synagogue. In Kasher, A., Oppenheimer, A. and Rappaport, U. (eds), *Synagogues in Antiquity*. Jerusalem: Ben Zvi Institute. pp. 31–51 (in Hebrew).

Schürer, E., Wermes, C. and Millar, A. 1979. *The History of the Jewish People in the Age of Jesus Christ (175 BC – AD 135), Vol. II*. Edinburgh: T. & T. Clark.

Schwabe, M. and Lifshitz, B. 1974. *Beth She'arim II: The Greek Inscriptions*. Jerusalem: Massada Press.

Sukenik, E.L. 1932. *The Ancient Synagogue of Beth'Alpha*. Jerusalem: Hebrew University.

Urbach, E.E. 1959. The Rabbinical Laws of Idolatry in the Second and Third Centuries in the Light of Archaeological and Historical Facts. *Israel Exploration Journal* 9: 149–65, 229–45.

Weiss, Z. and Netzer, E. 1996. *Promise and Redemption, A Synagogue Mosaic from Sepphoris*. Jerusalem: The Israel Museum Catalogue no. 378.

Chapter 5

The archaeology of Islam

Timothy Insoll

Introduction

Islam is a religion which is in many ways easier to assess in terms of archaeological visibility than some of the other world religions examined in this volume, such as, for example, Christianity or Hinduism. These are issues which have been considered both in Chapter 1 and elsewhere (see Insoll 1999), and is essentially due to the fact that Islam is composed of a uniform superstructure composed of the fundamentals of belief, what can be termed, 'structuring principles', with below this a diverse substructure of practices, cultures and their material manifestations, what can be termed, 'regional diversity'. Thus, it can be suggested, the presence of a Muslim should be recognisable in the archaeological record, for being a Muslim should generate certain types of material culture, specific to the faith, and reflecting its doctrines and requirements upon the believer. This, in turn, means that categories of archaeological evidence can exist, from the Atlantic to central Asia, which could indicate the presence of a Muslim community. Yet how these categories are manifest will be extremely diverse.

This chapter will examine the archaeological visibility of Islam through five categories of evidence: the mosque, the Muslim burial, dietary remains, the traditional domestic environment (with an especial focus on structures built of less durable materials), and finally, the community environment, the settlement. Other categories could have been included but again the reader is referred to Insoll (1999) for further details. The largely theoretical nature of the discussion will then be tested against material reality through considering the archaeological visibility of the Muslim community in Cambridge, England. But prior to presenting this material it is necessary to further consider whether Islam can indeed be treated as a single entity for the purposes of analysis.

Islam – unity and diversity

While acknowledging the overall existence of Islam as a structuring code to material culture, one stumbling block has been encountered, which also needs in part to be explained. This is the very existence of the notion of 'Islam' as compared to 'Islams', in other words the degree to which regional traditions, schools, sects and different nationalities within Islam and the Muslim world destroy, or at least encroach upon the idea of the cohesive whole, the ideal Muslim, from the Atlantic coast of Morocco to Indonesia, diversity which might be reflected in the archaeological record.

Antagonisms between universality and regionalism have been examined by various scholars. Eickelman and Piscatori (1990: xiii), for example, stress that 'universality competes with local communities and dogma with actualities', and that there is inherent danger in generating an essentialist view of Islam or being Muslim, with it being difficult to predict the practice and significance of Islamic faith in any given historical setting from the first principles of dogma or belief (1990: xxii, 18). By comparison Gellner has emphasised that it is the simplistic view to take 'Islam at face value' and naive to think that, 'because Muslim life is the implementation of one book and its prescriptions, therefore Muslim civilisation is homogeneous' (1981: 99). There is of course a departure point between ideals and realities, and in no way is Islam a bland uniformity across the whole of the Muslim world. Heterodoxy exists, as attested by the importance of Sufism in many areas, and by the existence of the two dominant creeds of Sunni and Shi'ah Islam (for an introduction to the origins of Islam, its requirements upon believers and component parts, omitted here for reasons of space, see Gibb and Kramers [1961], Waines [1995], Insoll [1999: 17–24]).

However, there also exists an underlying uniformity, otherwise the notion of the existence of a series of Islams, rather than a universal Islam, implies that the whole idea of a system of belief falls down, which is patently in opposition to the beliefs of the majority of Muslims, Sunni or Shi'ah. This raises the question of 'where then does one cease to be a Muslim?'. Where do you draw the line about what is acceptable if you adapt your own Islam just how you might like it? It sometimes appears as if the chipping away at the existence of an Islam in favour of various regional Islams is nonsense when one comes to consider the essential input of faith in a universal belief system, as compared to the observational rationality of usually Western social scientists. Furthermore, Gellner continues from the point quoted above, that, 'for all the indisputable diversity, the remarkable thing is the extent to which Muslim societies resemble each other'. The obvious existence of an Islam, even if only reduced to an acceptance of basic tenets, and thus of a Muslim, is reinforced by observational data from various parts of the Muslim world. In sub-Saharan Africa, for example, Muslims, though great local adaptation of Islam has taken place, are immediately recognisable as Muslims, both today, and in the past (Insoll 1996a, 1996b, 2000, in preparation). It is argued here that one Islam, rather than a series of disparate regional traditions, exists, which lends itself to archaeological investigation. Yet within this whole, of course, exists diversity, represented by different ways of life; nomadic and sedentary, town and country dweller, with ethnic, cultural and geographical factors, elements of non-observance, and varying interpretations and creeds.

Elsewhere (Insoll 1999: 12), I have suggested that it is possible to reconcile the problem of investigating universality and regionalism within the archaeology of Islam through drawing upon *Annales* theory. Namely, the conceptualisation of time at a variety of levels, long (*la longue durée*), medium (*conjonctures*) and short term (*evenements*) (Braudel 1972: 901). *La longue durée* is represented by the Islamic structuring codes, immutable elements of Muslim faith, whilst the *conjonctures* and *evenements*, either medium or short term, are represented by fashions, interpretations, and regionalism (though this can exist over the long term, it is still set apart from the essentials), which create the diversity apparent within the overall entity. However, such approaches are not directly transferable for various reasons, not least because it is not the purpose here to provide anything as presumptuous as 'general laws', or to shoehorn the evidence into fitting such theoretical 'straitjackets'. Rather, the concept of different scales of time or analysis is being borrowed, which as was explained before, serves to allow a division to be made between the unchanging elements of being Muslim, and within this, the diversity which exists and which is apparent in all areas of human endeavour, including religious belief, and its material remains.

The mosque

The obligation of prayer, one of the Five Pillars of Islam, is a structuring principle, an immutable element of being Muslim, whose material manifestation is the mosque. The second scale of analysis, that of cultural diversity as comprising regional traditions, fashions, and decorative and architectural trends is evident in the forms of the mosque. Thus, the mosque provides a useful example, the first category of material culture to be considered, of the archaeological visibility of Islam.

The criteria which define a mosque are simple: 'a wall correctly oriented towards the *qiblah*, namely the Black Stone within the Ka'bah in Mecca. No roof, no minimum size, no enclosing walls, no liturgical accessories are required' (Hillenbrand 1994: 31). Kuban (1974: 1) is even more minimalist when he mentions that, strictly speaking a mosque is not needed at all, as a Hadith records (Bukhari 7: 1), 'all the World is a *masjid*' (the place of prostrations). This negative statement would at first glance appear to be of little use in attempting to identify a Muslim community within the archaeological record. However, mosques of a form recognisable across the Islamic world developed rapidly after the establishment of Islam, as a structure for, and defined by, the requirements of prayer.

Prayer itself occurs at four levels; individually five times a day; congregationally at noon on Friday; communal (village or town prayer) at festivals; and at the level of the entire Muslim world. Material manifestations of these prayer requirements are: first, the prayer rug and a simple *masjid* or prayer hall, second, the *jami* or Friday (congregational) mosque, and third, the *musalla* (place of prayer), a common term, but sometimes used to specifically denote a place of prayer used at festivals. A physical embodiment of the fourth level of prayer does not exist, but pilgrimage to Mecca or *Hajj* can perhaps be seen as what Dickie terms, 'a congregation of all the Muslims of the World' (1978: 35). The actual act of prayer is also reflected in the form of the mosque, with the rectangular shape of the mosque sanctuary, the *haram*, reflecting the need to pray in rows parallel to the *qiblah*, the wall facing Mecca (Figure 5.1). Prayer is led by an adult male, the *Imam*, at the front. Whether women are allowed to pray in a mosque depends on doctrines followed and regional variation. Where women do pray in mosques they pray behind the men, often in a special section. Amongst the Shi'ah Friday congregational prayer is of less importance, though they have other special prayers beside the obligatory ones for various occasions (Momen 1985: 181).

The origins of the mosque and its component parts have been, and still are, much debated. However, general consensus sees the prototype in the Prophet's house in Medina. Here, a shelter of palm trunks and leaves was built on to one of the walls of the courtyard, initially on the side in the direction of Jerusalem, but following a revelation from God experienced by Muhammad the direction of prayer was changed to the side facing Mecca (Kuban 1974: 1–2). This simple structure was also built to aid in the creation of the *ummah*, the Muslim community, by functioning as a place for not only religious ceremonies, but also where social gatherings were held, religious teaching was undertaken and public proclamations were made (Gibb and Kramers 1961, Nasr 1993).

The one concern which can be isolated even in the first mosque, the Prophet's mosque, is the direction of prayer, which was ultimately fixed on Mecca and is perhaps the only universal which can be said to exist when considering the mosque as a structure. To the archaeologist this is of importance, as given a compass and an understanding of the position of Mecca in relation to the area under study, theoretically at least, the archaeological recognition of a mosque should be straightforward (however problems could arise when, for example, Mecca is due east as churches are aligned in the same direction, or as already mentioned, mosques are incorrectly aligned). Luckily, this task is facilitated by the fact that the vast majority of mosques do not only fulfil the simplest requirements of prayer,

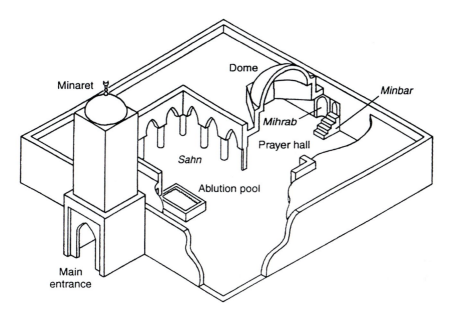

Figure 5.1 Stylised plan of mosque components in an ideal mosque (adapted from Chaudhuri 1982)

a correctly aligned *qiblah* wall, but incorporate various other features which in themselves form recognition criteria.

Primary amongst these and related to the question of orientation is the physical marker of the direction of prayer, the *mihrab*, an almost universal feature which is built into, or as a salient from, the *qiblah* wall, and forms the focus of the mosque sanctuary (Figure 5.1). From in front of the *mihrab* the prayers are led by the Imam, and although almost always a niche in form, it can be decorated in many ways. It is extremely unlikely that Muhammad's mosque had such a permanent indicator of prayer direction; the earliest *mihrab* niche at Medina dates from 705 (all dates are CE [Common Era] unless otherwise stated), though does not survive in its original form (Gibb and Kramers 1961: 343, Hillenbrand 1994: 46). Flat plaque-like *mihrabs* were also occasionally used in the early Islamic period. From the early eighth century the use of the *mihrab* spread; utilising single, or less frequently, double or multiple niches. The *mihrab* is therefore a critical indicator of the presence of a mosque, as the symbol of prayer direction in what would otherwise be a blank wall.

A variety of other features exist which could be present in a mosque, and which form further elements of the translation of the structuring principle of prayer into material culture. The *minbar*, introduced in the time of the Prophet, is a flight of sometimes movable steps placed next to the *mihrab*, from which the Imam preaches a sermon at Friday prayers. Another, and the best known visible feature of the mosque, is the minaret, which has been called the 'Symbol of Islam' (Bloom 1989) (Figure 5.1). Though common today, the original function, origins and introduction of the minaret in the eighth and ninth centuries have been the subject of debate; as a lighthouse, watchtower etc. (Gibb and Kramers 1961: 340–1, Bloom 1989, Hillenbrand 1994: 129–37). The importance of the minaret archaeologically is that in all its many forms it is a physical representation of the call to prayer. It is usually a tower, attached to or near the prayer hall containing a staircase leading to a balcony for the *muezzin* to make the call to prayer.

Further features of the mosque which might be found include an enclosed courtyard (*sahn*) attached to the sanctuary in which an ablutions area is situated, often centrally or near the entrance (Figure 5.1). Washing prior to prayer is obligatory, and thus a fountain, tap, or a pot of water should be provided for the use of worshippers, and would certainly be archaeologically recognisable. The entrance to the courtyard and thence to the sanctuary should also be mentioned. Frequently imposing and ornate, it serves as a portal between the world outside and the 'tranquil atmosphere within' (Frishman 1994: 41). A number of other features may or may not be present: a screened area for women; a raised and screened enclosure (*maqsura*) for the ruler or Imam; Qur'an stands and chests; and a *dikka*, a platform formerly used by the Muezzin to transmit responses to the prayers to the congregation before the advent of loudspeakers (Gibb and Kramers 1961, Kuban 1974, Dickie 1978).

With regard to the mosque it has proved possible to isolate a number of features which show the structuring principle in action. Furthermore, although a somewhat pessimistic position was initially taken, whereby the archaeological recognition of the mosque was stated to be orientation, it has also been shown that the archaeologist can be helped by the existence of a number of other features. For example, perhaps ninety per cent of mosques found will have a *mihrab*, and a descending scale of features which might be present can be proposed below this; minaret, ablutions area, *minbar*, defined threshold, and a variety of less common items inside what is usually a clutter free, clean prayer space lacking the paraphernalia associated with the places of worship of other world religions. Thus, it can be proposed that the requirements of the structuring principle lead to the existence of a number of largely unchanging features, which will in turn allow (and have on numerous occasions allowed) the archaeological recognition of the mosque. It is at the second scale of analysis, cultural diversity, that the existence of great variation in whether these features are present, and how they are organised and constructed, is apparent.

Cultural diversity is best exemplified by regional traditions, and these have been extensively covered elsewhere (see for example Hillenbrand 1994), and have also been usefully defined by Frishman and Khan (1994: 13) as falling into five basic categories and seven regional styles of mosque design (Arabian Heartland, Spain and North Africa; Sub-Saharan West Africa; Iran and Central Asia; Indian subcontinent; Anatolia; China; Southeast Asia). Within these categories numerous subtypes exist as defined by materials, decoration and differences in layout. With these must be considered the different types of mosque; Friday and ward mosques, collegiate, monastic, and tomb and cemetery mosques, not forgetting temporary mosques and places of prayer used for festivals and laid out by travellers and nomads. But, even allowing for this diversity, the structuring principle is almost always in operation, with minarets, thresholds, and *mihrabs* present. Moreover, although Frishman and Khan (1994: 12) deliberately exclude the mosques of the 'Modern Movement' as these take many forms, it is probable that in the vast majority the structuring principle will be in operation, above and beyond the most important requirement of correct orientation. This cultural diversity or regional traditions, can come and go, and the mosque can be adapted to suit context and fashion, but the structuring principle behind the mosque as a place of prayer, and the elements which result cannot be altered beyond certain limits.

The Muslim burial

The Muslim burial is subject to similar restrictions, and is another category of evidence, and one of primary importance, which might allow the recognition of a Muslim in the archaeological record. Throughout the Muslim world an essentially uniform funerary rite should be employed and should be straightforward, unostentatious and simple: 'the body is treated with a ceremonial which varies little in different parts of the Muslim world, and is nearly the same for men and women' (Hastings 1911: 501).

The funerary rites should entail washing the corpse immediately following death, sealing the body orifices and perfuming the body, which is then enveloped in the shroud or grave clothes. Burial is rapid and the ritual prayer or *salat* for the deceased is said either in the open in the cemetery or the mosque (frequently in the cemetery) or sometimes in the house of mourning. The stretcher or bier is carried to the place of burial by men, followed by the funeral procession. The corpse is lifted out of the bier and placed in the grave (a coffin is not usually used), the head in the direction of the *qiblah*, so that it lies on its right side with the face towards Mecca (sometimes supported in this position by bricks, or by a narrower grave-shaft). A confession of faith is said to the deceased which is believed to enable it to answer the questions posed by the interrogating angels Munkar and Nakir, and thus gain entry to paradise. The grave itself should be reasonably shallow to allow the deceased to hear the muezzin's call, but also deep enough to allow the corpse to sit up for its interrogation by Munkar and Nakir. Only the place where the head of the deceased is laid may be commemorated with a marker stone or piece of wood. However in reality great variety with regard to grave markers is found according to the Islamic legal school or sect followed and geographical area (Gibb and Kramers 1961: 89–90, 515–17, Hastings 1911: 501–2, Dickie 1978: 44–6, Simpson 1995: 241–2, 244–5).

Needless to say many exceptions to these rites occur; amongst the Shi'ah for example, Rogers (1976: 130) records that the corpse was sometimes buried with the feet in the direction of Mecca (and see Insoll 1999: 172–3). However, it is above ground that complications arise, and ideals and reality diverge, for it is the means of commemorating the dead – the funerary monument – which is subject to great variability, the 'regional diversity'. The early prohibitions on funerary architecture and commemoration of the dead possibly reflected the opposition to the pre-Islamic cult of the dead in the Arabian peninsula, and the fact that ornate tombs were considered 'symbols of worldly pomp' (Leisten 1990: 18). No special attention should be paid to the place of the dead, and they should not become the focus of worship, for all should be equal in death. Such ideals were retained by some sects until today but for others were relatively short-lived, even if disapproval for an ornamented or inscribed gravestone might persist in Muslim law (Simpson 1995: 247) (Figure 5.2). A variety of factors

Figure 5.2 Ottoman tombstones, Haydarpasha (Istanbul, Turkey) (photo T. Insoll)

contributed to a growth in the use of funerary architecture; these included the expansion of Islam beyond the Arabian peninsula and the ensuing cultural admixture, pre-Islamic survivals, and the desire to express power and authority, both secular and sacred (Hillenbrand 1994: 253–4).

Thus it can be seen that while certain exceptions have to be acknowledged (see Insoll 1999: 172–3), the treatment of the corpse prior to burial, the procedures for its actual interment, and its position within the grave, should be uniform, and vary little throughout the Muslim world. This should allow the archaeological recognition of a Muslim burial. A further 'structuring principle' allowing the archaeological recognition of a Muslim community can be proposed.

Muslim diet

Muslim diet should also be structured by religious law and in theory this should also provide another category of evidence which might indicate the existence of a Muslim community archaeologically. Issues of non-observance must be acknowledged, and differences between the Islamic schools of law recognised, but in general terms a number of binding rules exist. Three categories of food exist, *halal*, that which is lawful, *haram*, that which is prohibited, and *makruh*, that which is reprehensible, but which is not subject to the degree of prohibition as *haram*. Alcohol, spilt blood, pork, dogs, excrement, carrion, and milk of animals whose flesh is not eaten are forbidden, and a complex body of laws regulates in great detail which food is considered lawful and when exceptions concerning consumption can be made. Similarly, slaughter is subject to religious law, and an animal must be killed facing the *qiblah*, the name of God invoked and its throat cut (see Pellat 1971: 304–9, Gibb and Kramers 1961: 431–2, 556).

To the archaeologist studying a faunal assemblage it might in theory be possible to identify the remains generated by a diet structured according to these Muslim dietary laws. Pertinent questions which might be asked could include:

1   Are certain species absent in faunal assemblages, pigs and dogs for example, and is this a result of dietary avoidance?
2   Is a *halal* diet noticeable, i.e. through special butchery patterns, cut marks on bones, body parts and offal left over?
3   Are slaughter patterns different amongst herds owned by Muslims, as opposed to those of other religious groups?
4   Is the composition of a 'Muslim herd' different, and can this be recognised archaeologically?

Yet unlike the mosque or Muslim burial, it is difficult to advance beyond theory in considering the archaeological recognition of Muslim diet for when it is tested against archaeological data it is apparent that, to answer questions such as those posed above, an 'ideal' faunal assemblage is required, well-preserved and numerically abundant (see Insoll 1999: 96–9). In other words, it should be of a sort infrequently encountered by archaeologists. Thus, the structuring principle might operate, through the existence of the core dietary rules, but it is largely impossible to recognise, in this instance, the structuring principle, materially.

However, the importance of this example also lies in the fact that it raises awareness that diet, and therefore the archaeological remains, are not solely the residue of logical economic decisions; they too can be strongly affected by religious reasoning. Equally, the archaeological recognition of other components of a Muslim diet, such as drink and vegetable foodstuffs also raises problems. The ban on alcohol within Islam is well known, and this might in certain instances be archaeologically visible. Sadan (1991: 721) for instance, mentions that the use of certain receptacles is forbidden to Muslims, 'for ease with which they might be used to ferment liquids'. Nevertheless, observance of this proscription is by no means uniform. For example, physical evidence for the infringement of the prohibition on alcohol was found at Samarra in Iraq, where several tall pottery vessels dating from the mid-ninth century were found which were interpreted as wine flasks, and which led to the inference 'that there was a wine hall near the Caliph's harem at Samarra' (Talbot Rice 1971: 37).

More complex even is the recognition of the vegetable component of the Muslim diet. This is not subject to dietary law as is flesh and associated products, and thus cannot begin to be an archaeological indicator of a Muslim community in the same way, as staple food crops often remained unchanged in regions to which Islam spread. Botanical remains might however indicate the spread of crops associated with the Muslim world. Crops such as rice, sugar cane and wheat were widely diffused, but obviously they do not take on a Muslim identity! Rather at a precise point in time they can be said to be culturally associated with Islam, as Al-Hassan and Hill (1992: 212–13) discuss. For example, wheat was a staple food in Islamic agriculture in the mediaeval period, as compared to rye bread common in northern Europe, and sugar is a basic commodity which, 'owes much of its development and spread to the Islamic civilisation' (ibid.: 220).

Although only a cursory treatment of Muslim dietary law has been provided here, the importance of this fundamental area of Muslim life to the archaeologist interested in Islam has been emphasised, as have the difficulties in identifying religious influence on the material remains we encounter.

The traditional domestic environment

The domestic environment, at first glance, appears to provide an even more problematical category of evidence to consider – not only in terms of its archaeological visibility but also because, unlike the mosque, Muslim burial, or diet, it is not imbued with any overt religious importance. Yet when it is looked at in some detail it can be seen that it is not merely secular, but forms a further element which can be structured according to Muslim social requirements and therefore is another significant component of the archaeology of Islam.

The model for the Muslim household can be regarded as that of the Prophet, and the courtyard house built by the Prophet in the first year of the *hijrah* (622) in Medina as the first Muslim domestic structure. Although often seen as the progenitor of Muslim domestic space, it was in fact based on existing west Arabian architectural traditions, and the pre-Islamic architectural heritage must be acknowledged. The Prophet's house itself, as far as it has been reconstructed historically, consisted of a rectangular walled courtyard, in which livestock were kept, and on one or more sides of which were rooms for sleeping, storing goods, and for

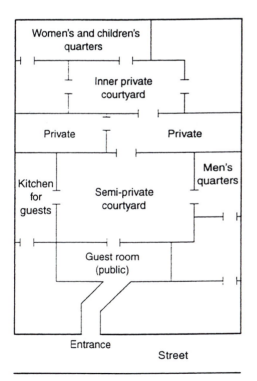

Figure 5.3 Stereotypical layout of an idealised Muslim courtyard house

each wife and her children. The house functioned as both a dwelling and a meeting place for believers (Cresswell 1932: 7, Marcais 1965: 113, Fentress 1987: 63).

Obviously, the concept of privacy was not invented by Muslims (see Insoll 1999: 64), but domestic space is referred to in both the Qur'an and the *hadith* (the traditions – the Prophet's sayings and doings), where the sacredness of the house is indicated, and strict rules to maintain domestic privacy are outlined (see Petherbridge 1978, Campo 1991). The primary and overriding concern is with privacy and the protection and seclusion of women (in certain cultural contexts referred to as purdah), and the sanctity of the family. Both wife and domestic space are to be protected and domestic life is linked to ideas of purity. To achieve this, physical space is often segregated into two spheres, be it in two halves of a tent, within a single or double courtyard, or spread over several palatial complexes (Figure 5.3). The private area for family life includes the harem, or women's quarters, which is the arena for domestic activities and from which all men except immediate male relatives (husbands, sons, brothers) are usually excluded. The second area forms a male-communal sphere usually referred to within the literature as 'public' or 'semi-public', and which can include a reception room or rooms, or area where guests (usually male) are entertained, and possibly separate men's living quarters. Numerous permutations are possible, and many devices can be used to ensure privacy.

Within the traditional courtyard house, the dominant permanent type which might be encountered archaeologically, privacy can be further maintained through a deliberate inward orientation of space. Exterior windows, which are usually few, are above street level, to avoid views inward, and the exterior walls are usually austere and undecorated and entered by a single door; a second (women's) door is sometimes present. Angled entrance ways are employed to deny the passer-by a view into the interior of the house, and guest rooms are placed close to the entrance so the family quarters are left undisturbed (Al-Azzawi 1969). Allied with the social requirements which Muslim domestic architecture might aim to satisfy, cultural and environmental factors must also be considered, and it is perhaps best to define traditional Muslim domestic architecture as a mix of varying local cultural, religious, social and environmental factors.

As with the other categories of evidence, regional diversity has to be acknowledged, but a common concern can be seen to run through the entire spectrum of Muslim domestic architecture, from the palaces of the rich, to the tents of the pastoralists. This, where observed (and this is and was frequent), is a preoccupation with maintaining privacy through gender segregation and the separation of the domains of public and private life. To the archaeologist, who for interpretative simplicity likes the existence of common codes or rules, the existence of these separate domains, however termed, is reassuring. But as with all the other categories of material culture discussed, exceptions do occur, and how space is demarcated can vary and need not necessarily be fixed. As Carsten and Hugh-Jones note, 'we should then be wary about describing the house as a structure of unchanging gendered oppositions' (1995: 41).

Yet, the existence of these public/private spatial domains means that a definable Muslim domestic space exists. However, we can recognise a Muslim domestic space not merely because of a spatial divide; furnishings, inscriptions, individuals, all create the image. But it is when we come to try and recognise a domestic space archaeologically, basing this identification solely upon the existence of these separate domains, that difficulties arise. A terraced house in Cambridge, England, for example, reduced to a ground plan or standing as an empty structure, and though perhaps inhabited by a Muslim family for many years, and formerly curtained or partitioned into separate areas, would defy identification. It is not possible to define a Muslim domestic space utilising plan alone; in this manner it could not be set apart from a Christian or Hindu domestic structure which shows privacy concerns. To repeat, not all Muslim domestic structures do or have ever maintained a public/private divide, and Muslims do not and have never maintained a monopoly on privacy. The only way in which the Muslim domestic structure could be archaeologically identified is if it is found in company with other categories of archaeological evidence. Thus we have identified a further important criteria for the archaeology of Islam, that to strengthen the identification of the former presence of a Muslim community archaeologically, it is necessary to recover several categories of evidence in association with each other.

Assuming that we are investigating the Muslim domestic environment as part of a complete package, the practical issues which might be of interest to the archaeologist can best be summarised as the axes of investigation; how can Muslim domestic space be visualised both horizontally and vertically in buildings, and how can the essential structuring principles be recognised in more ephemeral materials.

If we concentrate upon the latter aspect, it should be noted (though is often neglected) that both nomadic pastoralists and sedentary agriculturists living in structures built in less durable materials have obviously been attracted to Islam since the beginnings of the religion. The fact that such people frequently live in shelters constructed of ephemeral materials, cloth, skin or reeds for example, does not mean that they were excluded from structuring their domestic space according to Islamic custom.

Amongst the Bedouin of the Arabian peninsula, for example, the customary shelter, the textile 'black tent' is divided into men's and women's spaces (see Feilberg 1944, Faegre 1979). This separation is maintained through a dividing curtain. The men's side, usually the smaller, is covered with carpets and cushions for guests. Here also will be a hearth for preparing coffee and all the accompanying accoutrements. The larger women's side is the main living and working area, which will not usually be seen by any other man except the tent owner. Yet in other areas and with other ethnic groups explicit domestic spatial separation is not so clear. The Qashqa'i of the Zagros Mountains in Iran do not divide the tent structurally into male and female sections, though in practice such a division, of tasks and entertaining, does occur (Beck 1978: 356–8). However, although internal physical boundaries might not be created, manifestations of a concern with privacy may be present. One such feature can be the orientation of the tent or indeed of the whole camp. With the Qashqa'i, for example, although they might not subdivide the tent, the tents themselves are oriented so that no tent entrance faces another (Beck 1978: 357).

Although we cannot directly transfer from the past into the present, it is also reasonable to suggest that information gained from ethnography has some bearing upon the tented domestic environment in the past. It can be seen that variety is found, and the degree to which space is structured into public and private domains, male and female spaces, varies greatly, and in many instances no such demarcation exists at all. Once again we are largely concerned with an ideal, but where such a spatial separation exists could it be archaeologically recognisable? The archaeological recognition of a tented domestic space which has been structured by possible Muslim requirements is difficult, yet this is not an impossible undertaking. Whereas nomads are frequently attested archaeologically, evidence which might allow the recognition of a division of domestic space is more elusive. Recent research in southern Jordan isolated a number of features which could attest to this (Banning and Köhler-Rollefson 1992: 195). In recently occupied nomadic encampments near Beidha there were two hearths within the tents, the larger one placed in the centre of (or just outside) the tent (itself represented by an area cleared of stones and blanketed by sheep and goat dung) which was used by the women for cooking, and a smaller one used by men for coffee-making.

The existence of such features could illustrate that an internal division had existed within a tent, possibly reinforced by the patterning of domestic items and faunal remains within the demarcated area. To make such an identification more secure, physical evidence for the partition would be needed, such as lines of stones to hold a curtain in place. Avni (1992: 245) found that just such an arrangement was used to strengthen tents externally in pre-Islamic contexts in the Negev desert. Thus, it can be argued that in certain cases it should be possible to archaeologically recognise the former presence of a tented domestic space which had been structured according to different spatial domains, but to take this identification one stage further, to say it was structured by Muslim social codes, requires more than an outline of stones on the ground. Other categories of archaeological evidence are required as well.

The community environment

The final category of evidence to be considered, the Muslim community environment or settlement presents a further dimension, for it is a distinct entity, but it is also an agglomeration of mosques, houses, tombs, and many other types of structure not considered here. Furthermore, it too, as with the domestic environment, need not be (and usually is not) imbued with overt religious significance in the Muslim world, but equally functions in a socially important manner within Muslim life, and can be archaeologically recognisable as such.

The Muslim city has in the past provided a convenient unit of study, and based upon a limited number of examples, mainly drawn from North Africa and the Near East, wide ranging generalisations were made as to the overall character of the Muslim city everywhere. These studies were one of the first manifestations of the Orientalist approach, whereby the structure of the city was defined in terms of religious requirements, and a similar form was said to exist from Morocco to Indonesia. This process of the creation of a stereotypical Muslim city has been examined by a number of scholars, most notably Bonine (1977) and Abu-Lughod (1987), and more recently, region by region across the Muslim world (excluding sub-Saharan Africa, and south and Southeast Asia) by Haneda and Miura (1994). The stereotype created, based on North African or sometimes Syrian examples, comprised a standard kit of elements; the *medina*, or central urban entity, within which was the *casbah* or walled citadel, a city within the city containing the ruler's residence, mosque, barracks, stores etc. The *medina* would be walled with several gates, and perhaps surrounded by *rabad* or *rabat* – outer suburbs. The inhabitants lived in distinct quarters according to ethnic or economic background in groups of courtyard houses connected by winding alleyways and narrow streets, supposedly characteristic of the 'Oriental' or Islamic city (see Figure 5.4). The *medina* would also contain a number of core elements: the Friday mosque, other local mosques, *suq* or *suqs* (markets) arranged spatially according to the goods sold, baths, hostels for travellers, schools, shops, cemeteries perhaps (usually outside the city), and all the other prerequisites of urban life.

But is it necessary to deny completely the existence of any common features within Islamic cities or Muslim settlements, and to deny religion as a structuring principle to a greater or lesser degree? Perhaps as is now to be expected, it is here suggested that a 'mix and match' approach is advocated, whereby certain common features could be expected, but these will by no means be the same in every situation (if anything questions of scale will rule this out, a village will obviously not have all the facilities of the city). A complex of factors underlie the structuring of a Muslim settlement.

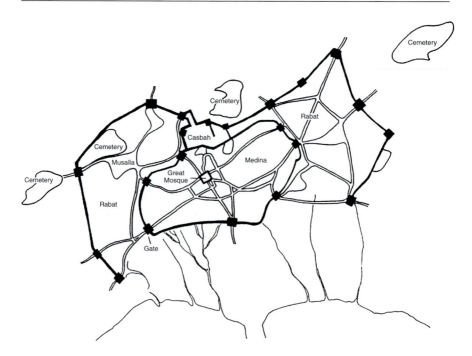

Figure 5.4 Stereotypical city layout based on Tunis (adapted from Hakim 1986)

Second, is a Muslim settlement, following the loose definition just proposed, archaeologically recognisable? It can be, but this does not mean that the sort of criteria just outlined will be found in every instance. Typological approaches are weak; not every city will have a walled citadel, surrounded by a *medina* and outer suburbs, defined by quarters of court-yard houses with an emphasis upon inward orientation, alongside ward mosques, with a central mosque/palace and administration complex either inside or outside of the citadel. *Suqs* need not be centrally placed and graded according to the trades or goods being sold and the degree to which they might be considered polluting. *Madrasahs* (religious schools), cemeteries, water-storage facilities, caravanserais, *hammams* (baths) and *maristans* (hospitals) need not all be present. Only in a few selective contexts, as in North Africa and Islamic Spain where a great degree of uniformity in city type appears to have existed, may near-complete examples of the model be found.

Yet it is true to say that many of these elements can be present, and that these constitute a Muslim city, as opposed to a non-Muslim one. It cannot be disputed that core characteristic elements exist, even if only reduced to their simplest form of a mosque and Muslim burials in a settlement, therefore allowing its identification as Muslim. It is these more basic criteria which are more likely to be applicable to smaller towns and villages, and which could allow their archaeological recognition. Certain criteria do exist which set apart a Muslim settlement from a non-Muslim one from Senegal to Saudi Arabia, from Kazakhstan to Indonesia. They are far from mirror images of each other, and are subject to many structuring factors other than religious requirements, but at the same time exhibit certain aspects in common which relate to a mutual religion.

A much looser structure is needed in assessing the Muslim settlement, and its archaeological recognition; some core features will be present, but a pre-ordained blue-print does not exist. Possible keys to identification might include all or any of the above, but even these changed over time. For example, it might be possible to say that narrow streets and alleyways with courtyard houses having largely blank facades and multiple dead ends were due to Muslim concerns with privacy and the protection of the family, but in some instances this might be due to the climate (providing shade), or as Bulliett (1975: 224) has suggested, to the existence of a society without wheels, rendering wider streets unnecessary. The invocation of a single factor to explain structuring features behind Muslim settlements is often impossible, but neither should economic or practical necessity be given precedence over social or religious needs. To repeat, which components are present and how they are manifest will vary, as will the structuring principles behind both the development and form of the Muslim settlement.

A case study: the Cambridge mosque and cemetery

Several categories of evidence have been isolated which can to varying degrees attest archaeologically to the former presence of a Muslim community. It is also evident that to this point specific archaeological examples have been largely omitted, and that discussion has remained on a theoretical note. It is now pertinent to bring in a case study, that of the Cambridge Muslim community and the possible archaeological visibility of their mosque and burials.

The Muslim community in Cambridge numbers some two thousand individuals, having grown rapidly from about seventy in 1973 (CEN 1973). The ethnic origins and social backgrounds of the community are diverse, with the majority from Pakistan and Bangladesh, and others from India, Turkey, Morocco, East Africa, and Saudi Arabia, for example. Some twenty converted European families also form part of the community. Shopkeepers, restaurateurs, engineers and many other occupations are represented (CEN 1990), and not surprisingly, considering that Cambridge is a university town, university students and staff, visiting scholars, and researchers, are well represented. The presence of the university and a

Figure 5.5 Former mosque at 175 Chesterton Road, Cambridge (photo T. Insoll)

large sector of high-technology industry does in fact mean that the Cambridge Muslim community is probably more mixed than in other medium-sized cities in Britain. However, although it might be convenient for the sake of academic procedure to break the community down into its component parts, it should be noted that the mosque authorities prefer to regard the community as one unit, superseding ethnic identities, thus, it could be said, acting in the true spirit of how the Muslim community should be conceived.

As well as growing in numbers over the past twenty-five years, the community has also grown in strength and in actions, mirroring processes apparent across the whole of Britain where the number of registered mosques has grown from 16 in 1966 to 452 in 1990, the latest figures found (Nielsen 1995: 45). Originally, in Cambridge, the incipient community used a room in the City Guildhall for prayers (CEN 1973), obviously not ideal, but which could be adapted, albeit temporally, as requirements dictated. In 1972 an ordinary terraced house of a type found

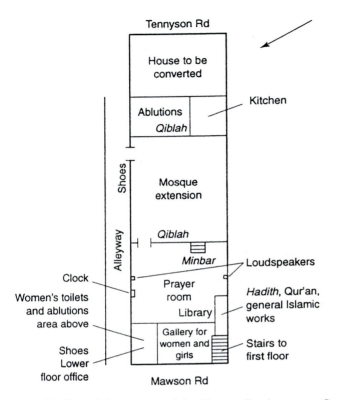

Figure 5.6 Plan of the interior of the Mawson Road mosque, Cambridge
(not to scale)

all over Britain, dating from the late Victorian period, was bought as a
more permanent place of community and prayer, number 175 Chesterton
Road, where the two small downstairs rooms were used as a mosque (see
Figure 5.5). Unfortunately, this was found to be unsatisfactory, as the house
was obviously built without the direction of Mecca as a primary concern,
a fact commented upon by a reporter from the local newspaper, the
Cambridge Evening News, 'those praying are in lines at an angle across the
room, facing the south-east corner' (CEN 1976). A further problem was
that planning permission to use the house as a mosque had not been
obtained, therefore the City Council served an enforcement notice, which
was given a stay of execution whilst another property was sought (CEN
1981a, b).

The third, and current, location for a place of prayer which was chosen
was originally a gospel hall, then a meeting house of the Plymouth Brethren,
and finally a social centre for the Co-operative Society. It began to be
used as a mosque in September 1982 (CEN 1982, 1988). Although still

not ideal, in many ways the new location, which became the Abu Bakr Siddiq Islamic Centre in Mawson Road, was much more suitable, primarily because the orientation is right, prayer can be said, by chance, on exactly the right alignment by making use of the original layout of the building, which is also, being a hall, relatively open and spacious. Second, the former choir or stalls area upstairs serves as a ready-made area for women. The necessary alterations have been minimal, as a local reporter again comments, 'those who look for minarets or listen for the distant sound of the imam . . . will however, be disappointed. The church hall-like building has mundane sloping roofs, while any sounds from the imam would be lost in the roar of nearby traffic' (CEN 29/11/85).

As Figure 5.6 shows, the interior of the mosque is plain and uncluttered. It is divided into two parts, the former church meeting hall which contains the cloakroom, women's area and one prayer hall where a *minbar* and copies of the Qur'an and other religious texts are stored, and adjacent to this a second prayer hall has been added in which the imam stands to lead Friday prayers, directed via a microphone relay throughout the building. Due east of the *qiblah* wall are the ablutions area and a kitchen. Entrance is via two ways, through the main western doorway, or via a passage which leads into the second prayer hall. Noticeably, a *mihrab* is absent. At normal daily prayers between thirty to fifty people are usually present, but for Friday prayers and at festivals these numbers increase dramatically, highlighting the lack of space. The primary disadvantages of the mosque which were cited were the general lack of space and the inconvenient position of the ablutions area; there was also a preference for a building aligned so more worshippers could be accommodated parallel to the *qiblah* (T. Ali pers. comm. 11/9/96). A programme of rebuilding is planned to solve these difficulties, and ideally the sentiments expressed in 1981 still hold true, to build a mosque 'in the classical style with a gold-decorated dome and a minaret' (CEN 1981b) – but finances are unlikely to allow this option, even if the planning authorities were amenable to such a suggestion.

The development of the Cambridge Muslim community over the past twenty-five years, and the resulting material culture, is important to the themes discussed in this volume in a variety of ways. First, and fundamentally, is the fact that this example shows that a Muslim sacred space, no different in ethos to that encountered in the perceived Islamic heartlands, is now to be found in a new environment. It is no longer possible to think of religions such as Islam as confined to specific places, religious diasporas have been established leading to the blurring of the edges of what were previously thought to be (erroneously) geographically religious monoblocs. Second, although the material culture translation of the church hall to the requirements for a mosque are minimal, this structure is unmistakably a mosque when one sets foot inside. Its function as the centre of worship

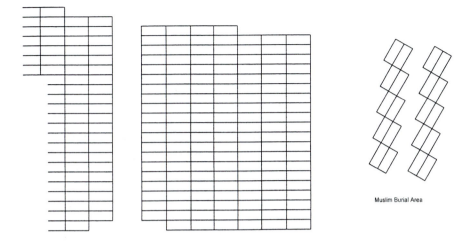

Muslim Burial Area

Figure 5.7 Plan of burial plots in Newmarket Road cemetery, Cambridge
        (not to scale)

remains the same as that evident in the Arabian peninsula. But how would
the archaeologist define this structure in the form it is today 200 years
hence? If the contents were complete, the identification would be immediate, but divest of these and levelled to its foundations it would be much more
difficult, only an empty space with an east–west orientation would remain,
no traces of *mihrab*, minaret or *minbar*, thus little differentiating it from any
other hall. In this respect it provides a sobering reminder of what can elude
the archaeologist, and illustrates what the archaeologist interested in world
religions, or any religion, has to contend with.

   More positive from an archaeological perspective is the burial ground
of the Cambridge Muslim community within the Cambridge City cemetery. The growth in the Muslim community has meant a burial ground
was also needed. This has had obvious material culture implications, clearly
visible in Figure 5.7 where the Muslim section of this cemetery is both
spatially separated and oriented in a different direction from the blocks
of non-Muslim, and, in the majority, Christian graves. This would be
recognisable archaeologically, even if all surface indications had gone, and
the presence of a Muslim community, bearing in mind the points made
about relying upon one category of evidence, would be recognisable.

Conclusions

This brief analysis of what might indicate the presence of a Muslim or Muslim community archaeologically has indicated to what extent the evidence can vary, and the often wide gap which exists between theory and practical, i.e. archaeological, reality. Yet although caution has to be exercised, the existence of distinct categories of evidence subject to what have been termed 'structuring principles' have been shown to exist, ranging from core features of mosques, Muslim burials, and dietary rules, to an emphasis upon privacy in the traditional domestic environment, and the possible presence of certain elements within a Muslim settlement, or what was better termed, the 'community environment'. The oft-quoted maxim, usually from a secular Western viewpoint, that 'Islam is more than just a religion but a way of life', has been shown to be rendered correct materially.

Yet it must also not be forgotten that much of what has been presented is an ideal scenario, an ideal Islamic material culture, and it is very unlikely that such a 'suite' of evidence would ever be found in totality. Exceptions to every proposed structuring principle can, and will occur, in all probability outweighing the residue of orthodox behaviour. People will be buried with gravegoods, not all Muslims lived in courtyard houses, mosques can be misaligned and built without a *mihrab*, alcohol was drunk, the list continues. Equally, traditional criteria are of little validity in many areas of the modern Muslim world, but people are still Muslims, and it is possible to be a Muslim with few outward manifestations. Archaeology can and does attest to this, and comparative studies illustrate how flawed it is to create an ideal Muslim, who just does not exist, except perhaps in the Arabian Nights, or in a Hollywood stereotype of this whereby a landscape studded with minarets, and peopled with characters wearing turbans, baggy trousers, and shoes with pointed toes curling up is created. Many Muslims do not live life according to Qur'anic prescript or the injunction of Islamic law. The notions of ideals and realities are both plainly apparent.

Thus, in the face of the problems outlined, it could be asked what was the purpose of the exercise if, for example, one of the main conclusions is the recognition of the fact that the gulf between ideals or 'structuring principles' and reality or 'cultural diversity' is largely insurmountable? This makes us consider the positive points which have also been isolated, not least the practical advantages of illustrating that it is possible to consider religion as exerting a possible influence over all areas of life, and thus the archaeology of religion as constituting the residue of this 'total picture'. All aspects of life, from birth in the domestic environment to death and burial, can be structured according to religious, and the resultant social, codes. Furthermore, to end as the volume from which this summary was drawn ended (Insoll 1999: 232), it has been shown how the archaeology of Islam is of relevance for all of us, both in offering a further dimension of material culture of which to be aware, as was illustrated through the Cambridge case study, but also because of the conceptual implications in an era where we are constantly reminded of the globalisation processes at work around us. The archaeology of Islam is not a Muslim archaeology but everyone's archaeology.

Note

Parts of this chapter were originally published in *The Archaeology of Islam*. They are reproduced here with permission from Blackwell Publishers.

References

Abu-Lughod, J.L. 1987. The Islamic City – Historic Myth, Islamic Essence, and Contemporary Relevance. *International Journal of Middle Eastern Studies* 19: 155–76.

Al-Azzawi, S.H. 1969. Oriental Houses in Iraq. In Oliver, P. (ed.), *Shelter and Society*. London: Barrie and Jenkins. pp. 91–102.

Al-Hassan, A.Y. and Hill, D.R. 1992. *Islamic Technology. An Illustrated History*. Cambridge: Cambridge University Press.

Avni, G. 1992. Survey of Deserted Bedouin Campsites in the Negev Highlands and its Implications for Archaeological Research. In Bar-Yosef, O. and Khazanov, A. (eds), *Pastoralism in the Levant. Archaeological Materials in Anthropological Perspectives*. Madison: Prehistory Press. pp. 241–54.

Banning, E.B. and Köhler-Rollefson, I. 1992. Ethnographic Lessons for the Pastoral Past: Camp Remains near Beidha, Southern Jordan. In Bar-Yosef, O. and Khazanov, A. (eds), *Pastoralism in the Levant. Archaeological Materials in Anthropological Perspectives*. Madison: Prehistory Press. pp. 181–201.

Beck, L. 1978. Women among Qashqa'i Nomadic Pastoralists in Iran. In Beck, L. and Keddie, N. (eds), *Women in the Muslim World*. Cambridge, Mass.: Harvard University Press. pp. 351–73.

Bloom, J. 1989. Minaret, Symbol of Islam. *Oxford Studies in Islamic Art* 7. Oxford: Oxford University Press.

Bonine, M.E. 1977. From Uruk to Casablanca. Perspectives on the Urban Experience of the Middle East. *Journal of Urban History* 3: 141–80.

Braudel, F. 1972. *The Mediterranean and the Mediterranean World in the Age of Phillip II*. London: Collins.

Bulliet, R.W. 1975. *The Camel and the Wheel*. Cambridge, Mass.: Harvard University Press.

Campo, J.E. 1991. *The Other Sides of Paradise. Explorations into the Religious Meanings of Domestic Space in Paradise*. Columbia: University of South Carolina Press.

Carsten, J. and Hugh-Jones, S. (eds). 1995. *About the House. Lévi-Strauss and Beyond*. Cambridge: Cambridge University Press.

CEN 1973. Moslems Plan Mosque in City House. *Cambridge Evening News*, 26 January.

CEN 1976. Terraced House is Mecca for City's Islamic Faith. *Cambridge Evening News*, 6 July.

CEN 1981a. Moslems in City can keep Spiritual Home. *Cambridge Evening News*, 12 February.

CEN 1981b. Cash Available for Building Mosque in City. *Cambridge Evening News*, 21 July.

CEN 1982. Muslims Find New Home. *Cambridge Evening News*, 6 September.

CEN 1985. Peaceful Haven where Muslim Faithful Meet. *Cambridge Evening News*, 29 November.

CEN 1988. Small Building is Spiritual Centre for County Muslims. *Cambridge Evening News*, 9 June.

CEN 1990. Untitled. *Cambridge Evening News*, 13 September.

Chaudhri, R.A. 1982. *Mosque. Its Importance in the Life of a Muslim*. London: London Mosque.

Creswell, K.A.C. 1932. *Early Muslim Architecture (Vol. 1)*. Oxford: Clarendon Press.

Dickie, J. 1978. Allah and Eternity: Mosques, Madrasas and Tombs. In Michell, G. (ed.), *Architecture of the Islamic World*. London: Thames and Hudson. pp. 15–47.

Eickelman, D.F. and Piscatori, J. (eds). 1990. *Muslim Travellers. Pilgrimage, Migration, and the Religious Imagination*. London: Routledge.

Faegre, T. 1979. *Tents. Architecture of the Nomads*. London: John Murray.

Feilberg, C.C. 1944. *La Tente Noire*. Copenhagen: National Museum of Ethnography.

Fentress, E. 1987. The House of the Prophet: North African Islamic Housing. *Archeologia Medievale* 14: 47–68.

Frishman, M. 1994. Islam and the Form of the Mosque. In Frishman, M. and Khan, H.-U. (eds), *The Mosque. History, Architectural Development and Regional Diversity*, London: Thames and Hudson. pp. 17–41.

Frishman, M. and Khan, H.-U. (eds). 1994. *The Mosque. History, Architectural Development and Regional Diversity*. London: Thames and Hudson.

Gellner, E. 1981. *Muslim Society*. Cambridge: Cambridge University Press.

Gibb, H.A.R. and Kramers, J.H. (eds). 1961. *The Shorter Encyclopedia of Islam*. Leiden: E.J. Brill.

Hakim, B.S. 1986. *Arabic-Islamic Cities. Building and Planning Principles*. London: Kegan Paul.

Haneda, M. and Miura, T. (eds). 1994. *Islamic Urban Studies. Historical Review and Perspectives*. London: Kegan Paul International.

Hastings, J. 1911. *Encyclopedia of Religion and Ethics*. Edinburgh: T. & T. Clark.

Hillenbrand, R. 1994. *Islamic Architecture. Form, Function and Meaning*. Edinburgh: Edinburgh University Press.

Insoll, T. 1996a. *Islam, Archaeology and History. Gao Region (Mali) Ca. AD 900–1250*. Cambridge Monographs in African Archaeology 39. BAR International Series 647. Oxford: Tempus Reparatum.

Insoll, T. 1996b. The Archaeology of Islam in sub-Saharan Africa: A Review. *Journal of World Prehistory* 10: 439–504.

Insoll, T. 1999. *The Archaeology of Islam* (Social Archaeology Series). Oxford: Blackwell.

Insoll, T. 2000. (with other contributions). *Urbanism, Archaeology and Trade. Further Observations on the Gao Region (Mali) The 1996 Fieldseason Results*. BAR S829. Oxford: British Archaeological Reports.

Insoll, T. Forthcoming. *The Archaeology of Islam in Sub-Saharan Africa* (Cambridge World Archaeology). Cambridge: Cambridge University Press.

Kuban, D. 1974. *Muslim Religious Architecture*. Leiden: E.J. Brill.

Leisten, T. 1990. Between Orthodoxy and Exegesis: Some Aspects of Attitudes in the Shari'a Toward Funerary Architecture. *Muqarnas* 7: 12–22.

Marcais, G. 1965. Dar. *The Encyclopedia of Islam (Second Edition. Volume 2)*. Leiden: E.J. Brill. pp. 113–15.

Momen, M. 1985. *An Introduction to Shi'i Islam. The History and Doctrines of Twelver Shi'ism*. Oxford: George Ronald.

Nasr, A.M. 1993: The Structure of Society in Pre-Islamic Arabia and the Impact of the Hijra: A Traditional Archaeology. In Netton, I.R. (ed.), *Golden Roads. Migration, Pilgrimage and Travel in Medieval and Modern Islam*. Richmond: Curzon Press. pp. 3–10.

Nielsen, J. 1995: *Muslims in Western Europe*. Edinburgh: Edinburgh University Press.

Pellat, Ch. 1971. Hayawan. *The Encyclopedia of Islam (Second Edition, Volume 3)*. Leiden: E.J. Brill. pp. 304–9.

Petherbridge, G.T. 1978. The House and Society. In Michell, G. (ed.), *Architecture of the Islamic World*. London: Thames and Hudson. pp. 193–208.

Rogers, M. 1976. *The Spread of Islam*. Oxford: Elsevier.

Simpson, St J. 1995. Death and Burial in the Late Islamic Near East: Some Insights from Archaeology and Ethnography. In Campbell, S. and Green, A. (eds), *The Archaeology of Death in the Ancient Near East*. Oxford: Oxbow Books. pp. 240–51.

Talbot Rice, D. 1971. *Islamic Painting. A Survey*. Edinburgh: Edinburgh University Press.

Waines, D. 1995. *An Introduction to Islam*. Cambridge: Cambridge University Press.

Chapter 6

The archaeology of Christianity in global perspective

Paul Lane

> Christianity stands or falls with the tie that binds it to its unique historical origin. It originates at a definite historical moment and at all subsequent points in its history it explicitly and elaborately refers back to that moment.
>
> Connerton (1989: 46)

Introduction

In the space of roughly two thousand years, Christianity has grown from being a marginal sect restricted to a minor province on the eastern margins of the Roman world, to being one of the largest world religions with followers spread across all five continents. Perhaps inevitably, given its current geographical extent and the diverse cultural backgrounds of its many believers, Christianity today is characterised as much by its internal division into different denominations and sects as it is by any single, shared set of beliefs. Significantly, these differences lie not just in variations in liturgy and practice between one branch and another, but also in terms of origins, belief and matters of theology. Moreover, while organisations such as the World Council of Churches seek to create a sense of harmony and to heal rifts between different sections of the Church, the number of branches of Christianity continues to grow at an ever increasing rate (in 1999, for example, there were at least 33 recognised denominations [Peterson 1999]). In the light of this, any attempt to write an 'archaeology' of Christianity faces a number of problems, not least of which is trying to find an all-encompassing definition of the fundamentals of the Christian faith. For, without such an understanding although it may be possible to identify correctly aspects of Christian iconography and other material symbols, in the absence of supporting literary sources the chances of unravelling what these symbols meant to the individuals who either encountered or deployed them seem positively remote.

To this dilemma must be added a further problem, namely, that a great many archaeologists, as with the world at large, have tended to equate

Christianity with Western Christianity, and, more generally, with Western beliefs and ideology. There are, of course, good grounds for such a perception, since the global economic expansion of Western European societies from the fifteenth century onwards has played a major role in the expansion of Christianity and its adoption by millions of individuals in other parts of the world. Equally, those values which are generally held to characterise Western civilisation are, and have always been, closely bound up with the beliefs, ethics and views on morality associated with the Protestant and Roman Catholic traditions. Yet, as anyone, for example, who is familiar with any of the numerous so-called 'African' churches will be aware, belief in a Christian God and in the resurrection of Christ need not in any way betoken acceptance of any or all of the values that have come to be associated with Western civilisation.

Trying to account, in totality, for the spiritual values of the many and varied branches of Christianity and their material expressions is well beyond the scope of the chapter (for examples of regional studies that combine historical, archaeological and art historical sources, see Gerster 1970, Graham 1998, Morris 1997, Pound 1999, Pringle 1992, 1998, Rodwell 1981, Thomas 1971). It is, nevertheless, perhaps possible to address some of the problems of interpretation that are posed by this diversity by first deliberating on how the adoption of and adherence to a particular set of religious beliefs come to be manifested in the daily workings of a society and the everyday practice of its members. To put this another way, religious buildings and iconography, burials, and the physical trappings of religious orders and the clergy are all important material expressions of Christianity which bear testimony to its practice, and are as worthy of archaeological study as any other class of physical remains. However, such studies, if conducted in isolation and without due reference to the broader contexts in which such material symbols operated, are unlikely to be able to proffer any meaningful insight into the reasons why Christianity has had so much appeal to so many widely differing populations over the last two millennia, or how the adoption of this faith impinged on their lives. In their place are required more nuanced, contextual and landscape oriented approaches which link the overtly religious material elements of these societies with the quotidian, and an abandonment of the 'checklist' type of approach that has characterised so many previous attempts at the archaeological investigation of religion.

Archaeological approaches to the study of Christianity

The archaeological study of Christianity has had a rather chequered history. Typically, the primary concerns have been with the archaeological recognition of the adoption of Christianity in particular geographical settings, and with detailed description of the physical and iconographic characteristics of Christian art, architecture and archaeological remains in those contexts where the prevalence of Christian beliefs can generally be assumed. Moreover, at least until recently, much of this work has been largely text-driven such that archaeological methods were used principally as a means of verifying written historical sources, with interpretation of the evidence being more or less guided by specifically Christian treaties.

While such approaches have considerable value, and the integration of written and archaeological data remains an essential component of current research, in the majority of cases these earlier approaches made little effort either to explain the processes of conversion to Christianity, or to account for the occurrence of particular material expressions of Christian belief. Instead, reliance was placed on the definition of relevant traits which might betoken the adoption of Christianity in any given context. The use of such lists has been especially common in studies of Roman Britain, for example, at least since Radford's (1968) suggestion that the presence in early Romano-British contexts of inhumation burials, aligned east–west and lacking grave-goods could well be indicative of the adoption of Christian beliefs.

More recent research, however, has shown that while checklists can prove helpful in the task of interpreting particular archaeological contexts, they rarely, if ever, have universal applicability. Thus, for example, it has been established that in some parts of Britain the practice of burying the dead without grave-goods was not unknown during the pre-Roman Iron Age, and hence its occurrence within Romano-British times need not betoken the adoption of Christianity (Leech 1980). Equally, certain Christians may well have been buried with grave-goods, as has been attested in a variety of better documented cases from other parts of the world. By the same token, it is also recognised that a much wider range of evidence from Romano-British contexts can be regarded as potential indicators of a conversion to Christianity than those recognised by Radford. Watts (1989), for example, has shown that from the mid-fourth century CE onwards, there is an increased presence of infant burials in extra-mural cemeteries, and this marks a significant shift in burial practice from earlier centuries when infants were typically disposed of within domestic and urban deposits, rather than in formal graves. This change in practice, she argues, arose from differences in belief between Christians and pagans as to whether infants possessed a soul.

The complexity and unevenness of conversions to Christianity in Britain during the fourth and fifth centuries CE are also evident from other contexts and classes of material, such as the mixed sacro-religious symbolism found in the so-called 'ambivalent' floor-mosaics and wall-paintings which contain combinations of Christian and pre-Christian imagery and motifs

(Black 1986). A similar diversity is also evident in the earliest Romano British churches, such as those at Silchester, Richborough and Icklingham, which exhibit little consistency in either their layout or architectural features. They also contain traits, such as the presence of an apse or font, which were by no means unique to Christianity (Cookson 1987).

Interpreting Christian burials and iconography

The difficulty of linking the occurrence of particular archaeological traits with the introduction and adoption of new religious beliefs has often been compounded by the lack of consistency in such attempts. This is well illustrated in a recent study by Almut Schülke (1999) of changing archaeological approaches to the study of Christianisation in south-western Germany between the Rhine and Danube rivers. Occupied by a people known as the Alamanni, this area lay beyond the limit of the Roman Empire, and little is known from historical sources of the process of Christianisation here save that it was probably complete by the end of the seventh century, well after the imposition of Merovingian authority. Archaeological evidence for Christianity includes a number of wooden churches of sixth- and seventh-century date, of which some have associated burials, and isolated examples of Christian iconography. By far the most important source of information, however, comes from the numerous cemeteries of late fifth- to late seventh-century date known as *Reihengräberfelder*. Typically, these contain many inhumation burials, often oriented east–west, some of which lack grave-goods while others are replete with such objects including ones with Christian symbols. The latter include decorated crosses made from gold foil (Figure 6.1), that were placed on the face or chest of the corpse, and various artefacts such as fibulae, belt-buckles, and sword-knobs decorated with crosses, fish and other Christian motifs (ibid.: 80–3).

As Schülke's review indicates, archaeological approaches to the interpretation of this evidence have undergone a number of important changes. In the mid-nineteenth century, when the first interpretations were published, it was assumed that the *Reihengräberfelder* were pagan cemeteries because of the presence of grave-goods. Subsequently, any grave with an east–west orientation was interpreted as a Christian burial, whereas the inclusion of grave-goods was seen as a syncretic fusion with earlier 'traditions'. Moreover, the co-existence of burials containing artefacts decorated with Christian symbols and those with seemingly non-Christian items was taken as evidence of a degree of tolerance between pagan and Christian Alamanni. During the early part of the twentieth century there was another interpretative shift, with the consequence that qualitative and quantitative variations in grave-goods between individual burials came to be regarded, primarily, as indicators of social rank rather than religious belief. Graves found to contain objects decorated with Christian symbols, such as the

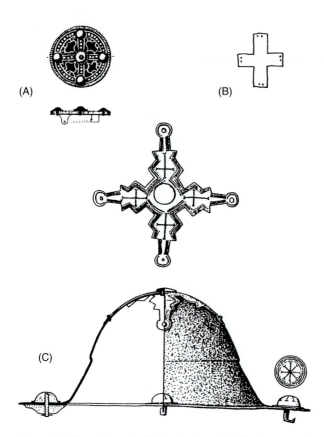

Figure 6.1 Examples of a Christian brooch (A), decorated cross (B) and shield boss (C) found in Alamanni graves (Reprinted by permission of Sage Publications Ltd from Schülke, A. 'On Christianization and grave-finds' in *European Journal of Archaeology* 1999: 84, Fig. 3 © Sage Publications Ltd)

decorated crosses, were still interpreted as being Christian burials, but now principally because of an unverified assumption that it was members of the Alamannic elite who were the first to adopt the new religion. Conversely, burials which lacked grave-goods but were nevertheless aligned east–west (and thus, could be said to fit most closely the ideal style of Christian burial), have been virtually disregarded in discussions on the presumption that they represented the graves of servants and other less well-off members of society. However, as Schülke points out, objects decorated with Christian symbols could as easily have been placed in pagan burials for a whole variety of reasons, thereby calling into question the reliance on the presence of such items to infer Christianisation (ibid.: 86–93).

Table 6.1 Socio-symbolic referents of different burial localities in the southern Netherlands, c. mid-sixth to mid-eighth century CE (after Theuws 1999)

Type of locality used for burial	Phase I	Phase II	Socio-symbolic referents
Discrete, communal cemetery	X	X	Old, local co-resident group, pre-Christian ancestors
Farmyard cemetery		X	Individual household, new claims to land
Basilicae chapel		X	Commemoration of individual land-owner, allegiance to land-owning elite
Major church or other cult centre		X	New Christian community

As this example suggests, burial practices are also related to wider strategies of social power and the construction of identity (Parker Pearson 1982), and in a community exposed to new or changing religious beliefs a number of different options may present themselves. Consequently, families and households may find it expedient to pursue a variety of different strategies so as to maintain their ties with, and influence within, different social spheres. This point has been well illustrated by the recent work of Frans Theuws on the Merovingian landscapes of the southern Netherlands during the seventh to thirteenth centuries (1999), where the use of different burial locations had different symbolic connotations (Table 6.1).

Mission, conversion, and the 'colonisation of consciousness'

One of the reasons why the checklist style of approach to the archaeological identification of Christianity (if not necessarily of other religions) works only partially, has to do with the nature of conversion, and more specifically, the complex pattern of approaches to it and the responses that these can engender. Since its very beginnings, 'Mission', or the act of bringing the Gospels to non-Christians and converting them to the Faith has been a fundamental aspect of Christian religion. 'Go ye therefore and teach all nations', St Matthew instructs believers at the end of his 'great commission', 'baptising them in the name of the Father, and of the Son and of the Holy Ghost' (*Matthew* 28:19). However straightforward this may seem, the work of Christian missionaries from that of St Paul onwards has always been selective and conditioned by both the interpretations of the individuals engaged in this process, and broader historical and political issues. Thus,

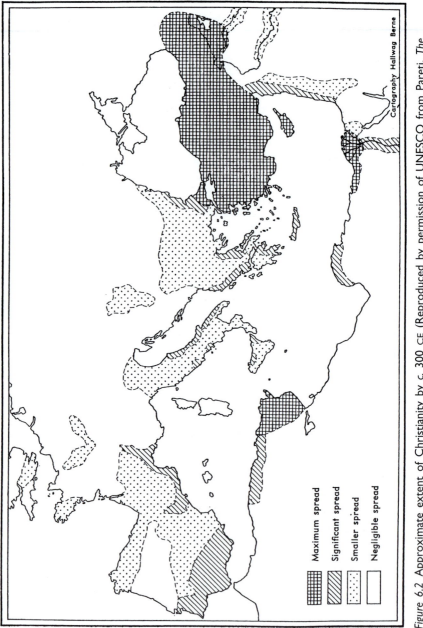

Maximum spread

Significant spread

Smaller spread

Negligible spread

Figure 6.2 Approximate extent of Christianity by c. 300 CE (Reproduced by permission of UNESCO from Pareti, *The Ancient World. Part III: From the beginning of the Christian era to c. AD 500* 1965: 874, Map 17 © UNESCO)

Cartography Hallwag Berne

for instance, during the first few centuries of Christian expansion, new converts were mostly drawn from the urban proletariat in towns throughout Syria, Palestine, western Europe and North Africa (Figure 6.2). This may have been partly due to the revolutionary appeal of Christ's message and that of his disciples to under-privileged members of urban communities, especially as the religious elites of the day occupied positions of social and economic power. Anxieties created by the economic and political uncertainties of the second and third centuries may also have eroded local attachment to the Classical pantheon, and belief in the efficacy of the Graeco-Roman gods. There is ample evidence from the Roman provinces, for example, of syncretic fusion of Classical and local, indigenous religions. It is conventional to consider such changes in terms of processes of acculturation and religious accommodation. While these are potentially valid interpretations, as Jane Webster (1997) and Elizabeth Graham (1999) have argued recently with reference to, respectively, Celto-Roman and Maya–Spanish interaction, such mixing of traditions and practices may have arisen from strategies of resistance to colonialism. Thus, it is equally plausible that similar motivations lay behind the adoption of Christianity by early converts in Palestine and North Africa.

Nevertheless, the focus on urban communities by the early evangelists, and the subsequent concentration of ecclesiastical power in such centres was influenced by additional factors such as their ease of access. Related to this was the perception that urban dwelling was a defining characteristic of citizenship and adherence to 'Roman' values, and correspondingly that country peasants were less 'civilised' (Fletcher 1997: 15–16). The word 'pagan', after all, is derived from the Latin term *paganus*, meaning 'country dweller' (Morris 1997: 51). There were also recursive consequences to this focus on urban communities by the early missionaries, since, with a few exceptions (most notably in parts of Egypt, such as the areas around Alexandria), resistance to Christianity was often greatest in the countryside (cf. Momigliano 1963).

Despite certain common similarities, such as an initial appeal to the more marginal members of society, this early phase of missionising differs from the situation in later centuries in at least two important respects. In the first place, Christian worship in the first few centuries CE lacked distinctive spatial referents and accompanying architecture and material culture. Emphasis was placed, instead, on the act rather than the place of worship. Although a basic orthodoxy and ecclesiastical hierarchy had emerged by the end of the first century (Peterson 1999), in the absence of sacred spaces and appropriate material symbols no clear break had yet been made from Christianity's religious and ritual antecedents. As discussed in the following two sections, this situation began to change during the fourth century with radical and profound consequences for the development of Christianity as a world religion.

Second, although most of the areas where Christianity first took root were under Roman colonial rule, the work of the early Christian missionaries and bishops was not part of the colonial project and until the fourth century was often perceived by the Roman authorities as in opposition to it. This contrasts, for instance, with the situation in many parts of Africa during the first few decades of work by various European and American missions in the second half of the nineteenth century. For, although the first Christian converts in most communities were drawn from the ranks of the more marginal members of rural communities, such as former slaves, alienated youth, women fleeing unhappy marriages and refugees (Spear 1999), this was not the initial intention of the missionaries. Great effort and money was expended from the very beginning in trying to persuade the ruling elite of African societies to adopt Christian beliefs, although not always successfully.

Moreover, conversion is not a one-way process, but instead involves the dynamic interaction between the bearers of the Christian message and their potential converts. More often than not, the two sides had different motives, aspirations and perceptions of what Christianity had to offer both on a personal level and in terms of potential, broader societal benefits. It is also evident that as 'individuals adopt new beliefs, practise old rituals, and consider new shared experiences as part of becoming Christian, Christianity undergoes conversion by being continually transformed' (Graham 1998: 29). Maya–Spanish interaction and the missionisation of the Yucatan, central America, by Franciscan friars during the sixteenth century provide a case in point. In broad terms, a tripartite, developmental sequence can be defined (Hanson 1995, and references cited therein). During the initial phases of missionary activity, friars established sacramental links with local communities and began selecting suitable sites for their mission stations. However, largely because such visits were brief, the archaeological visibility of this 'Entrada phase' is low and rarely distinguishable from more general evidence (in the form of imported ceramics and other items of European manufacture), of Maya–Spanish interaction. During the subsequent 'Mission phase', doctrinal instruction commenced, for which simple, thatched chapels (or ramada) were built or modified from existing structures as at Lamanai and Tipu in Belize (Graham et al. 1989). These combine Mayan and European elements. Even more suggestive of a fusion of traditions, however, is that these early Christian buildings all appear to have been sited within or immediately adjacent to the monumental core of the pre-Hispanic settlement, and in the case of Lamanai, directly over a fifteenth-century temple (Hanson 1995, Graham 1998).

The final 'secularisation phase', during which the majority of the indigenous population adopted Christian values and practices, may well have occurred only in the larger urban centres, from which the next generation of Franciscan friars would ultimately set out on their proselytising missions. The main archaeological correlates of this phase include the building of more permanent and elaborate churches and the addition of a formal mission complex, as has been attested in the Mexican towns of Mani and Tizimin (Hanson 1995). In the smaller, more peripheral settlements, however, such as Tipu and Lamanai, the earlier, simple ramada churches were also often rebuilt or replaced with more substantial, larger structures, while at the same time there appears to have been an increase in the number of burials within and around these structures (Graham *et al.* 1989, Graham 1998). What is most remarkable, however, is that there is clear evidence from several sites that sections of the community continued to practice the 'old', i.e. Mayan, religion alongside the Franciscan missionaries and their converts. At Tipu, for example, excavators found the remains of two temples, complete with offerings and built in the Postclassic style, in the immediate vicinity of, and clearly contemporary with, the Christian church (ibid.). Initially interpreted as indicative of apostasy and resistance to colonial rule, Elizabeth Graham has recently argued that the evidence might be better understood as Mayan absorption of Christian beliefs into their own cultural traditions (1998: 52–4). It is also evident that, on occasion, sixteenth-century missionaries in Mexico failed to control *Aztec* appropriations of The Word, as well (Figure 6.3).

The documentary and material records of the interaction between various Tswana communities of southern Africa and members of the non-conformist London Missionary Society (LMS) during the nineteenth and early twentieth centuries provide another example of the archaeological complexities of religious conversion. Here, conversion to Christianity came to be regarded as a civilising mission, which sought to colonise Tswana consciousness 'by planting the seeds of bourgeois individualism and the nuclear family, of private property and commerce, of rational minds and healthily clad bodies, of the practical arts of refined living and devotion to God' (Comaroff and Comaroff 1992: 200).

Under such circumstances, changes in the quotidian, secular aspects of a society's material traditions may be better indicators of the adoption of Christian beliefs than the presence of churches or east–west aligned burials. The available documentary and photographic evidence (see Comaroff and Comaroff 1991, 1997), gives the impression that in the Tswana case (see also similar examples from West Africa [Meyer 1996, 1997] and the Pacific [e.g. Hilliard 1974, Boutilier *et al.* 1978]) this is precisely what happened – namely, that round 'huts' were replaced by square 'houses'; hoe agriculture carried out by women was supplanted by plough agriculture under the control of men; female domestic labour became a key factor in local economies; European clothing and household objects were adopted to replace Tswana styles; and settlements were transformed in response to changing patterns of authority.

Figure 6.3 Overlooking this font in the great early Colonial church of Xochimilco, near Mexico City, a prehispanic sculpture of a human skull maintains the Aztec association of death with life (photo N. James)

The archaeological record of Tswana encounters with European mission-aries, on the other hand, is rather more ambivalent. To be sure, the remains of early mission stations and churches have survived (Figure 6.4); objects of European manufacture, such as cutlery and china table-ware make a sudden appearance alongside Tswana forms; new modes of burial and gender relations become evident, and so on (Hall 1997, Reid *et al.* 1997, Lane 1999). Nevertheless, the material record for the period *c.* 1850–1930 also has many elements in common with that of pre-contact Tswana settlements. The organisation of space remains steadfastly Tswana in character, to the extent that the placement of LMS missions and churches was not allowed to disrupt this pattern, even among communi-ties, such as the Bangwato, where there was royal support for their presence. Likewise, there is often clear evidence for continuity in vernacular archi-tecture and evident reluctance to abandon the traditional circular form of

Figure 6.4 The LMS 'African Church' at Phalatswe (Old Palapye), Botswana, built
c. 1891–3 (photo P. Lane)

houses in the face of concerted pressure from the European missions (Reid
et al. 1997, Lane 1999).

The differing patterns of continuity and change in domestic architecture
and burial practices, and the fluctuating position of churches and mission
stations within these settlements, 'were all elements of a material discourse
over power, authority and religion' (Reid *et al.* 1997: 389). Like other
discourses, these were situated communications grounded in specific contexts of use and the historical conditions of their production (cf. Barrett
1988). In other contexts of Christian evangelism and under other historical
conditions, different discourses would have emerged (e.g. Edwards 1999).
It is precisely for these reasons that using lists of key traits to identify the
adoption of Christian beliefs is so unreliable.

Churches and the archaeology of 'cult'

Over the past 30–40 years, 'church archaeology' has become a distinct
and significant sub-discipline with a clearly defined set of procedures and
methodology (Addyman and Morris 1976, Rodwell 1981) and evolving
research priorities (Blair and Pyrah 1996). In Britain, where the field is
especially well developed, the initial impetus came in response to the devas-
tation caused to urban centres by bombing raids during the Second World

War, and the major rebuilding programmes launched in the 1950s and 1960s to redress this. Early emphasis was placed on rescue excavation and recording, with analytical and theoretical approaches developing later. The study of the increasing number of churches made redundant by shrinking congregations and shifting patterns of worship, followed. In due course, living churches and their graveyards also became the legitimate focus of archaeological enquiry. The immediate consequences of this work were twofold – much better chronological resolution for the establishment, expansion and the phasing of changing fashions of church building, and, second, the emergence of new perspectives on Britain's ecclesiastical architecture which challenged many of the premises of earlier studies (Rodwell 1997). As methods of excavation and structural recording have become more sophisticated, so researchers have become more conscious of the potential significance of graveyards, construction methods, building materials and their geographical origins, landscape setting and the broader role of the Church within mediaeval and post-mediaeval society (e.g. James 1997, Morris 1997).

The importance of these kinds of approaches to an understanding of the history of churches and their environs cannot be overstated. However, it is also necessary to examine their religious importance as places of worship, and the symbolic meanings of liturgical space (e.g. Graves 1989, Gilchrist 1999: 83–7). One strategy for addressing such issues is through the use of a more generic approach to the 'archaeology of cult', such as that proposed recently by Renfrew and Bahn for the study of prehistoric examples. In this scheme, 'cult' is defined as 'the system of patterned actions in response to religious beliefs' (1991: 359). However, in order to distinguish religious and ritual practices from similar secular activities, it is also important to acknowledge that the focus of any religious worship is of a supernatural or transcendent nature. Thus, minimally, cult activity encompasses four components – focusing religious attention on the supernatural; creating and maintaining boundaries between the human and spirit worlds; the presencing of a deity or deities, or some other transcendent force; and, the performance, by celebrants, of acts of worship and offering to the supernatural. Each of these different components can entail a variety of physical forms and material expressions, which in turn can serve as potential archaeological indicators (Table 6.2), although it is unlikely that more than a few of these will be present in any particular archaeological context (ibid.: 359–60).

Churches, and their associated structural features, artistic embellishments, and artefactual and burial assemblages are probably the most obvious indicators of a Christian cult. An important feature of Christian churches, which distinguishes them from the cult places of the two major religions from which the first Christians sought to differentiate themselves, is that they serve simultaneously as congregational meeting-places and

Table 6.2 A scheme for studying the 'archaeology of cult' (after Renfrew and Bahn 1991: 359–60), with particular reference to Christian sites and monuments

Focusing of attention	*Boundary zone between this world and the next*	*Presence of the deity*	*Participation and offering*
Archaeological indicators			
Sacred place – e.g. holy well, saint's birth place	Architectural features used to separate or hide certain areas, or in conspicuous display – e.g. altar rail, rood screen	Use of a cult image or representation of deity in abstract form – e.g. crucifix, Virgin and Child	Acts of worship such as prayer depicted in the art or iconography of decorations or images
Special building – e.g. church	Fixtures, equipment and facilities related to concepts of purity, cleanliness and/or pollution – e.g. baptistery, font, floor plastering	Iconographic symbols of deities and associated myths – e.g. wall paintings, mosaics, decorative motifs on artefacts	Physical and/or spatial evidence for use of devices for inducing religious experience – e.g. choir stalls, organ, incense burners
Fixtures and equipment that act as attention-focusing devices – e.g. altar, shrines, bells, communion chalice		Use of related or similar symbols on funerary architecture and offerings – e.g. decorated headstones	Special votive deposits suggestive of animal or human sacrifice; or physical traces of offerings of food or drink – rare in Christian settings
Repeated use of ritual symbols (redundancy) in/around sacred area			Other material objects used as votives; these can often be hidden, broken or placed in special deposits
			Evidence for great investment of wealth reflected in the equipment used, size and ornamentation of structures, nature of offerings – e.g. mediaeval cathedrals

houses of divine residence (Morris 1997: 4). In both Judaism and the Graeco-Roman pantheic tradition these functions were allocated to different spaces. In Judaism, separate buildings – synagogue and temple – were used (see Hachlili, this volume), whereas in the Classical tradition places of religious worship were generally separated into a public enclosure, or temenos, and a holy shrine or temple accessible only to priests or priestesses intimately associated with the cult (ibid.).

Initially, Christianity existed as a sect within Judaism, which remained the dominant indigenous religion of Palestine even under Roman rule. Some of the early followers of Jesus, and perhaps even some of his disciples, may have been members of the underground, quasi-political party known as Zealots which actively sought to overthrow Roman rule, by force if necessary. Early converts to Christianity continued to attend synagogues, and emphasis was placed mostly on the act of worship conducted by small groups of initiates, rather than on the establishment of sacred places. Private houses of members of the Christian community were simply adapted for use as a place of worship. Known as *domus ecclesia*, these typically consisted of a large room in a normal dwelling where prayers, communal meals and rituals were held. Sometimes additional rooms were incorporated, one for use as a baptistery (baptisterium) and the other for candidates (catechists) awaiting baptism. Examples of such buildings are rare, although one possible candidate is the large, roughly 21 m² structure dated to between the first and fourth centuries and known traditionally as the House of St Peter, found beneath a later mid-fifth-century octagonal church at Capernum (Corbo 1984).

This situation changed during the fourth century, following the assumption of Constantine I as Emperor, and the official sanctioning of Christianity as a recognised religion. Although Constantine only became a Christian shortly before his death, and scholars have long debated whether he ever truly converted (González 1984), certain of his actions and events during his rule (306–337 CE), had a profound influence on the development of Christianity. In particular, after assuming complete control over the western Roman Empire, Constantine issued a proclamation in March 313 known as the Edict of Milan, calling for the end of Christian persecution. By 324, he had also extended his authority across the eastern half of the Empire, and as a direct consequence initiated the Christianisation of Roman Palestine, and its transformation from Provincia Palestine to Terra Sancta – the Holy Land (Patrich 1998: 471).

Central to this process was the construction of a number of imperial churches beginning around 326 CE, following those established in the previous decade in Rome and Tyre. These were, the Church of the Holy Sepulchre in Jerusalem (also known as the Church of the Resurrection), the Church of the Nativity in Bethlehem, the Church of Abraham's Oak at Mamre, near Hebron, and the Eleona Church on the Mount of Olives.

Work also began on numerous other smaller and less prestigious churches across Palestine, simultaneously providing a new context for Christian worship and sanctifying other points in the landscape as 'holy places' (Tsafrir 1993).

These early, local Byzantine churches in Palestine can be divided, architecturally, into four types – basilicas; chapels; cruciform churches; and churches of central circular (rotunda), or octagonal plan (Patrich 1998: 478). Basilica churches, which were by far the most common form, comprise a long, rectangular central hall divided longitudinally by two, or more rarely four, rows of columns, so as to create a central nave and flanking aisles. One end of the building, typically the east, was designated as the bema, or chancel, with an apsidal end-wall supporting a half-dome roof. This latter area formed the sanctuary, and access to it was restricted to priests. It contained the altar, usually on a raised dais, and was generally decorated with mosaics and wall paintings depicting Jesus and scenes from his life. Another feature of the chancel was a narrow flight of steps leading up to the ambo, or pulpit, situated just within the nave. Other parts of the interior, as well as the sanctuary, were also richly decorated with wall paintings and mosaics depicting scenes from the Bible and Christian symbols. Additional features would have included chandeliers, incense burners and candle-holders (Tsafrir 1993).

Although the imperial churches endowed by Constantine exhibit certain elements of the basilica form, all had a more centric plan, created by the inclusion of an octagonal or circular structure at the chancel end. These commemorative churches, or martyrium type as they are also known, were inspired by the monumental mausolea constructed for Roman emperors and other high-ranking individuals. They were intended to fulfil the dual functions of providing a place of worship and sanctifying a holy place in the Christian landscape (Tsafrir 1993, Wilkinson 1993b). At the Church of the Nativity in Bethlehem, for example, this latter role was achieved by the construction of a large octagon (a Christian symbol of perfection) over the cave in which Christ is said to have been born. In the floor at the centre of this, was an opening around which was a balustrade and walkway (ambulatorium), from which the faithful could gaze down on the place of the nativity. In the apex of the roof, and immediately above the one in the floor, was an opening, or oculus, which directed daylight into the cave (Tsafrir 1993: 8).

Even without the benefit of written sources, it is evident that various architectural and decorative elements in both the imperial churches, and the simpler, local examples can be interpreted in terms of Renfrew and Bahn's criteria as aspects of a religious cult. Thus, for instance, the oculus in the Church of the Nativity offers a prime example of the use of architectural devices to focus the attention of worshippers, in this case on a ritually significant and symbolically charged place within the sacred

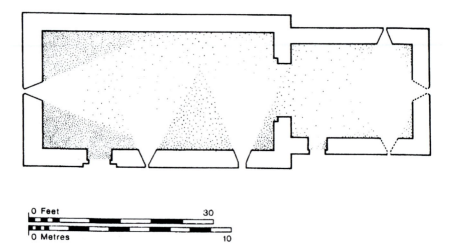

0 Feet   30

0 Metres   10

Figure 6.5 Example of the use of natural light to emphasise key areas of the ritual space of a church interior, St Mary, Stainburn, N. Yorks (Reproduced with permission from J.M. Dent Ltd from Morris *Churches in the Landscape* 1997: 299, Fig. 92)

topography of the Holy Land. Parenthetically, the use of particular openings and their specific alignment so as to highlight holy areas within church interiors, was by no means restricted to Palestine or the Byzantine era, as examples from mediaeval parish churches in Britain demonstrate (Figure 6.5). More generally, elements such as the chancel rail or sanctuary step, traces of which have been found in several excavated local churches throughout Palestine, e.g. 'Agur, 'Ain Karem, Hadat, and Shavei Zion (Avi-Yonah 1976), served to mark the symbolic boundary between heaven (chancel) and earth (nave). Mosaics in the area of the chancel depicting crosses, chi-rho symbols and other elements of Christian iconography that mark the presence of the deity, are also well documented in these early churches (e.g. 'Ain Hanniya, 'Evron, Ozem) as are actual crosses (e.g. Mishmar-Ha'emeq, Roglit) (ibid.). Similarly, as contemporary descriptions of early Christian liturgy confirm, because of its position just within the nave, every time a priest mounted the pulpit steps from the chancel to read the lesson, a visual reaffirmation that the Scriptures were indeed a gift from Heaven was provided (Wilkinson 1993a: 19).

Transformations of sacred space

With the exception of the cruciform type, which was a Byzantine introduction, Roman prototypes provided the main architectural inspirations for these early churches (Patrich 1998). Although certain elements were borrowed from Roman funerary architecture and imperial palaces, it was civil architecture, and especially the type of basilica associated with the forum, which exerted the greatest influence. The reason for this was that the Christian church (and also the Jewish synagogue), was intended for public use. As already mentioned, this contrasted with the ritual practices within the Classical tradition, in which only the cult priests had access to the temple while worshippers were confined to the temenos outside. Thus, as Tsafrir has observed, by 'choosing the basilica and not the temple form the Christians' were in effect emphasising 'the distinctions between their religious practices and those of paganism' (1993: 3).

However, given that Christianity originated as a sect within Judaism, early Christian liturgy was more closely modelled on Jewish rites than on those of the Classical tradition (Table 6.3). Consequently, the early churches also had certain aspects in common with Jewish synagogues and temples. Thus, for example, in both religions the symbolism of the two principal ritual spaces (in Christian churches, the nave and sanctuary/chancel, in Jewish temples, the Holy of Holies and the place of the Tabernacle), was identical. In some early churches, this is even reflected in the proportions of the different parts relative to those of corresponding areas in contemporary Jewish structures. As, for example, in the church at 'Ain Hanniya,

Table 6.3 Comparisons of Jewish and Early Christian liturgies
(after Wilkinson 1993a: 18)

Liturgical sequence	Jewish synagogue service	First part of the Christian Sunday assembly
Entry	Occasional procession to place the Scriptures in position	Entry of bishop to Sanctuary and of the book of Gospels
Prayer	Call to prayer The Shema: 18 benedictions and petitions	Greeting Prayer of preparation
Readings	The Law [Psalm?] The Prophets	The Law Psalm The Prophets
		Psalm Reading from New Testament Hymn Gospel
	Sermon	Sermon
Blessings	Blessing (if priest present)	Blessing or those about to be dismissed

where the sanctuary has the exact same proportions as the place of the Tabernacle in the Temple in Jerusalem (Wilkinson 1993a).

The spatial organisation of Ethiopian churches provides an even clearer case for links with Judaism. The size and form of these vary from the large rectangular and octagonal forms found in the major centres (such as Aksum) and the unique rock-hewn churches at Lalibela, to the many small, circular churches typically found in Ethiopian villages and various monasteries, such as those on the islands of Lake Tana. Nevertheless, irrespective of their form, all Ethiopian churches have the Ark of the Covenant, or *tabot* in Ethiopian centrepiece. All churches have a threefold division modelled on the Jewish temple (Pankhurst 1955: 168–70). The outside ambulatory, called *qene maḥlet*, where hymns are sung and the cantors (*Debteras*) stand, corresponds with the *ḥāṣer* of the Tabernacle or *'ulām* of Solomon's Temple. The outer chamber, or *qeddest* where communion is administered to the populace is equivalent to the *qodeš* of the Tabernacle or *hekāl* of the Temple. The innermost part is the *mäqdäs* where the *tabot* is kept and is accessible only to priests (and traditionally the king), corresponds with the *qodeš haqqodāšīm* of the Tabernacle or *debīr* of the Solomonic Temple (Ullendorff 1967: 88).

One area of difference between Jewish and Christian religious rituals is the Christian emphasis placed on baptism as the means by which individuals are admitted into the Faith. No obvious parallel exists in Jewish liturgy (Wilkinson 1993a). The novelty of this practice is clearly reflected by the extreme variation in the positioning of the font and baptistery in the plans of many early churches in Palestine (Figure 6.6). In due course, the positioning of the font and/or baptistery was standardised, and in the Western tradition at least, came to be located towards the western end and to one side of the nave. Aside from baptism, water was also needed for ritual ablutions and cleansing vessels used in the Eucharist and it was not uncommon for early churches to be built in proximity to springs or wells, and even for these features to be incorporated within the churchyard or church itself. While there were utilitarian reasons for this, especially in arid areas such as in Palestine and north-east Arabia (on the latter area, see Langfeldt 1994), such associations were often symbolically loaded. Specifically, in Christian thought water has a number of connotations which centre around concepts of purity and cleansing. Moreover, the act of baptism is held to signify a spiritual rebirth of the individual following his or her ritual death by actual or symbolic immersion in water.

Water and watery places, however, were also important in many pre-Christian religions throughout the world. Across much of western Europe, for example, there is extensive evidence, in the form of hoards of metalwork and other kinds of votive offerings deposited in rivers, lakes, sea lochs and marshy areas and around springs, as well as the placing of monuments, that suggests the widespread and long-standing ritual significance

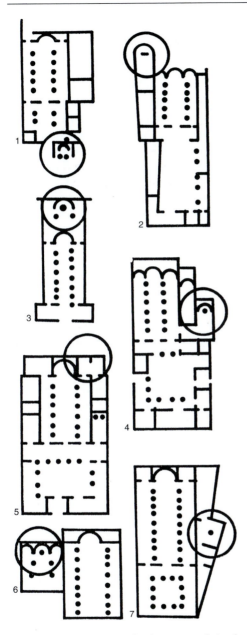

Figure 6.6 Variations in the locations of the font and baptistery (circled) in early
Palestinian churches: 1) Avdat North. 2) Beth Yeraḥ. 3) Imwas North.
4) Shivta North. 5) Kuris. 6) Susita Cathedral. 7) Mamshit East.
(Reproduced with permission from the Israel Exploration Society from
Wilkinson, J., 'Christian Worship in the Byzantine Period' in Tsafiri, Y.,
Ancient Churches Revealed 1993: 18)

of such areas (e.g. Bradley 1993, Richards 1996). The inclusion of existing sacred springs and wells in Christian sites, as for example at the aptly named Wells Cathedral (Rodwell 1984), therefore, indicates that the syncretic fusion of Christian and earlier traditions often went far beyond the adoption of material forms to include the deliberate assimilation of pre-existing beliefs (for another example of this see Kate Prendergast's [1999] recent review of the pagan origins of Christmas). This was not always the case, however. In Scania in southern Sweden, for example, the long-standing pagan practice of making lake and bog-offerings appears to have been abandoned in the sixth century, before the introduction of Christianity. This change in ritual practice roughly coincided with the introduction of timbered halls as the most prominent type of building in local settlements, and thus could be related to changes in the local social structure, which may in turn have laid the foundations for the subsequent adoption of Christian beliefs by the elite (Fabech 1999: 459).

The appropriation of pre-existing sacred places by early Christian communities was not restricted merely to those associated with water, but appears to have been a common strategy of religious conversion over the centuries. Many of the first churches in Palestine, including three out of the four imperial churches erected under Constantine, for example, were built on the sites of pagan shrines (Patrich 1998). In the same vein, as Richard Morris has observed, the 'Celtic attachment to particular land-scape features, regarded as abodes of deities, provided a lattice of points across the landscape, some of which, at least in Gaul, were redefined and incorporated within the new Christian geography' (1997: 51). Thus, for example, several churches in former Gaulish towns, including those of Arles, Angers and Sens, have traces of Roman temples beneath them (Morris 1997: 50).

Of course, the assimilation of pre-existing ritual spaces was not the only approach employed, and there is ample evidence for the deliberate, physical destruction of shrines and other sacred monuments, especially in Egypt and Syria during the first few centuries of Christian expansion (Fletcher 1997). Moreover, as examined in the following section, the influence of a world religion 'upon spatial use goes far beyond merely dictating the nature of places of prayer. Public and private buildings, landscapes, gardens, and city or town plans can all be influenced by religious or sacred considera-tion' (Insoll 1999: 1). It is important to stress, also, that whereas in the early phases of Christianisation in different parts of the world local styles and symbols were often assimilated by the Christian Church and commu-nity, as liturgy developed and the religious hierarchy consolidated its power distinctly Christian material traditions emerged (see below). An excellent example of this is provided by Emma Loosley's (1999) recent study of changes in early Syriac liturgy and its architectural consequences in north-western Syria. In that area, after the seventh century, there was a change

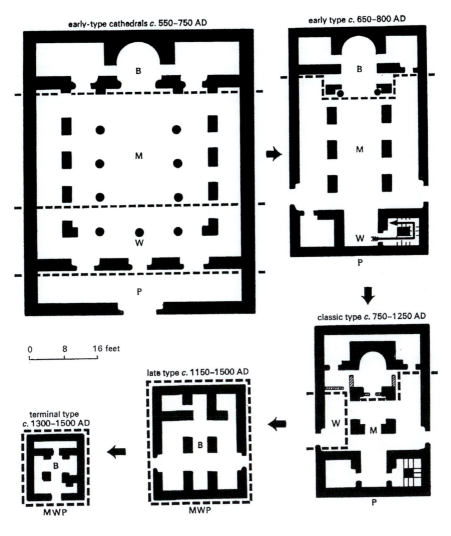

Figure 6.7 Architectural developments and changing sizes of churches in Nubia, c. sixth–sixteenth century (Reproduced with permission from the American Research Center for Egypt from Adams 1977: 475, Fig. 72)

in the liturgy and the earlier intimacy between the clergy and the congregation, in which the spatial organisation of the church served as a mnemonic device, was lost. As a direct consequence of this, the bema-type of church disappeared. The reasons for these changes are undoubtedly complex, but, as Loosley argues, one probable cause was the rise in prominence of monasteries and their attendant schools, which from the sixth to the seventh century began to assume greater control over determining what constituted orthodox practice, and what might amount to heresy.

Neither is this an isolated example. In Nubia, for example, where Christianity was introduced by missionaries from Egypt in 543 CE, and rapidly became the state religion, the first churches are large, spacious structures modelled on those in Egypt. Over the next 100–200 years, distinctively Nubian forms developed. Although somewhat smaller, they still retained a sizeable nave. By the twelfth century, when Islam was already growing in importance, not only had they become significantly smaller (Figure 6.7), but, more notably, 'the entire church had . . . become the sanctuary, accessible only to the clergy and a few privileged members of the laity' (Adams 1977: 477). Although the reduction in size may be partially attributable to diminishing congregations, just as in Syria it was also symptomatic of a growing gulf between clergy and laity and the growing control over doctrine by the monasteries (ibid.).

Monasticism and pilgrimage

The establishment of Christianity as the state religion of the Roman Empire and the corresponding creation of a 'Holy Land' had a number of far-reaching consequences. Among these were the emergence of monasticism and a pilgrimage tradition. The origins of both can be attributed partly to the decline in persecution of Christians. Specifically, as the numbers of Christian martyrs diminished, other means of expressing individual dedication evolved. Many of the early monastics, for example, lived as hermits in remote, desolate places where they freely and gladly suffered a number of privations in celebration of Jesus Christ. In due course, these 'holy men' were joined by small groups of like-minded followers thereby giving rise to the first monasteries. In turn, because of their association with devotees of Christ, these sites rapidly became important nodes in the sacred landscapes of Palestine and other areas of the eastern Mediterranean. As more and more places with Christian associations were sanctified and assimilated within these ritual topographies, so a tradition of embarking on journeys to visit them as an act of devotion developed. Since the pilgrimages were also often long and arduous, the physical act of pilgrimage quickly came to be seen as a metaphor for the spiritual hardships and sacrifices regarded as a necessary component of becoming a true Believer.

According to Christian tradition, Anthony of Egypt, a Coptic peasant farmer who became a desert hermit around 270 CE, is generally regarded as the founder of monasticism. The first monastery, however, was probably established by Pachomius, one of Anthony's followers, at Tabennisi around 320 CE (Peterson 1999: 69). The practice soon spread throughout the eastern Mediterranean, and two types rapidly emerged. These were the hermitage or laura type of monastery, where monks lived a more or less solitary existence spent in prayer, and the more communal form, or coenobium, in which monks placed more emphasis on collective participation in a life of prayer, work and celebration of the liturgy.

As befits their status as places of spiritual contemplation, laurae tended to be located in remote, isolated places. The monastery of Debra Damo (Figure 6.8) in the Tigre region of Ethiopia provides an excellent example of this kind of isolated setting. Founded around 500 CE, by Za-Mika'el, one of the so-called Nine Saints who are held to have been responsible for most of the early proselytising in Ethiopia (Gerster 1970: 71, see also Pankhurst 1955: 140–66), the monastery sits on the summit of a flat-topped mountain, and can only be reached by a plaited leather rope that hangs some 15 m down the side of a near-vertical cliff immediately below the main gateway. Comparable isolated monasteries are known throughout the Holy Land, especially in the Negev and the Sinai desert. Most of these consisted of little more than a collection of individual cells, often converted

Figure 6.8 The monastery of Debra Damo, Ethiopia (photo N. Chittick, copyright BIEA, reproduced with permission)

from caves, grouped around the founder's original shelter and a small chapel. Each monk was assigned his own cell, and spent the week there in prayer and solitary contemplation (Cohen 1976). On the Sabbath, the monks would come together for a communal meal and prayers. Some of the larger hermitages, such as the Great Laura or Mar Saba situated in the Judean desert east of Bethlehem, also contained a tomb in which the founder was buried. The presence of such features tended to reinforce the holiness of the site, such that in due course many became the focus of Christian pilgrimage (Binns 1999). Coenobia, on the other hand, were rather more complex architecturally. In the first place, and unlike the laurae, virtually all of the architectural components were enclosed within an external wall. Like laurae, a coenobium contained prayer cells for the monks, a church and refectory. However, other elements, such as hostels, storerooms, and stable blocks were also common, and some even had a hospital. Because the monks often engaged in agriculture, farm buildings, oil- and wine-presses and irrigation works are also often situated outside the main enclosure (Patrich 1994).

By the seventh century, monastic traditions were well established across Europe as far west as Ireland and the Iberian peninsula. As in the east, both types are known. Over time, however, some of the eremitic type were transformed as a consequence of their growing importance as places of pilgrimage and were eventually converted into coenobic communities (as happened in the case of the monastery at Debra Damo). An excellent example of this is provided by the evolving history of the monastery on the island of Iona off the west coast of Scotland, founded by the Irish monk St Columba in *c.* 563 CE. Judging from surviving documentary evidence, notably the seventh-century account of St Columba's life known as 'Adomnan's Vita', the initial construction was very simple, comprising little more than a number of turf- and timber-built cells, a burial ground and wooden church within an earthen bank and ditch, or vallum. Recent research at the site suggests that, contrary to earlier interpretations, parts of this latter feature may have been built during the first or second century, and thus considerably pre-date the founding of the monastery (McCormick 1993).

It is generally held that the earliest monastic structures at the site were concentrated in the area where the later Benedictine Abbey was erected (Ritchie 1997). The archaeological evidence for this is scanty, however, and certainly open to alternative interpretations. One of the more convincing traces consisted of a low, stone-walled square structure containing a number of large granite slabs. This was interpreted by the excavators as a prayer cell, possibly even that used by Columba himself (Fowler and Fowler 1988). Some 50 m or so to the east, immediately adjacent to the west front of the Abbey are the remains of another early structure, known as St Columba's Shrine. This appears to have been a free-standing mortuary chapel originally, but probably post-dates the original foundation of the monastery (Redknap 1979).

More targeted archaeological investigations, with rather less reliance being placed on the documentary sources, are clearly needed to resolve some of these uncertainties. Nevertheless, it is clear that over the ensuing centuries of use, Iona's exceptional importance as a pilgrimage destination had recursive consequences on the spatial organisation and reorganisation of the island's ritual topography. As Jerry O'Sullivan has observed, this can be seen along two main trajectories, namely, that of the original settlement and the broader ecclesiastical landscape setting. In terms of the former, during the early mediaeval period the main transformations, such as the construction of the mortuary chapel referred to above, and the addition of three stone crosses nearby, seem to have been directed towards enhancing the sanctity of this 'inner space' (1998: 7–8). Even the later addition of the Abbey church could be said to fulfil a similar role. The steady accretion of numerous satellite churches, cemeteries and crosses in the surrounding landscape, on the other hand, seems to have been more closely associated with amplification of the primary monastic site so as to create a topological narrative, or spatial topophilia to use Tuan's term (1980), of St Columba's life and that of the monastic community he founded.

Similarly inscribed, mythologised landscapes grew up around other pilgrimage sites. In some cases, the placement of individual elements was designed to channel pilgrims through an idealised set of journeys intimately associated with the Biblical and/or later Christian history of the site. As, for example, around the monastery of St Catherine on Mount Sinai, where a combination of paths, prayer niches, chapels and other shrines was ordered so as to lead pilgrims to the alleged sites of the burning bush, Elijah's cave and the point where Moses received the ten commandments (Coleman and Elsner 1994). The emphasis placed by the Byzantine Church on the construction of shrines dedicated to significant Biblical events may also account for the discovery of a wooden memorial (or memorials), dating from the sixth to ninth centuries, on Mount Ararat in Turkey (Taylor and Berger 1980), which Christian fundamentalists have preferred to interpret as the remains of Noah's Ark.

At other pilgrimage locations, instead of Biblical narratives, the natural topography was used to recreate aspects of the life of the saint to whom the site was dedicated. An example is provided by the layout of the pilgrim roads and their associated monuments leading up to the summit of Mount Brandon on the Dingle peninsula in south-west Ireland. The area around the mountain appears to have been associated initially with a local saint, Maolcethair (Harbison 1994). In the ninth century, however, the landscape became a spiritual focus of a broader cult centred on the Irish saint, Brendan the Navigator. Brendan is best known for his many missionary voyages made in a skin boat, or curragh, to various islands along the north European Atlantic seaboard, that probably included the Faroes, Iceland and possibly Greenland. Here, pilgrims followed a route (known as the Saint's Road), that was only approached from the sea and passed various stone crosses, churches and boat-shaped oratories. Thus, in a sense, they re-enacted elements of Brendan's voyages, and metaphorically shared in the hardships he endured and the progress of his mission.

Time and the emergence of a Christian core

Much of the discussion thus far has focused on spatial and material changes arising as a consequence of the introduction and adoption of Christianity in different parts of the world. Particular attention has been given to the transformation of sacred domains at spatial scales ranging from individual buildings to the broader landscape. It needs to be noted, however, that the adoption and spread of Christianity did not just affect sacred spaces. The rise of Christian pilgrimage during the Middle Ages, for example, had a number of widespread impacts on local economies and infrastructure across Europe, partly as a consequence of the need to accommodate and provision the thousands of individuals who were engaged in these activities. It also generated a whole new industry of the manufacture, trade and acquisition of souvenirs and relics (Stopford 1994). The economic power and influence of the larger monastic institutions was even more consequential and has been the focus of numerous studies (e.g. Gilchrist and Mytum 1989, Coppack 1990, Kinder 1998). Neither should we forget that many of the monasteries 'founded by . . . exiled holy men had something of the character of mission stations' (Fletcher 1997: 94), and as a result their influence tended to spread further and further afield with the passage of time. For instance, as well as founding the monastery at Iona, St Columba established communities at Derry and Durrow in Ireland. The monks of Iona were also instrumental in converting Oswald and Oswy, both of whom became rulers of Northumbria, which in turn opened the way for the founding of a monastery at Lindisfarne by Bishop Aidan. In due course, Aidan's disciples founded their own monasteries at Lastingham, Lichfield, Barrow-on-Humber, and Ripon, whence subsequent generations of monks extended their missionary endeavours to other parts of Britain and mainland Europe (Fletcher 1997: 160–80).

As this example suggests, each Christian site and artefact, be it an impressive cathedral, pilgrimage site, stained glass effigy or simple grave, has its own 'genealogy', which links it with other Christian objects and spaces and so bestows on it a certain legitimacy. The periodic need to appropriate or invent such a genealogy for a particular landscape, tradition or category of object, as for example in the case of mediaeval relics (Sox 1985, Geary 1986), merely underlines their significance to the global expansion of Christianity. The adoption of Christianity, in other words, necessarily entails a colonisation of time as well as space. The most obvious manifestation of this can be seen in the use of Christ's Nativity, following the meeting of General Council held at Nicea in 324 CE, to provide a linear calendar against which to date events in the past, present and future. Although linear notions of time are by no means exclusive to either Christianity in particular, or world religions in general (for discussions of the anthropology of time, see Gell 1992), as Paul Connerton explains: 'Calendars make it possible to juxtapose with the structure of profane time a further structure, one qualitatively distinct from the former and irreducible to it, in which the most notable events of sacred time are assembled together and co-ordinated' (1989: 65).

The most important characteristic of 'sacred time' in any religion is that it is held to be eternal (Eliade 1957). Consequently, the invariant recurrence of different ceremonies within daily, seasonal and annual ritual cycles is not simply a matter of regulation and imposing order but is central to the reaffirmation of their sanctity (Rappaport 1986: 20). Repetition, whether of the rituals themselves, or the individual acts and utterances of which they are made up, as both Rappaport and Connerton observe, is thus a pivotal component of religious practice.

Repetition, however, is also central to the creation of material traditions and thus, in this sense, all physical objects, structures and landscapes can be said to be imbued with their own particular temporality and cultural biography (*pace* Ingold 1993, see also Lane 1994). As the different examples discussed above illustrate, to acquire a Christian status, places and objects need to be tied to particular individuals, practices and/or events of the past. This may be achieved in a fairly explicit manner, as for instance with the pilgrimage sites of Iona and Mount Sinai. In other circumstances, the linkages are more indirect and may rely on a deeper understanding of Christian symbols and iconography. What is also evident is that over time, the choice of historical referents tends to change. In the early phases of Christianisation, whether in the Holy Land in the first few centuries CE, or parts of Africa and the Pacific a hundred-and-fifty years ago, Christian buildings, holy places and associated rituals frequently incorporate elements of pre-existing practices and religious beliefs. It is perhaps for this reason that the archaeological traces of Christianity in such circumstances are often so nebulous and subject to alternative interpretations. As each denomination developed its own distinctive canon, however, so the lives of saints, martyrs and most especially that of Jesus Christ became the main source of value and legitimacy. Sites, symbols and settings could now be placed within a truly 'Christian' time frame, and through either real or invented associations began to acquire Christian genealogies.

Conclusions

Archaeology, with its sister disciplines, is well placed to document the geographical distribution of such varied and changing cycles of the material expression of Christian belief, and to place each development in chronological order against a linear scale measured in years AD. Less certain, however, is the discipline's abilities to understand how Christians may interpret this evidence, as recent and past controversies over the history, use and management of Christian sites and monuments bear witness (e.g. Stewart 1998, Coleman and Elsner 1999, Moreland 1999). These are, of course, complex issues, that have as much to do with issues of politics and control of resources as they do with religious belief. Nevertheless, at the root of such debates lie different conceptions of time although both emanate from the same Christian tradition. For the scientific community, the date of an object as measured against a linear scale, and its associations of manufacture, use and deposition provide the critical indicators of its authenticity. From a religious, Christian perspective these are, at best, of secondary importance (see, for example, the comments by Prof. Pierluigi Bollone on the relevance of C14 dating of the Turin Shroud, cited in Chippindale 1987: 6). Instead, it is the sanctity of the object as evidenced by its adherence to a canonical form and genealogy of Christian associations that is the main source of value. Reconciling such differences may also be unattainable, since it is a fundamental of Christian belief that God, in the form of Jesus Christ, intervened in history for humankind's salvation – a fact that is reaffirmed in each symbol of the cross, in each Christian artefact and building, and which it is the vocation of all Christians to remember and commemorate in their acts of devotion. In the face of such belief, it would seem that at best, archaeology can only provide a parallel text, a parallel history of one of the world's most powerful religions.

Acknowledgements

The initial seeds from which this chapter has evolved were planted during participation in the University of Botswana – University of Stockholm Landscape History in Botswana project, funded by SAREC. I am grateful to the project directors Mats Widgren and Alinah Segobye for encouraging me to become involved. I would also like to thank the editor of this volume, Tim Insoll, for his patience during the preparation of this chapter, and for his helpful comments, along with those of two anonymous reviewers, on an earlier draft. Thanks are also due to Nick James and Niall Finneran for their help with sources, and to Skye Hughes for her continuing support. Any remaining errors or omissions are my responsibility alone.

References

Adams, W.Y. 1977. *Nubia, Corridor to Africa*. London: Allen Lane.

Addyman, P. and Morris, R. (eds). 1976. *The Archaeological Study of Churches. CBA Research Report 13*. London: Council for British Archaeology.

Avi-Yonah, M. 1976. Churches. In Avi-Yonah, M. (ed., English edition), *Encyclopedia of Archaeological Excavations in the Holy Land, Vol. I*. London: Oxford University Press. pp. 303–13.

Barrett, J.C. 1988. Fields of Discourse: Reconstituting a Social Archaeology. *Critique of Anthropology* 7: 5–16.

Binns, J. 1999. The Concept of Sacred Space in the Monasteries of Byzantine Palestine. In Insoll, T. (ed.), *Case Studies in Archaeology and World Religion*. BAR S755. Oxford: Archaeopress. pp. 26–32.

Black, E.W. 1986. Christian and Pagan Hopes of Salvation in Romano-British Mosaics. In Henig, M. and King, A. (eds), *Pagan Gods and Shrines of the Roman Empire*. Oxford: Oxford University Committee for Archaeology Monograph 8. pp. 147–58.

Blair, J. and Pyrah, C. (eds). 1996. *Church Archaeology: Research Directions for the Future. CBA Research Report 104*. York: Council for British Archaeology.

Boutilier, J.A., Hughes, D.T. and Tiffany, S.W. (eds). 1978. *Mission, Church and Sect in Oceania. ASAO Monograph 6*. Lanham, Md: University Press of America.

Bradley, R. 1993. *Altering the Earth*. Edinburgh: Society of Antiquaries of Scotland.

Bradley, R. and Williams, H. (eds). 1998. The Past in the Past: the Reuse of Ancient Monuments. *World Archaeology* 30/1.

Chippindale, C. 1987. Editorial. *Antiquity* 61: 4–9.

Chitty, D.J. 1966. *The Desert a City: An Introduction to Study of Egyptian and Palestinian Monasticism under the Christian Empire*. Oxford: Oxford University Press.

Cohen, R. 1976. Monasteries. In Avi-Yonah, M. (ed., English edition), *Encyclopedia of Archaeological Excavations in the Holy Land, Vol. III*. London: Oxford University Press. pp. 876–85.

Coleman, S. and Elsner, J. 1994. The Pilgrim's Progress: Art, Architecture and Ritual Movement at Sinai. *World Archaeology* 26: 73–89.

Coleman, S. and Elsner, J. 1999. Archaeology and Christian Space at Walsingham. In Insoll, T. (ed.), *Case Studies in Archaeology and World Religion*. BAR S755. Oxford: Archaeopress. pp. 128–38.

Comaroff, J. and Comaroff, J. 1991. *Of Revelation and Revolution, Vol. 1: Christianity, Colonialism and Consciousness in South Africa*. London: University of Chicago Press.

Comaroff, J. and Comaroff, J. 1992. *Ethnography and the Historical Imagination*. Oxford: Westview Press.

Comaroff, J. and Comaroff, J. 1997. *Of Revelation and Revolution, Vol. 2: The Dialectics of Modernity of a South African Frontier*. London: University of Chicago Press.

Connerton, P. 1989. *How Societies Remember*. Cambridge: Cambridge University Press.

Cookson, N. 1987. The Christian Church in Roman Britain: A Synthesis of Archaeology. *World Archaeology* 18: 426–33.

Coppack, G. 1990. *Abbeys and Priories*. London: Batsford/English Heritage.

Corbo, V.C. 1993. The Church of the House of St. Peter at Capernum. In Tsafrir, Y. (ed.), *Ancient Churches Revealed*. Jerusalem: Israel Exploration Society. pp. 71–6.

Edwards, D. 1999. Christianity and Islam in the Middle Nile: Towards a Study of Religion and Social Change in the Long Term. In Insoll, T. (ed.), *Case Studies in Archaeology and World Religion*. BAR S755. Oxford: Archaeopress. pp. 94–104.

Eliade, M. 1957. *The Sacred and the Profane: The Nature of Religion*. New York: Harcourt, Brace and World.

Fabech, C. 1999. Centrality in Sites and Landscapes. In Fabech, C. and Ringtred, J. (eds), *Settlement and Landscape: Proceedings of a Conference in Århus, Denmark, May 4–7 1998*. Århus: Jutland Archaeological Society. pp. 455–73.

Fletcher, R. 1997. *The Conversion of Europe: From Paganism to Christianity 371–1386 AD*. London: Fontana Press.

Fowler, E. and Fowler, P.J. 1988. Excavations on Torr an Abba, Iona, Argyll. *Proceedings of the Society of Antiquaries of Scotland* 118: 181–201.

Geary, P. 1986. Sacred Commodities: The Circulation of Medieval Relics. In Appadurai, A. (ed.), *The Social Life of Things*. Cambridge: Cambridge University Press. pp. 169–91.

Gell, A. 1992. *The Anthropology of Time: Cultural Constructions of Temporal Maps and Images*. Oxford: Berg.

Gerster, G. 1970. *Churches in Rock: Early Christian Art in Ethiopia*. London: Phaidon.

Gilchrist, R. 1999. *Gender and Archaeology: Contesting the Past*. London: Routledge.

Gilchrist, R. and Mytum, H. (eds). 1989. *The Archaeology of Rural Monasteries*. BAR 203. Oxford: British Archaeological Reports.

González, J.L. 1984. *The Story of Christianity, Vol. 1, The Early Church to the Dawn of the Reformation*. San Francisco: Harper and Row.

Graham, E. 1998. Mission Archaeology. *Annual Reviews in Anthropology* 27: 25–62.

Graham, E., Prendergast, D.M. and Jones, G.D. 1989. On the Fringes of Conquest: Maya–Spanish Contact in Colonial Belize. *Science* 246: 1254–9.

Graves, C.P. 1989. Social Space in the English Medieval Parish Church. *Economy and Society* 18: 297–322.

Hall, S. 1997. Material Culture and Gender Correlations: The View from Mabotse in the Late Nineteenth Century. In Wadley, L. (ed.), *Our Gendered Past: Archaeological Studies of Gender in Southern Africa*. Johannesburg: Witwatersrand University Press. pp. 209–19.

Hanson, C.A. 1995. The Hispanic Horizon in Yucatan: A Model of Franciscan Missionization. *Ancient Mesoamerica* 6: 15–28.

Harbison, P. 1994. Early Irish Pilgrim Archaeology in the Dingle Peninsula. *World Archaeology* 26: 90–103.

Hilliard, D.L. 1974. Colonialism and Christianity: The Melanesian Mission in the Solomon Islands. *Journal of Pacific History* 9: 93–116.

Ingold, T. 1993. The Temporality of the Landscape. *World Archaeology* 25: 152–74.

Insoll, T. 1999. Introduction. Research Foci in Archaeology and World Religions. In Insoll, T. (ed.), *Case Studies in Archaeology and World Religion*. BAR S755. Oxford: Archaeopress. pp. 1–4.

James, N. 1997. The Archaeology of Churches. In Hicks, C. (ed.), *Cambridgeshire Churches*. Stamford: Paul Watkins. pp. 196–208.

Kinder, T. 1998. *L'Europe Cistercienne*. Paris: Editions Zodiaque.

Lane, P. 1994. The Temporal Structuring of Settlement Space among the Dogon of Mali: An Ethnoarchaeological Study. In Parker Pearson, M. and Richards, C. (eds), *Architecture and Order: Approaches to Social Space*. London: Routledge. pp. 196–216.

Lane, P. 1999. Archaeology, Nonconformist Missions and the 'Colonisation of Consciousness' in Southern Africa, *c.* 1820–1900. In Insoll, T. (ed.), *Case Studies in Archaeology and World Religion.* BAR S755. Oxford: Archaeopress. pp. 153–65.

Langfeldt, J.A. 1994. Recently Discovered Early Christian Monuments in Northeastern Arabia. *Arabian Archaeology and Epigraphy* 5: 32–60.

Leech, R. 1980. Religion and Burials in South Somerset and North Dorset. In Rodwell, W. (ed.), *Temples, Churches and Religion in Roman Britain, Vol. 1.* BAR 77. Oxford: British Archaeological Reports. pp. 329–66.

Loosley, E. 1999. The Early Syriac Liturgical Drama and its Architectural Setting. In Insoll, T. (ed.), *Case Studies in Archaeology and World Religion.* BAR S755. Oxford: Archaeopress. pp. 18–25.

McCormick, F. 1993. Excavations on Iona in 1988. *Ulster Journal of Archaeology* 56: 78–108.

Meyer, B. 1996. Modernity and Enchantment: The Image of the Devil in Popular African Christianity. In van der Veer, P. (ed.), *Conversions to Modernities: The Globalization of Christianity.* London: Routledge. pp. 199–230.

Meyer, B. 1997. Christian Mind and Worldly Matters: Religion and Materiality in Nineteenth-century Gold Coast. *Journal of Material Culture* 2: 311–37.

Momigliano, A. (ed.). 1963. *The Conflict between Paganism and Christianity in the Fourth Century.* Oxford: Oxford University Press.

Moreland, J. 1999. The World(s) of the Cross. *World Archaeology* 31: 194–213.

Morris, R. 1983. *The Church in British Archaeology. CBA Research Report 47.* London: Council for British Archaeology.

Morris, R. 1997 [1989]. *Churches in the Landscape.* London: Phoenix.

O'Sullivan, J. 1998. More Than the Sum of the Parts – Iona: Archaeological Investigations 1875–1996. *Church Archaeology* 2: 5–18.

Pankhurst, S. 1955. *Ethiopia: A Cultural History.* Woodford Green, Essex: Lalibela House.

Pareti, L. (assisted by P. Brezzi and L. Petech) 1965. *The Ancient World. Part III: From the Beginning of the Christian Era to c. AD 500.* London: George Allen and Unwin.

Parker Pearson, M. 1982. Mortuary Practices, Society and Ideology: An Ethnoarchaeological Study. In Hodder, I. (ed.), *Symbolic and Structural Archaeology.* Cambridge: Cambridge University Press. pp. 99–113.

Patrich, J. 1994. *Sabas, Leader of Palestinian Monasticism. A Comparative Study in Eastern Monasticism, Fourth to Seventh Centuries. Dumbarton Oaks Studies 32.* Washington DC: Dumbarton Oaks Research Library and Collections.

Patrich, J. 1998. Church, State and the Transformation of Palestine – The Byzantine Period (324–640 CE). In Levy, T.E. (ed.), *The Archaeology of Society in the Holy Land.* London: Leicester University Press. pp. 471–87.

Peterson, R.D. 1999. *A Concise History of Christianity.* Second edition. London: Wadsworth.

Pound, N.J.G. 1999. *A History of the English Parish.* Cambridge: Cambridge University Press.

Prendergast, K. 1999. Chronos, Saturn, Mithra: Archaeology and the Pagan Origins of Christianity. In Insoll, T. (ed.), *Case Studies in Archaeology and World Religion.* BAR S755. Oxford: Archaeopress. pp. 175–81.

Pringle, D. 1992. *The Churches of the Crusader Kingdom of Jerusalem: A Corpus, Vol. 1.* Cambridge: Cambridge University Press.

Pringle, D. 1998. *The Churches of the Crusader Kingdom of Jerusalem: A Corpus, Vol. 2.* Cambridge: Cambridge University Press.

Radford, C.A.R. 1971. Christian Origins in Britain. *Medieval Archaeology* 15: 1–12.

Rappaport, R.A. 1986. *The Construction of Time and Eternity in Ritual. The David Skomp Distinguished Lectures in Anthropology.* Indiana: Indiana University, Department of Anthropology.

Redknap, M. 1979. Excavation at Iona Abbey, 1976. *Proceedings of the Society of Antiquaries of Scotland* 108: 228–53.

Reid, D.A.M., Lane, P.J., Segobye, A.K., Börjeson, L., Mathibidi, N. and Sekgarametso, P. 1997. Tswana Architecture and Responses to Colonialism. *World Archaeology* 28: 96–118.

Renfrew, A.C. and Bahn, P. 1991. *Archaeology: Theories, Methods and Practice.* London: Thames and Hudson.

Richards, C. 1996. Henges and Water. *Journal of Material Culture* 1: 313–36.

Ritchie, A. 1997. *Iona.* London: Batsford/Historic Scotland.

Rodwell, W.J. 1981. *The Archaeology of the English Church.* London: Batsford.

Rodwell, W.J. 1984. Churches in the Landscape: Aspects of Topography and Planning. In Faull, M.L. (ed.), *Studies in Late Anglo-Saxon Settlement.* Oxford: Oxford University Press. pp. 1–23.

Rodwell, W.J. 1997. Landmarks in Church Archaeology: A Review of the Last Thirty Years. *Church Archaeology* 1: 5–16.

Schülke, A. 1999. On Christianization and Grave-finds. *European Journal of Archaeology* 2: 77–106.

Sox, D. 1985. *Relics and Shrines.* London: Allen and Unwin.

Spear, T. 1999. Towards the History of African Christianity. In Spear, T. and Kimambo, I.N. (eds), *East African Expressions of Christianity.* London: James Currey. pp. 3–24.

Stewart, C. 1998. Who Owns the Rotonda? Church vs. State in Greece. *Anthropology Today* 14(5): 3–9.

Stopford, J. 1994. Some Approaches to the Archaeology of Christian Pilgrimage. *World Archaeology* 26: 57–72.

Taylor, R.E. and Berger, R. 1980. The Date of 'Noah's Ark'. *Antiquity* 54: 34–6.

Theuws, F. 1999. Changing Settlement Patterns, Burial Grounds and the Symbolic Construction of Ancestors and Communities in the Late Merovingian Southern Netherlands. In Fabech, C. and Ringtred, J. (eds), *Settlement and Landscape: Proceedings of a Conference in Århus, Denmark, May 4–7 1998.* Århus: Jutland Archaeological Society. pp. 337–50.

Thomas, A.C. 1971. *The Early Christian Church of North Britain.* Oxford: Oxford University Press.

Tsafrir, Y. 1993 The Development of Ecclesiastical Architecture in Palestine. In Tsafrir, Y. (ed.), *Ancient Churches Revealed.* Jerusalem: Israel Exploration Society. pp. 1–16.

Tuan, Y.-F. 1980. *Topophilia.* New York: Prentice Hall.

Ullendorf, E. 1967. *Ethiopia and the Bible.* London: Oxford University Press.

van Rooden, P. 1996. Nineteenth-Century Representations of Missionary Conversion and the Transformation of Western Christianity. In van der Veer, P. (ed.), *Conversions to Modernities: The Globalization of Christianity.* London: Routledge. pp. 65–88.

Watts, D.J. 1989. Infant Burials and Romano-British Christianity. *The Archaeological Journal* 156: 372–83.

Webster, J. 1997. Necessary Comparisons: A Post-Colonial Approach to Religious Syncretism in the Roman Provinces. *World Archaeology* 28: 324–38.

Wilkinson, J. 1993a. Christian Worship in the Byzantine Period. In Tsafrir, Y. (ed.), *Ancient Churches Revealed*. Jerusalem: Israel Exploration Society. pp. 17–22.

Wilkinson, J. 1993b. Constantine Churches in Palestine. In Tsafrir, Y. (ed.), *Ancient Churches Revealed*. Jerusalem: Israel Exploration Society. pp. 23–7.

Chapter 7

Ethics and the archaeology of world religions

Anders Bergquist

Introduction

This chapter is an attempt to diagnose the conflicts that arise between archaeologists and museum curators on the one hand, and those who speak for (or claim to speak for) communities of religious belief/practice on the other. It will be argued that conflicts over the excavation, study, conservation, and display of religiously sensitive material remains are best understood as instances of conflict between competing systems of meaning in a pluralist society, and that they are only resolved when there is a 'negotiated consent' or a capacity for 'bilingualism of discourse'. These terms will be explained in what follows. The examples are drawn largely from the archaeology of Judaism and Christianity and from western Europe, but specialists in the archaeology of other religions and regions may test the analysis offered here against examples taken from their own field of study.

Religion, archaeology, and the sacred

It will be impossible to escape terms such as 'sacred' and 'profane', but we have to be sensitive to their complexity. The notion of 'sacredness' can only operate *within* a religious system. It is a concept that may be attached to places, persons, times, or objects. For an archaeologist, conflict may therefore arise over the disturbance of a sacred place, the disturbance of human remains that are held to be sacred (either because of who they were in life, or because of the respect that a particular religious system has for any human remains), the conduct of archaeological work on sacred days or at sacred seasons (e.g. excavating on the Sabbath), and the excavation, conservation, and display of sacred objects. 'Sacredness' is also a concept capable of gradation. Within a religious system, places, persons, times, and objects are commonly graded in hierarchies of sacrality which may be very elaborate, and the location of a place, person, time, or object within that hierarchy will have important implications for the degree and nature of the conflict that arises with respect to it (Jenson [1992], for example, shows how the grading of places, persons, times, and objects on a scale from profane to sacred is a key structuring principle of the ritual and cultural system set out in the biblical book Leviticus).

The concept of 'archaeology' also requires comment. Here it will be helpful to start from a minimum definition of 'archaeology' as a set of techniques of enquiry – excavation, typology, photogrammetry, radio-carbon dating, etc. In this perspective, archaeology ceases to be a discipline in itself, and is seen as a set of techniques that may be placed at the service of a whole range of disciplines – economic history, demography, anthropology, history of religions, etc. Archaeology becomes a means to an end, a way of pursuing 'something else'. We may note in passing that many conflicts between archaeologists themselves about the nature and purpose of archaeology are really conflicts between the 'something elses' – 'my something else is interesting and important, yours is not'. Different aspects of archaeological technique may raise different issues of conflict. Excavation is a non-repeatable destructive experiment, which requires disturbance of place, and it takes place within a limited span of time. The conservation and display of artefacts, or of human remains, is not intrinsically limited in time, and need not be destructive – although it may include the removal of a sample for radiocarbon dating or DNA analysis. It is not surprising that the custodians of the Turin Shroud should have delayed permission for radiocarbon dating, until the dating technology had improved to the point where only a small sample needed to be taken (Damon *et al.* 1989: 611). Those who are familiar with the complex interdenominational politics of the Church of the Holy Sepulchre in Jerusalem will realise that it was a triumph of negotiated consent to secure permission for a photogrammetric survey of that most sensitive Christian site, the traditional Tomb of Christ (Biddle 1999). Permission for any invasive procedure at this site will be even harder to obtain. Finally, the application of any archaeological technique of enquiry will generate information, which may appear to confirm the beliefs and/or practices of a religious community, and be welcomed by it, or which may appear to subvert those beliefs and/or practices, and be experienced as threatening. This too will affect the nature of the conflicts that may arise.

'Religion' is a third concept that requires comment. Religions are complex adaptive systems. Leaving aside the fundamental question whether they are 'adaptive' in the sense that they are to be explained as part of the cultural equipment with which the human species adapts to its environment (Burkert 1996, Rappaport 1999), they are certainly adaptive in the sense that they develop in relation to their environment, and are in processes of long-term change. Judaism is a good example. In the time of Jesus of Nazareth, there was a wide variety of Judaisms (e.g. Sanders 1992). The defeat, by the Romans, of successive Jewish revolts between 66 CE and 135 CE, and especially the destruction of the Temple in 70 CE, radically reduced the possible ways of articulating Jewish practice. The destruction of the Temple effectively ended the institutions of priesthood and animal sacrifice, and the various cultural and political establishments that depended upon them (see Hachlili, this volume). The triumph of Rome put an end to the political hopes of the Zealots, and destroyed the radical separatist community that left us the Dead Sea Scrolls. Only the legal and halakhic traditions of the Pharisees survived, to be developed through Mishnah and Talmud into the various schools of mediaeval rabbinical Judaism.

The same point could be made by exploring the consequences for Judaism, as a religious system, of the Enlightenment, or the Holocaust, or the creation of the Jewish state of Israel. Christianity is, similarly, a complex system involved in processes of long-term change; Hopkins (1999) has recently drawn attention to the huge gap between what a Late Antique Christian would take for granted as normative in Christian practice, and what a typical present-day western European Christian might expect (see Lane, this volume). Major world religions are varied within themselves, and typically marked by diverse schools or communities of belief and practice; and the trend of the long-term process of adaptive change is often towards increased internal variety (but not always; Judaism as it developed after the year 70 CE was initially a narrowing of the spectrum; mediaeval Catholic liturgy tended to become more standardised over time). The long-term historical process of a religion may even end in its extinction. It is significant that specifically religious objections are not raised to the excavation of the sacred places or sacred objects of a 'dead' religion: Etruscan artefacts, or Dacian temples, or Graeco-Roman altars. This is confirmation that the ethical issues are not intrinsic to places or objects that have been held sacred, but are issues of conflict between *current* discourses.

Modern revivals of 'dead' religions are a fascinating case, precisely because they beg the question of how it will be determined whether a religious discourse is current or not. Present-day British Druids are the product of a romantic eighteenth- and nineteenth-century revival, and are not historically continuous with any religion of pre-Roman Britain (Piggott 1974). The noisy summer solstice confrontations at Stonehenge can be construed as attempts by modern Druids to assert their right to be taken seriously as a current religious discourse, attempts which are resisted by the historically sophisticated community of archaeologists (Chippindale *et al.* 1990 offer a fascinating cross-section of these competing voices). But to say that the excavation of a Graeco-Roman temple does not raise *religious* objections is not to say that it is value-neutral. Conflicts over what is appropriate in the archaeology of religions are closely intertwined with conflicts over what political causes one's archaeological enquiry might be used to support or resist, or how museums should behave in a post-colonial age. It would be unrealistic to suppose that we can disentangle ethical issues arising from the 'sacredness' of a site or artefact from issues arising from their 'political charge', even if they are logically distinct. Yigael Yadin's presentation of his work at Masada (1966) is a classic example of the intertwining of the religious and the political; Meskell (1998) has brought together similar examples from eastern Mediterranean and Middle Eastern archaeology.

The point that religions are systems of meaning in process of adaptive change has an important bearing on the question sometimes raised, whether archaeologists should undertake work which could disturb the foundation of a religious community's belief/practice. This anxiety is unfounded. Two mirror-image observations are in order:

(a) When archaeological enquiry leads to conclusions congruent with the claims of a religious community, archaeologists do well to be suspicious. The work of the Franciscan scholars Bagatti and Testa on a range of early Christian sites, including Nazareth and Capernaum, is instructive. Their religiously motivated desire to fashion a link between their archaeological evidence and events or places recorded in the New Testament has led them to press their evidence too hard: it is not impossible, but simply difficult, to sustain the proposition that a structure with early Christian graffiti excavated at Capernaum is the house of the Apostle Peter (Bagatti 1971, Taylor 1993 [this structure is now preserved under a glass floor at the centre of the late 1980s Roman Catholic church at Capernaum, a neat example of the coincidence of religious veneration with archaeological display]). The difficulty is the same as that involved in the attempt of the distinguished Roman epigraphist Margherita Guarducci to identify the remains of St Peter – the evidence is pressed beyond what the archaeological community would think possible (Guarducci 1989, Bergquist 1991). But there is no *ethical* issue at stake here, only one of ordinary scholarly judgement. Guarducci's interpretation, like Bagatti and Testa's, has straightforwardly to compete in the market place of archaeological interpretation.

(b) When archaeological enquiry leads to conclusions contrary to the claims of a community of faith, then it is important not to underestimate the robustness and adaptability of religious discourse. All religions are involved in processes of long-term adaptation; the archaeological evidence is simply part of the environment within which a religion will change. There is no need for archaeologists to have tender consciences because radiometric dating techniques show the world to have been created long before 4004 BCE. Those who are committed to believing in Archbishop Usher's seventeenth-century chronology will find ways of continuing to do so – they will argue, for instance, that

God has deliberately inserted misleading evidence into the fabric of creation to test the faith of the faithful (see Insoll, this volume). It is an intriguing thought-experiment to wonder how Christianity would develop if a group of archaeologists were able to prove (*per impossibile*) that a particular set of bones excavated in Jerusalem were indubitably the bones of Jesus of Nazareth. Certain materialist articulations of the doctrine of the resurrection would become unsustainable, but Christians would go on believing in the resurrection of Jesus: the religious system would adapt to this new feature of its environment.

Case studies

We may now examine some particular cases, to see how conflicts between archaeologists and religious practitioners can be construed as conflicts between different discourses or systems of meaning. We may consider first persons, and then objects. Anyone who watches the reactions of the general public in a gallery of Egyptian funerary archaeology will realise that difficulties surrounding the display of human remains begin as questions about the recognition and evaluation of human identity. There are two variables: whether the remains create a strong sense of human identity or not, and what kind of value is placed upon them. The average Roman or Anglo-Saxon skeleton does not create a strong sense of human identity, and, being scarcely persons, their display is seldom controversial. The Late Neolithic/Chalcolithic body discovered on the Hauslabjoch in the Tyrolean Alps in 1991 ('Ötzi the Iceman') is better preserved, and it has been possible to reconstruct in some detail his clothing, his diet, and the circumstances of his final journey in the Alps (Spindler 1994). This makes it impossible to escape a strong sense of his personhood, which has led to public controversy over the permanent museum display of his remains in Bolzano (Malone and Stoddart 1998: 4).

Archaeologists are less likely to be troubled by the display of human remains than members of the general public. This is partly because (like funeral directors) they work with them regularly; at a deeper level, it is because they have learned to invest them with a new kind of value. Human remains become data which contribute to the mass of knowledge and insight which the archaeologist is building up, and data are intrinsically good. This valuing of the human remains within a new scientific system of meaning outweighs the widespread initial instinct to leave the dead undisturbed. When people do not inhabit a frame of reference within which this new value can be given to human remains, so that there is nothing to set against the initial instinct to leave the dead undisturbed, and/or when that initial instinct is religiously reinforced (either in respect of all human remains, or in respect of these particular remains because they have a special significance within a religious system), then it will be harder to negotiate consent for excavation and display. Conflict will persist until the balance of values can be struck differently. Hubert (1988) has helpfully gathered together numerous examples of this kind of conflict, especially in Australian and North American archaeology; the conflict is frequently articulated around a demand that archaeological evidence be 'reburied' (Layton 1988 includes several essays on this theme).

The excavation of Jewbury, the Jewish burial-ground of mediaeval York, has become literally a textbook example of consent withheld (Rahtz 1991: 46–9). Excavations in 1983 recovered an extensive sample of the medi-aeval Jewish population of the city: clearly material of considerable scientific value. There was no significant protest within the city; that is, for the people of York the balance was struck in favour of the 'scientific' value of the human remains. The Beth Din (i.e. religious court) of the Chief Rabbi in London was informed of the excavation, but took the official view that the burials were not Jewish; the orientation was unusual, and there were no artefacts or inscriptions to prove beyond doubt that this was a Jewish cemetery. This opinion ran entirely counter to the expert opinion of the historians and archaeologists of mediaeval York, and may be seen as a move by the Beth Din to avoid a contest between 'scientific' and 'religious' discourses. The excavation then came to the attention of orthodox Jewish circles in Gateshead. In the face of their vigorous protests, which also led the Chief Rabbi to change his mind, the bones had to be reburied before they had been studied. For the Jewish objectors, the prohi-bition on disturbing human remains was religiously reinforced, and they struck the balance in favour of leaving the evidence in (even, returning it to) the ground.

The withdrawal of consent at Jewbury can be contrasted with the less well-known excavation of several near-contemporary Christian bodies at St Albans Abbey (Biddle and Kjølbye-Biddle 1980). Before dissolution in 1539, this was one of the richest and most powerful Benedictine houses in England. In 1978 the Abbey, no longer a monastic house but now the cathedral of an Anglican diocese, set about building a new chapter house on the site of the chapter house of the mediaeval abbey. During excava-tions, the remains of several mediaeval abbots and other important persons were recovered. It was possible to identify them precisely, from epigraphic and literary evidence. They provide a skeletal sample of unusual value to a mediaevalist – precisely identified, and belonging to a very particular stratum of mediaeval society. They had names familiar from the medi-aeval chronicles of St Albans – Paul of Caen (who built the great Norman tower), John de Cella, Robert of the Chamber (who was not an abbot, but was accorded the privilege of burial in the chapter house because he was the father of a Pope). These were, in short, well-known historical personalities, but no objections were raised to the excavation and meticulous analysis of their bones (Figure 7.1). Once the archaeologists

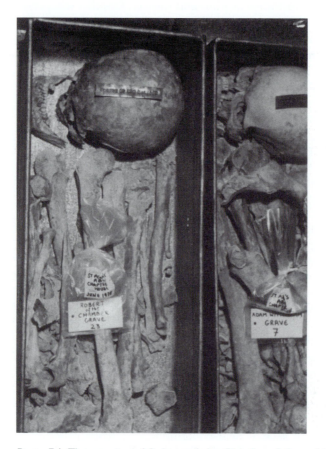

Figure 7.1 The remains of Robert of the Chamber, father of Pope Adrian IV
(courtesy The Cathedral and Abbey Church of St Alban)

had done their work, the same remains were reburied in front of the High
Altar of the cathedral, under a magnificent new carved memorial slab
(McKitterick and Cardozo 1992). The office of Vespers of the Dead was
sung by monks from Benedictine houses across the country; the Cardinal
Archbishop of Westminster, himself a Benedictine, presided over the service
(Figure 7.2). This is a striking example of what one may call 'bilingualism
of discourse'. The same human remains are handled within two different
systems of meaning, one 'scientific' and one 'religious'. In this instance, it
is worth remarking that the meanings are successive: first the excavation
and analysis, then the reburial. The display of human material may prove
more problematic than its excavation, because display renders the 'scientific' meaning permanent (assuming that the display is in a museum; display

Figure 7.2 Vespers of the Dead are sung by Benedictine monks as the mediaeval abbots of St Albans are reburied (courtesy The Cathedral and Abbey Church of St Alban)

is also a religious technique, as innumerable Christian saints in glass coffins testify).

When a 'sacred' artefact is placed in a museum display, it is separated from its use within a religious system. Take the example of Orthodox icons. These are artefacts which were produced to function in very precise ways within a religious system, as points of connection between this contingent world of space and time, and the eternity inhabited by God and the saints. Orthodox Christians are taught to think of icons as windows in the walls of a church, through which the believer can look into, and communicate with, the saints in eternity. In the course of Byzantine history, theologians developed an immensely sophisticated account of how icons are able to function in this way (see Evdokimov 1972 for a classic exposition). Icons are now likely to be seen in museums or galleries, where they have been detached from their setting in churches and in the liturgies enacted in churches: they are no longer to be read religiously, but in cultural-historical terms, or in aesthetic terms of 'art' and 'beauty' that would be alien to their makers. The question is therefore, 'who shall determine the frame of reference within which icons shall be read, and by what right?' Although icons are a good example, the same issue arises in relation to any artefact that was originally made to function within a religious system. At first sight, the argument that 'we made them first' or 'this is what they were originally made for' may appear decisive – but what are the rights of the prime manufacturer?

It may be helpful to make a comparison with a well-worn question in literary theory, namely, how far does authorial intention determine the meaning of a text? Perhaps it seems obvious that a text means what its author intends it to mean, but once a text has been published, it takes on a life of its own, and may prove to sustain meanings and implications unintended by the author. Neither the intentionalist insistence that it is authorial intention alone that determines the meaning of a text, nor the insistence of the reader-response school that a text can mean anything that a reader chooses to make it mean, does justice to the complex way in which the meaning of a text is negotiated through the simultaneous operation of three forces. The author's intention (1) counts for something, and so does the way (2) in which an individual reads the text, but that individual reception will be conditioned by (3) the history of the ways in which the text has already been read. This analogy suggests that the argument which one might summarise as, 'we (religious practitioners) determine the meaning of this artefact because we made it, and we made it to function in certain ways within our religious system', is not decisive. The meaning of the artefact has to be negotiated between what it was meant to mean, what it has meant in the past, and what it might mean now; there is no a priori way of adjudicating between competing claims of meaning. If a religiously charged artefact is to be displayed, there will need to be this kind of negotiation, or at least the possibility of reading the same artefact simultaneously within two or more different systems of meaning – 'bilingualism of discourse'.

Conclusions

'Religious meaning' is a construct, but then so are 'archaeological meaning' and 'scientific meaning'. A case has to be argued for the value of archaeological enquiry; it cannot simply be assumed. Consent has to be negotiated for the excavation of religiously charged places, persons, and objects, and archaeologists will inevitably sometimes find themselves caught up in conflicts between different systems of meaning which they are practically unable to resolve. In a contemporary Western context where traditions are fragmented, meaning is fragmented, and there is bound to be confusion over the handling of 'sacred' material evidence. This commentary has offered elements of a typology of conflicts in the archaeology of religions, and a diagnosis – rather than a resolution – of the issues at stake. But this limitation is not surprising. The problem of the relationship between archaeological and religious discourse turns out to be part of a much larger problem, of how a single society or a single world handles plural meaning. That is a problem which religious leaders, politicians, and cultural historians all find intractable (e.g. Sacks 1990). It is not surprising that archaeologists should also be perplexed by it.

References

Bagatti, B. 1971. *The Church from the Circumcision. History and Archaeology of the Judaeo-Christians.* Jerusalem: Franciscan Printing Press.

Bergquist, A.K. 1991. *Bone fide?* Guarducci on the Bones of St Peter. *Antiquity* 64: 412–13.

Biddle, M. 1999. *The Tomb of Christ.* Stroud: Sutton Publishing.

Biddle, M. and Kjølbye-Biddle, B. 1980. England's Premier Abbey. The Medieval Chapter House of St Albans Abbey, and its Excavation in 1978. *Expedition* 22: 17–32.

Burkert, W. 1996. *Creation of the Sacred: Traces of Biology in Early Religions.* Cambridge, Mass.: Harvard University Press.

Chippindale, C. *et al.* 1990. *Who Owns Stonehenge?* London: Batsford.

Damon, P.E. *et al.* 1989. Radiocarbon Dating of the Shroud of Turin. *Nature* 337: 611–15.

Evdokimov, P. 1972. *L'Art de l'Icône: Théologie de la Beauté.* Paris: Desclée De Brouwer.

Guarducci, M. 1989. *La Tomba di San Pietro: una Straordinaria Vicenda.* Milan: Rusconi.

Hopkins, K. 1999. *A World Full of Gods: Pagans, Jews and Christians in the Roman Empire.* London: Weidenfeld & Nicolson.

Hubert, J. 1988. A Proper Place for the Dead: A Critical Review of the 'Reburial' Issue. In Layton, R. (ed.), *Conflict in the Archaeology of Living Traditions.* London: Unwin Hyman. pp. 131–66.

Jenson, P.P. 1992. *Graded Holiness: A Key to the Priestly Conception of the World.* Sheffield: Journal for the Study of the Old Testament Press.

Layton, R. (ed.). 1988. *Conflict in the Archaeology of Living Traditions.* London: Unwin Hyman.

McKitterick, R. and Cardozo, L. 1992. *Lasting Letters: An Inscription for the Abbots of St Albans.* Cambridge: Cardozo Kindersley Editions.

Malone, C. and Stoddart, S. 1998. Editorial. *Antiquity* 72: 1–16.

Meskell, L. (ed.) 1998. *Archaeology under Fire: Nationalism, Politics, and Heritage in the Eastern Mediterranean and Middle East.* London: Routledge.

Piggott, S. 1974. *The Druids.* Harmondsworth: Penguin.

Rahtz, P. 1991. *Invitation to Archaeology.* Second edition. Oxford: Blackwell.

Rappaport, R. 1999. *Ritual and Religion in the Making of Humanity.* Cambridge: Cambridge University Press.

Sacks, J. 1991. *The Persistence of Faith: Religion, Morality, and Society in a Secular Age.* London: Weidenfeld & Nicolson.

Sanders, E.P. 1992. *Judaism: Belief and Practice.* London: SCM Press.

Spindler, K. 1994. *The Man in the Ice.* London: Weidenfeld & Nicolson.

Taylor, J.E. 1993. *Christians and the Holy Places: the Myth of Jewish-Christian Origins.* Oxford: Clarendon Press.

Yadin, Y. 1966. *Masada: Herod's Fortress and the Zealots' Last Stand.* London: Weidenfeld & Nicolson.

Chapter 8

Gender in the archaeology of world religion?

Rachel MacLean

Introduction

Whilst the archaeology of world religions and the role of gender in those religions are dauntingly vast and complex subjects, once one begins to consider the role of gender in the archaeology of world religions or the archaeology of religious gender, the field of study narrows somewhat. This is unsurprising. As this volume illustrates, the archaeological study of living religions has, until very recently, largely occurred outside the archaeo-logical mainstream; furthermore, the explicit consideration of gender in archaeology is a relatively recent development, still evolving from its feminist origins (see Gilchrist 1999 for an introduction to the history and current state of gender archaeology). It is, therefore, not impossible, at present, to discuss such a potentially enormous subject area in this necessarily short commentary. This chapter, whilst intended primarily as a review of the current situation concerning gender in archaeological studies of the five world religions discussed in this volume, considers, in addition, the role that gender has played in archaeological approaches to religion. It suggests that the absence of gender in many studies is the result of an absence of people and their communities, that archaeological studies of religions have not always recognised the complex and disparate nature of historically specific religious communities, but have often been focussed upon other issues in which the identity of the worshipper (or heretic) was viewed as redundant – e.g. the attempt to identify sacred locations (Keller 1965), and the recording of detailed architectural developments (Buxton 1971, Higuchi and Barnes 1995). It further suggests that the role played by gender in discussions of prehistoric religion in European archaeology, and the rise of the Mother Goddess cult, is in part a reaction to the andro-centric archaeological approach to historical religion.

Gender and religion are both emotive subjects. Is it possible, or indeed desirable, to attempt some degree of objectivity when considering their relationship? Insoll has, in his introduction to this volume, considered the issue of religious subjectivity, and the explicitly feminist stance adopted by the first archaeologists writing on gender issues (see Conkey and Spector 1984, Moore and Scott 1997) has clearly been both necessary and rewarding. Gilchrist, in summarising the short history of the archaeology of gender (1994: 2–8), stresses the nature of gender as something which is socially created and historically specific. Similarly, the author, being herself 'socially created and historically specific', explicitly acknowledges her own gendered and religiously distinct identity. An expert neither on gender in archaeology, nor on archaeological studies of religion, she is an archaeologist brought up as a woman within a Western Christian tradition. On a personal level religion has always been experienced as fundamentally gendered and fundamentally exclusive. This chapter attempts to move beyond personal experiences in its review of current archaeological studies of the world religions, but will return firmly to this excluded position in its final discussion of the influence of historical religious gender in the archaeological debate of European prehistoric religion.

Gender and world religion

There is an enormous literature on the subject of gender in religion, and it is impossible to consider this without acknowledging the influence of the Western Christian tradition. The experience of female exclusion from religion, and the androcentric nature of Western academia, have resulted in many studies which seek to examine the role played by women as something absent from general religious debate (Sharma 1987, Loades 1990) – 'women', for example, appears in the index of *A Handbook of Living Religions* (Hinnells 1991) as a separate category, but there is no mention of 'men'. Much of this work is culturally and historically specific (e.g. Sheils and Wood 1990, *Manushi* 1989), and much, whilst considering other religious traditions, clearly results from the Western Christian viewpoint (e.g. Webster 1984). Indeed, so great is the subject area that it is obviously naive to ask the questions necessary for this study; is gender important in the five religions? do the religions distinguish between genders? do the practitioners? do they see two distinct genders, or a more complex pattern? As stressed by Gilchrist (1994: 2–8), gender must be seen as culturally and historically specific, therefore we cannot provide simple answers to these questions. Within the five religions there are a plethora of differing contemporary interpretations and beliefs, and hence of attitudes to gender. When one considers the great time depth necessary for this archaeological study the extent of the many different realities which may have existed is virtually infinite.

Recognising the impossibility of the task, it nevertheless remains necessary, in order to initiate any sensible discussion, to attempt to isolate certain general characteristics. In Judaism (though not in Reform Judaism), there is a clear division between the male and female sphere. Woman is seen, 'as a "helpmeet opposite" man . . . public religion, e.g. synagogue worship, the office of rabbi and torah study, is essentially a male preserve. Women's role is primarily as a wife and mother, who is not bound to keep all the commandments as the male is' (Hinnells 1995: 561). This division between the public and male and the private, or domestic, and female, is also continued (though again with notable exceptions) in both Christianity and Islam (Insoll 1999: ch. 3). Christian women, moreover, were deemed to be equated with sin by St Augustine in the fifth century. In the main-stream of these three monotheistic religions God, himself, is male-gendered, though more complex ideas of male, female and genderless attributes are contained within all three.

Hinduism, by contrast, is a religion of diversity. Its innumerable gods reflect all shades of gender, as do its practitioners, and shrines are located in public temples, in the home, and throughout the landscape (see Chakrabarti, this volume). Indeed, not only is Hinduism clearly gendered, but also sexualised. The *linga*, the most basic image of Shiva and a main object of worship (Hinnells 1995: 272–3), represents the power of primeval sexual completeness in its depiction of a phallus resting in a vagina. Erotic sexual imagery is also part of the Hindu tradition, being used, for example, to indicate the supreme bliss of the union of *atman* (the individual soul) and *brahman* (the impersonal absolute) which is a fundamental element of Hinduism. Hinduism is concerned with all elements of society playing their correct role and remaining in their correct place, *dharma*, and the roles of men and women are distinguished; high-caste Hindu women, for example, must always remain subject to male authority, and their true place is in the home (Flood 1996: 65–6). However, the very complex caste system which governs Hindu society is perhaps of greater importance than gender division. This system and the many rituals of Hinduism serve to allow a great number of possible roles for its practitioners, with women and men participating on many different levels.

Buddhism is the only religion of the five which is, essentially, non-theistic. Moreover, its concern with the individual's attempt to transcend earthly suffering and achieve enlightenment, and its espousal of universal equality and charity, should leave little to distinguish between the genders. However, divine beings (*bodhisattvas*) do play an important role in Buddhism and, in general, these are male, women are reborn in masculine incar-nations once they reach the Pure Land of the Amitabha Buddha (Frédéric 1995: 220).

Gender and the archaeology of world religion

As we have seen, attitudes to gender differ between the five religions, although, perhaps unsurprisingly given their historical relationship, Judaism, Christianity and Islam similarly make a clear distinction between the male, public arena of religion, and the female, private and domestic role. In contrast, Hinduism is characterised by a much greater variety of potential genders and gender roles, whereas gender, in Buddhism, appears to be of lesser importance, though women may be considered further from the sacred. These, however, are only general conclusions which necessarily recognise a much greater variability in actual practice, and once we begin to consider the archaeology of these religions the great depth of time involved allows even greater potential variability. Very different scholarly trends have emerged for each religion, reflecting their various characters, or the differing perceptions of their character by various academic traditions. These are issues which are discussed in detail in other contributions to this volume. Gender has been an issue in various archaeological studies of these religions, and the differing role played by gender in the religions and the different attitudes to gender displayed by individual archaeologists and academic traditions have similarly resulted in distinct emphases emerging in the study of each religion.

Archaeological studies of Christianity tend to focus upon the architectural and the Biblical, solid scholarship and the convoluted search for historical 'proofs' (see Insoll, this volume). There are, in fact, many archaeological studies of Christianity which have had a particular gender focus. Being historically a publicly male religion, many Christian buildings were, or have been viewed as, male spaces and hence studies of these buildings have been studies of male religious communities, of monasteries and similar religious institutions (e.g. Braunfels 1972, Coppack 1990). In Gilchrist's study, *Gender and Material Culture* (1994), she explicitly aims to redress this imbalance, using the archaeological (and historical) record to examine the role played by women's religious communities in Late Mediaeval England and to compare it with that played by similar male communities. Working in an academic tradition which has frequently ignored female participation, and examining a religion which often sharply distinguishes the male and female her priority is to rediscover neglected elements of a past community, and as such her work provides one of the best examples of the radical influence of gender theory in this previously androcentric field.

As was suggested in the introduction to this chapter, absence of gender in most cases actually reflects an absence of the recognition of the multifaceted nature of societies. Religions do produce communities in which membership may be restricted by sex, age and occupation, and thus archaeological studies of particular communities have provided much of the information on gender roles in Christianity. However, a more general picture of a religious community emerges from studies of Jewish burial grounds, which have allowed the recognition, not only of male and female burials, but also of adults and children, various social classes, and of family groups (see Hachlili this volume, Hachlili and Killebrew 1983, 1999). Whilst there will always be problems with using burial evidence to examine the living communities that they represent (see Parker Pearson 1999), communal cemeteries do provide a good basic introduction to a particular religious community, reflecting the many sections of the group which may not be visible in the archaeological remains of public worship. Judaism, like Christianity, has seen a distinction between the male and public and the female and private, and thus archaeological studies of religious build-ings have tended to ignore the role of women (though women's synagogue buildings have been recorded at some locations [Codreanu-Windauer 1999: 151]). Furthermore, the absence of a monastic tradition in Judaism has prevented the clearly gendered studies which are possible for Christian communities, and thus there can be no similar studies of groups of reli-gious men and women. Rather, with its history of cultural assimilation and associated need to define a distinct Jewish identity, it is not only neces-sary, but far easier for archaeological studies of gender in Judaism to focus on the religious community as a whole and upon the interaction of its various sub-sections.

In Islam, as in Christianity and Judaism, there is the clear distinction between the male and public and the female and private. However, it is possible to argue that in Islam the great value placed upon the privacy and seclusion of female, domestic space gives it a religious significance which is absent in the other two religions. Studies of this female space, therefore, can indicate the role played by women in past Muslim commu-nities. Islam has been viewed by Western academics, and particularly by feminist academics, reacting to our own experience of female exclusion, as an extreme example of male power and female oppression. However, studies of male and female space, such as that of Donley-Reid (see Donley 1982, Donley-Reid 1990), who used archaeological and ethnographic evidence to examine the relationship between gender and space in the eighteenth-century Swahili communities of the north Kenyan coast, reveal a much more complex relationship. Ideas of space and gender relations have been enthusiastically embraced by archaeology (e.g. Hastorf 1991, Lane 1998), as a relatively straightforward method of recognising the pres-ence and functioning of gendered communities in the past. Archaeological studies of Islam, which have tended towards the purely art historical (see Insoll 1999 and this volume), have very rarely considered the nature of the Islamic community, yet it is Islam which has also inspired some of the most sensitive explorations of public and private religious life (see for example Campo 1991).

Archaeologists have reacted very differently to Hinduism. The very fact that it has a multitude of Gods, both male and female, prevents the projec-tion of a Western experience on to the archaeological evidence. The sheer diversity of Hinduism appears to have acted, archaeologically, as some-thing of a conceptual barrier (see Chakrabarti this volume), yet has also ensured that aspects of religious gender are an integral part of much evidence of Hinduism in the archaeological record. Material found at Harappan sites dating from 4,000 years ago include female terracotta figurines and seals showing ithyphallic, seated figures, which have been interpreted as early representations of the Mother Goddess and male gods such as Siva, and phallic and vulva-like stones which have been interpreted as *linga* (Marshall 1931, Flood 1996: 27–30), objects reflecting the long history of the sexualised nature of Hindu religion.

'The history of Hinduism', writes Flood (1996: 20), 'is the history of a male discourse . . . women's self-perceptions and experience have generally been "written-out" of the tradition'; perhaps archaeology can provide us with a broader picture. Archaeological studies of this material cannot be seen to exclude the activities and beliefs of women, as is generally the case with Judaism, Christianity and Islam, yet neither do they provide the insight into the activities of religious groups that was also possible. To a certain extent, the identity of the worshipper becomes obscured by the vast range of religious behaviours possible. Moreover, the role played by caste in Hindu society has already been discussed, and it would be wrong to look simply for gender in the past without also looking for evidence of caste. In a recent study into the archaeological visibility of caste at the urban site of Anuradhapura in Sri Lanka for the period 350 BCE – CE 200, Coningham and Young (1999) examined the spatial distribution of craft waste and faunal remains. Though they concluded that formal caste-based divisions had not been observed rigidly, and that caste, at this period, may have been more complex and flexible than is the case today, as with Donley-Reid's study of the Islamic Swahili, their work highlights the potential of such spatial approaches for understanding more of the various elements and functioning of religious communities in the past.

In the *World Archaeology* volume, 'Buddhist Archaeology' (1995), Barnes stresses the intrinsic relationship between Buddhism and the state, 'its philosophical basis was developed by a member of a ruling clan . . . other rulers supported his disciples in order to enhance their own *karma*' (1995: 178–9). It is hard to move much beyond this level of discussion when considering Buddhist archaeology, which has often been restricted to the clearing of monuments (see Coningham this volume). Whilst it is possible to see the actions of individuals, both male and female, and of communities, in the past, particularly in the inscriptions which detail the donors of Buddhist monuments (e.g. Lahiri 1999: 33, Marshall *et al.* 1940: 34), we gain limited understanding of social relationships from such evidence. Buddhism, like Christianity, has a monastic tradition, with both male and female renounceants, but, like Christianity, studies of religious complexes tend to be studies of male communities – there is at present only one suggested convent (Coningham, this volume, Dutt 1962: 134). It is difficult not to conclude that Buddhist archaeology remains, essentially, an archaeology of monuments, of *stupas* and monasteries, much as Christian archaeology has been in the past. Unlike Christianity, however, which, through its fundamental distinction between the roles of men and women has produced studies which examine clearly gendered religious communities, Buddhism with its less clearly defined gender roles has yet to foster similar reactions.

Gods and goddesses/goddesses and gods

In Western Christianity, and in Western academia, gender has, historically, been used as a method of division and exclusion, keeping public power in the hands of men and relegating women to the secondary and the domestic. Academics began reacting to this historical exclusion in the nineteenth century, suggesting that matriarchal societies may have existed in prehistory (Bachofen 1861, Morgan 1877), a reaction which culminated in the late twentieth-century development of radical gender archaeology, and the increasing recognition that archaeology should adopt 'a more holistic study of the meaning and experience of sexual difference in the past' (Gilchrist 1999: 146). This historical religious androcentrism has only recently been addressed by studies such as those of Gilchrist (1994), which question previous assumptions of past male and female religious roles. Instead, the sense of religious exclusion has pushed archaeologists back into prehistory in search of an equivalent female role in religion. Bachofen's original argument for an early European matriarchy was partly based upon finds of prehistoric human figurines which he interpreted as goddess figures (Ehrenberg 1989: 63). These figures, which are found at several locations in Europe and date from the Palaeolithic to the Bronze Age, do often exhibit characteristics which enable them to be sexed, and the female figures and other depictions of women (e.g. the reliefs and wall paintings at Catal Huyuk) have been seen as evidence for the worship of a Mother Goddess throughout Europe for this considerable time period (see Mellaart 1967, Gimbutas 1974, 1989).

The Mother Goddess argument, having long ago abandoned any pretence of cold objective discussion, is 'the genie that will not go back into the bottle. It immediately finds that most fertile of pastures in which to seed, that of angry feminism' (Leeder 2000: 12). It has generated emotional and bitter argument from both sides (e.g. Meskell 1995, Christ 1997), yet has succeeded only in proposing a prehistoric religious sexual reversal, in establishing 'a new "truth" about what happened "in the beginning" which mirrors the old fundamentalisms of conventional religion' (Goodison and Morris 1998b: 13). It can be seen, surely, as an expected reaction to women's past experience of Western religion and academe. A female archaeologist writing today can say that she felt, as a child, that the Christian fundamentalist church saw little difference between Ishtar, Eve, the Virgin Mary and the whore of Babylon, 'it was all one antipatriarchal plot that had to be anathematised' (Leeder 2000: 3). She argues that these figures actually represent a deep need for female representation in the Divine. This need for female representation, both spiritually and intellectually, is the driving force behind the ever growing Mother Goddess cult. Whilst more rational analysis of the evidence for female divinities in historically and culturally specific contexts is now beginning, and is proving rewarding (Goodison and Morris 1998a), until women no longer feel excluded from their religious past (and present) the great Mother Goddess will simply continue to grow ever more fertile.

Conclusions

This commentary has, of necessity, dealt with a potentially enormous subject rather abruptly. Yet the lack of gender awareness in many archaeological studies of the world religions has prevented this abruptness from distorting the overview of the current situation. Despite the fundamental role played by gender in Judaism, Christianity and Islam, studies which explicitly recognise this are few, though those which have done appear to be all the more successful (e.g. Gilchrist 1994, Donley-Reid 1990). In contrast, archaeological studies of Hinduism, with its many potential gender roles and religious behaviours, neither exclude nor reveal clear gender roles, and the importance of caste may prove dominant. Buddhism, which has no clearly defined gender roles, presents a different problem. Archaeological attitudes to gender in religious communities are, in many cases, strongly influenced by the attitudes of the Western Christian and academic traditions to gender, and in particular the historical exclusion of women. These experiences of androcentrism continue to push archaeologists, thealogians (as opposed to theologians), and feminists towards the 'rediscovery' of a parallel gynocentric past, in which the all-powerful Judaeo-Christian God was preceded by an all-powerful Mother Goddess.

The lack of gender in archaeological studies of the world religions results from an absence of people and an absence of communities. Tringham (1991) tells a story in her paper, 'Households with Faces: the Challenge of Gender in Prehistoric Architectural Remains', of being asked to envisage the prehistoric south-east European households she was studying, to give them faces. She describes it as an 'Aha' experience, and realised that 'until, as an archaeologist, you can learn to give your imagined societies faces, you cannot envisage gender . . . and you cannot *think* of your prehistoric constructions as really human entities with a social, political, ideological and economic life' (ibid.: 93–4). Simply sexing gods does not help us deal with issues of a community's religious life, we need to begin attempting to see the faces of the believers.

References

Bachofen, J. 1961. *Das Mutterecht*. Basel: Benno Schwabe.

Barnes, G.L. 1995. An Introduction to Buddhist Archaeology. *World Archaeology* 27: 165–82.

Barnes, G.L. (ed.). 1995. Buddhist Archaeology. *World Archaeology* 27(2).

Braunfels, W. 1972. *Monasteries of Western Europe*. London: Thames and Hudson.

Buxton, D.R. 1971. The Rock-Hewn and other Medieval Churches of Tigre Province, Ethiopia. *Archaeologia* 92: 1–42.

Campo, J.E. 1991. *The Other Sides of Paradise. Explorations into the Religious Meanings of Domestic Space in Paradise*. Columbia: University of South Carolina Press.

Christ, C. 1997. *Rebirth of the Goddess*. New York: Routledge.

Codreanu-Windauer, S. 1999. The Medieval Jewish Quarter of Regensburg and its Synagogue: Archaeological Research 1995–1997. In Insoll, T. (ed.), *Case Studies in Archaeology and World Religion*. BAR S755. Oxford: Archaeopress. pp. 139–52.

Coningham, R. and Young, R. 1999. The Archaeological Visibility of Caste: An Introduction. In Insoll, T. (ed.), *Case Studies in Archaeology and World Religion*. BAR S755. Oxford: Archaeopress. pp. 84–93.

Conkey, M.W. and Spector, J. 1984. Archaeology and the Study of Gender. *Archaeological Methods and Theory* 7: 1–38.

Coppack, G. 1990. *Abbeys and Priories*. London: Batsford/English Heritage.

Donley, L. 1982. House Power: Swahili Space and Symbolic Markers. In Hodder, I. (ed.), *Symbolic and Structural Archaeology*. Cambridge: Cambridge University Press. pp. 63–73.

Donley-Reid, L. 1990. A Structuring Structure: the Swahili House. In Kent, S. (ed.), *Domestic Architecture and the Use of Space*. Cambridge: Cambridge University Press. pp. 114–26.

Dutt, S. 1962. *Buddhist Monks and Monasteries of India*. London: George Allen and Unwin.

Ehrenberg, M. 1989. *Women in Prehistory*. London: British Museum Publications.

Flood, G. 1996. *An Introduction to Hinduism*. Cambridge: Cambridge University Press.

Frédéric, L. 1995. *Buddhism*. Paris: Flammarion.

Gero, J.M. and Conkey, M.W. (eds). 1991. *Engendering Archaeology: Women and Prehistory*. Oxford: Blackwell.

Gilchrist, R. 1994. *Gender and Material Culture: The Archaeology of Religious Women*. London: Routledge.

Gilchrist, R. 1999. *Gender and Archaeology*. London: Routledge.

Gimbutas, M. 1974. *The Gods and Goddesses of Old Europe*. London: Thames and Hudson.

Gimbutas, M. 1989. *The Language of the Goddess*. London: Thames and Hudson.

Goodison, L. and Morris, C. 1998a. *Ancient Goddesses*. London: British Museum Press.

Goodison, L. and Morris, C. 1998b. Introduction. Exploring Female Divinity: From Modern Myths to Ancient Evidence. In Goodison, L. and Morris, C., *Ancient Goddesses*. London: British Museum Press. pp. 6–21.

Hachlili, R. and Killebrew, A. 1983. Jewish Funerary Customs during the Second Temple Period in Light of the Excavations at the Jericho Necropolis. *Palestine Exploration Quaterly* 115: 109–32.

Hachlili, R. and Killebrew, A. 1999. *Jericho, The Jewish Cemetery of the Second Temple Period*. Jerusalem: The Israel Antiquities Authority Reports no. 7.

Hastorf, C.A. 1991. Gender, Space and Food in Prehistory. In Gero, J.M. and Conkey, M.W. (eds), *Engendering Archaeology: Women and Prehistory*. Oxford: Blackwell. pp. 132–59.

Higuchi, T. and Barnes, G. 1995. Bamiyan: Buddhist Cave Temples in Afghanistan. *World Archaeology* 27: 282–302.

Hinnells, J.R. (ed). 1991. *A Handbook of Living Religions*. London: Penguin.

Hinnells, J.R. (ed.). 1995. *The Penguin Dictionary of Religions*. London: Penguin.

Insoll, T. 1999. *The Archaeology of Islam*. Oxford: Blackwell.

Keller, W. 1965. *The Bible as History. Archaeology Confirms the Book of Books*. London: Hodder & Stoughton.

Lahiri, N. 1999. Bodh-Gaya: An Ancient Buddhist Shrine and its Modern History (1891–1904). In Insoll, T. (ed.), *Case Studies in Archaeology and World Religion. The Proceedings of the Cambridge Conference*. BAR S755. Oxford: Archaeopress. pp. 33–43.

Lane, P. 1998. Engendered Spaces, Bodily Practices in the Iron Age of Southern Africa. In Kent, S. (ed.), *Gender in African Prehistory*. Walnut Creek, Calif.: Altamira, pp. 179–203.

Leeder, C. 2000. The Resurrection of the Godshe. Unpublished MA essay, University of Manchester.

Loades, A. (ed.). 1990. *Feminist Theology: A Reader*. Louisville, Ky: SPCK.

Manushi (Indian Feminist Journal). 1989. *Women Bhakta Poets*. 50, 51, 52.

Marshall, J. (ed.). 1931. *Mohenjodaro and the Indus Civilization*. London: Arthur Probsthein.

Marshall, J.H., Foucher, A. and Majumdar, N.G. 1940. *The Monuments of Sanchi*. Delhi: Archaeological Survey of India.

Mellaart, J. 1967. *Catal Huyuk*. London: Thames and Hudson.

Meskell, L. 1995. Goddesses, Gimbutas and 'New Age' Archaeology. *Antiquity* 69: 74–86.

Moore, J. and Scott, E. (eds). 1997. *Invisible People and Processes: Writing Gender and Childhood into European Archaeology*. London: Leicester University Press.

Morgan, L.H. 1877. *Ancient Society*. New York: World Publishing.

Parker Pearson, M. 1999. *The Archaeology of Death and Burial*. Stroud: Sutton Publishing.

Sharma, A. (ed). 1987. *Women in World Religions*. Albany, N.Y.: University of New York Press.

Sheils, W.J. and Wood, D. (eds). 1990. *Women in the Church*. Oxford: Blackwell.

Tringham, R. 1991. Households with Faces: The Challenge of Gender in Prehistoric Architectural Remains. In Gero, J.M. and Conkey, M.W. (eds), *Engendering Archaeology: Women and Prehistory*. Oxford: Blackwell. pp. 93–131.

Webster, S. 1984. Harim and Hijab: Seclusive and Exclusive Aspects of Traditional Muslim Dwelling and Dress. *Women's Studies International Forum* 7: 251–7.

Chapter 9

Death, being, and time

The historical context of the world religions

Mike Parker Pearson

Introduction

We all want to know what happens when we die. Perhaps this question lies at the core of our humanity along with the multitude of ways in which the human species has attempted to answer it during the last 100,000 years or more. This human quest has been both intensely personal and exaggeratedly institutional. Our realisation of 'being in the face of death' is a muse of both philosophy and religion, and has been a motivation for building the most stunning monuments as well as the inspiration for religious movements that have animated many millions. The greater part of this journey through the human religious experience is entirely undocumented other than through archaeological remains from prehistory. What can we say about the ways in which that experience has changed in the last 100,000 years or even in just the last 10,000? The initial answer is 'not very much'. The archaeological record before 10,000 BP is extremely fragmentary and partial and, even after that date, how are we to explore aspects of the mind and its ideals when all that survive are material things? And yet there may be ways around this dilemma. Beliefs and faiths that have moved spiritual mountains have also constructed edifices of enduring permanence, size and complexity. We might describe this materialisation of the ideal as the *technology of belief*.

This chapter examines the context of the world religions within the wider currents and transformations of human religious thought over the last 5,000 years. Any archaeology of the world religions contextualises them: by removing them from history's centre stage and relegating them to a short period of the recent human past, archaeologists can focus on their transience and fluidity. The world religions will, of course, continue to loom large in our consciousness because of their propagation within historically documented time and because most are vibrant and powerful traditions whose ideologies will profoundly affect the intellectual context of archaeological thought for a very long time to come.

The world religions have largely come into being only in the last 3,000 years of human existence. Claims can be made for the beginnings of Judaism a thousand years earlier, for Hinduism and Jainism to have their roots in Harappan culture of six millennia ago, and for Shinto to have developed from ancestor cults of a similar antiquity (Smart 1998). Despite these comparatively early beginnings, it is in the brief period between 2,600 and 1,400 years ago that most of the world religions emerged. They represent a remarkable historical moment in the expression of human consciousness which requires rather more contextualisation within the greater stream of human religious experience than it currently receives. Even in the most recent synthesis of the world's religions (Smart 1998), those pre-dating the rise of the world religions merit the attention of only 22 out of over 600 pages.

Technologies of belief

The theory of archaeological evidence as a 'ladder of inference' – with technology the most inferable and belief systems as the least accessible – may have constrained archaeological enquiries into prehistoric religion for much of the twentieth century but the current of theoretical changes in archaeology since the 1960s has moved us elsewhere. The negative empiricism represented by the 'ladder of inference' approach compartmentalised aspects of social life which have to be considered as embedded; technology has a social and ideological dimension and vice versa. More useful is the notion of technologies of belief, that the spiritual is actualised in material form or that the word is made flesh. The ideal world of belief is not wholly lost to the gaze of the prehistorian even though it may be seriously obscured. More promisingly, most of the contexts excavated by archaeologists – graves, temples, shrines, special deposits and even domestic buildings – were formed through people's spiritual beliefs in some way or another.

Our reflexive relationship with material culture is such that we build our beliefs and, in doing so, we objectify these beliefs as external fact and reality. No world religion has as its aim the accumulation of earthly wealth and yet even the most world-renouncing – Buddhism – manifests itself through monumental architecture. Within our complex relationships with material culture, the human species cannot be considered to think independently of practice or to act independently of thought. The quest for understanding religious belief prior to writing and the world religions is worth attempting because it resided not merely in people's minds but in their practices which left material traces in the form of monuments, representations and funerary deposits.

It was Aristotle who said that 'men create the gods after their own image' (cited in Morris 1987: 111). For Marx: 'Man makes religion, religion does not make man ... Man is the world of Man, the state, society. This state, this society, produce religion, a reversed world consciousness, because they are a reversed world. Religion is the general theory of that world, its encyclopaedic compendium, its logic in popular form, its enthusiasm, its moral sanction, its universal ground for consolation and justification. It is the fantastic realization of the human essence because the human essence has no true reality' (Marx and Engels 1957: 37–8). Once we understand some of Marx's more subtle ideas about the historical specificity of all conceptions, religious and otherwise, we can bypass his more mechanistic formulations of production determining the religious and ideological superstructure. The fundamental point is that religion is not a creature of the economy (Childe 1951) nor is it 'a fantastic reflection in men's minds of those external forces which control their daily life' (Engels 1878 in Marx and Engels 1957: 131). The relationship between the religious and the social is not one of simple reflection but a reflexive relationship grounded in historical circumstances in which the spiritual is shaped by the material conditions of existence.

Just as religious systems cannot develop without externalised representations in material form, so particular modes of religious belief have only become possible within certain social formations. This is not to say that religious beliefs are determined by the social and economic infrastructure. Rather, each brings the other into being. It is not simply that the Pharaohs built the pyramids and the pyramids then built the Pharaohs (Huntington and Metcalf 1979) – the Pharaohs also created the deities who were used to support the power of the Pharaohs.

Late Victorian theories of the origin and evolution of religion

Speculations about the origins and development of prehistoric religion abounded a hundred years ago. Theories of 'primitive religion' lay at the heart of the emergent discipline of social anthropology before they vanished forever in the face of the synchronic and ahistorical theoretical movements of functionalism and structuralism (Evans-Pritchard 1965: 101). The search for an evolutionary development of human religious thought is present by the early nineteenth century in Hegel's three essential phases: the religions of nature (including magic, Hinduism, Buddhism and the Chinese religions), the religions of spiritual individuality (the Greek and Roman religions and Judaism), and the final phase of a higher synthesis of god and world (*Aufgehoben*) which he believed Christianity to be (Hegel 1956).

Nineteenth-century theories evolved as scholars began to place newly encountered peoples into a hierarchical framework between savage and civilised. Laid before them in geographical terms, so they thought, was the entire history of the human species whose earliest phases were represented by 'survivals'. For Comte and others, fetishism (the worship of inanimate things and animals) was conceived as the most primitive religion, succeeded by polytheism and eventually monotheism.

By the end of the nineteenth century new evolutionary formulations abounded, untrammelled by any attention to archaeological evidence and conceived of as ahistorically evolutionary in character. Engels (1878 in Marx and Engels 1957) hypothesised that humans first worshipped the forces of nature, which became personified as the first gods, social forces in the form of polytheism and eventual monotheism. Müller (1898) similarly saw nature as the foundation of earliest beliefs, initially through worship of nature's majestic attributes – the heavenly bodies – which became personified as deities. Edward Tylor (1871) worked from the notion that religion in its barest form is the belief in spiritual beings. The basis of all religion was animism: all contemporary societies, he argued, had developed complementary notions of 'spirit' and 'soul'. Such beliefs had arisen out of experience of dreams (immaterial manifestations), from experience of death (the departure of the life-force), and from visions and ecstatic out-of-body experiences. The experience of death and dreams thus provided humanity with the empirical basis for inferring the existence for every person of 'a life and a phantom'. Although Tylor's ideas were later challenged, it has been suggested that part of the reason why studies into the origin of religion came to an end was because there has never been a better theory (Morris 1987: 101). Animism was the 'groundwork' which was found in all religion past and present. From animism developed ancestor worship, with departed spirits surviving as disembodied entities capable of possessing the bodies of the living. Belief in spirits as gods who controlled the elements then followed. This polytheism was ultimately joined by monotheism, the belief in a single god which characterised Christianity, Judaism and Islam.

During the same period Herbert Spencer developed similar ideas (1876). He reasoned that death and dream experiences would have led to a conceptualised duality between body and soul/spirit. Thus the first supernatural entities perceived by the human mind were ghosts. The ghosts of founding ancestors or other important people might develop into divinities which were worshipped. Whereas animism was Tylor's origin point, Spencer concluded that 'ancestor worship is the root of every religion' (1876: 411).

Later variations on these ideas were those of Wilhelm Schmidt and Robert Marett. Schmidt (1983 [1931]) considered that since there were monotheistic beliefs among the supposedly most 'primitive' Andaman Islanders and Tasmanians, and among many other small-scale societies, then monotheism had been the earliest form of religion. Marett's proposal (1909) of a 'preanimist' or 'dynamist' phase prior to animism drew from the Melanesian concept of *mana*, to infer that religion began with belief in non-personal sacred forces before evolving into beliefs in personal spirits, polytheism and eventually monotheism.

Whereas Tylor had considered magic, religion and science as capable of co-existing, Sir James Frazer proposed that they were evolutionary stages: magic, religion and science in ascending order (1913: 304, 1925: 57). Magic was the ultimately unsuccessful attempt to coerce nature through spells and sacred formulae whereas religion sought to propitiate super-natural forces rather than compel them. In order to provide empirical support for this theory, he characterised Australian Aboriginal beliefs as magical and pre-religious; such a notion is, of course, wholly erroneous since Aboriginal belief systems are very complex.

Emile Durkheim argued that Aboriginal religious complexity was out of all proportion to the simplicity of their hunting and gathering lifestyle. Yet these beliefs, which he characterised as totemism, embodied the 'elementary form' of religion: the totemic clan cult, in which clan ancestors were worshipped in the form of a clan totem (1915). Underlying totemism, Durkheim reasoned, was a quasi-divine principle or force – the totemic principle – which is incarnated within each individual as the soul. He may have had a better grasp of the evidence than Frazer but his view was still evolutionary, employing a dichotomy of 'elementary' and 'complex' forms. Durkheim disposed of the earlier theories concerning the originary roles of ancestor cults and deified natural phenomena. He pointed to the empirical evidence: not only were developed cults of the dead a feature of state societies such as China, Rome and Egypt rather than of simple tribal cultures but also deified forms of nature amongst Aboriginals and others were often the least majestic aspects – rabbits, lizards and witchetty grubs. Durkheim's arguments restored concepts akin to those of Marx, that religion is something eminently social and that conceptions of divinity have a social origin (Morris 1987: 119). In Marx's words, it is not our consciousness that determines our being but our social being that determines consciousness (Evans-Pritchard 1965: 77).

Speculating from a minimum of archaeological evidence, these Victorian scholars attempted to construct evolutionary sequences for the origin and early development of religion by proposing so-called primitive societies' beliefs as archetypal stages in the emergence of the human consciousness. Such theories seem laughable today because of their implicit assumptions and racist chauvinism but they were radical and progessive in their day. Individuals such as Edward Tylor were asserting the 'psychic unity of humankind', that people shared a common humanity regardless of culture, in contrast to the many racialist theories of the time that posited 'primitives' as child-like in their cognitive abilities. Second, many of these writers were themselves agnostics or atheists who were keen to promote the ideas of a secular society free of religious tyranny and compulsion. By examining the origins and evolution of religion they were, by and large, subverting notions that Christianity or any other world religion was the natural or highest condition to be achieved by humanity. Secularism and science lay as the evolutionary prize to be gained, the highest achievement of human development.

Curiously this particular late Victorian episode of evolutionary anthropology is no longer discussed within archaeological writings but still features in textbooks of social anthropology (Evans-Pritchard 1965, Hendry 1999). More recent social anthropological enquiries into the origins and evolution of religion include writings by James (n.d., 1957, 1960), Bellah (1964) and Godelier (1977). Godelier's approach has been characterised as a mere echo of the ideas of the Victorian anthropologists (Morris 1987: 326). If archaeologists have broadly avoided social anthropological theories of religious evolution, they have been keen to utilise the anthropologists' evolutionary schemes of social organisation (from savagery to barbarism to civilisation and latterly from band to tribe to chiefdom to state) – schemes which are still current despite much criticism (Rowlands 1989). Most recently Rappaport (1999) has attempted a new evolutionary synthesis but this lacks a true historical dimension.

Death, being, and time

Thus far, the various arguments and models for the prehistory of religion have been placed in as small a nutshell as possible. Broader treatments can be found in many works (Evans-Pritchard 1965, Morris 1987, Smart 1969, 1998). The main reason for this brief review is to clear the ground for a new foray into the field, reassessing the archaeological evidence to avoid the pitfalls and blind alleys that were previously encountered by nineteenth-century anthropological theories and their adherents. The starting point is the human experience of death and its centrality for religious belief.

The fact of death has been called 'the only fact we have' (Baldwin 1962). It is the only certain generalisation about the human condition and yet billions consider that they will continue an existence in some form or other after their death. Whilst some of those nineteenth-century anthropologists of religion recognised that the process of dying might have helped to form people's spiritual beliefs they seem not to have realised that the development of a consciousness of 'being in the face of death' may have served as midwife of both religion and philosophy. More recently, philosophers such as Heidegger (1962), Schütz (1967), Becker (1973) and Baumann (1993) have considered how the knowledge of our impending death directs our projects towards comprehension of the eternal mystery of our own personal extinction:

> the idea of death, the fear of it, haunts the human animal like nothing else; it is a mainspring of human activity – activity designed largely to avoid the fatality of death, to overcome it by denying in some way

that it is the final destiny for man . . . the fear of death is indeed a universal in the human condition.

(Ernest Becker 1973: ix)

the whole system of relevances which governs us within the natural attitude is founded upon the basic experience of each of us: I know that I shall die and I fear to die . . . It is the primordial anticipation from which all the others originate. From the fundamental anxiety spring the many interrelated systems of hopes and fears, of wants and satisfactions, of chances and risks which incite man within the natural attitude to attempt the mastery of the world, to overcome obstacles, to draft projects, and to realize them.

(Alfred Schütz 1967)

The awareness of death and our attempts to transcend it have haunted humanity for thousands of years. It is the last five millennia that are under review here, thereby returning the various world religions to the stream of history from which they have been removed. That removal has not only been performed by scholars seeking to focus on the specific historical circumstances of particular world religions but has also been implicit in the agendas of the religious movements themselves, which recast notions of time – new beginnings and ends – to break with the religious traditions of earlier times.

Changing conceptions of the supernatural in the last 5,000 years

This study is mainly but not wholly concerned with the Old World and predominantly with the region where Africa, Europe and Asia intersect, the crossroads or bottleneck of land which has occupied a formative position in world prehistory (Sherratt 1996, 1997) and out of whose arid landscapes have emerged Zoroastrianism and the religions of Abraham – Judaism, Christianity and Islam. Just why these religions emerged in this area is not our concern here. Rather, the archaeological evidence from the region allows a clear vista from the beginnings of farming through the emergence of the Mesopotamian and Egyptian states to the formation of these and other world religions.

This author has suggested elsewhere that the religions of the earliest Neolithic farming communities in this part of Eurasia were not centred on mother-goddess worship but on ancestor cults (Parker Pearson 1999: 157–64; see also Cauvin 1972). The 'little people' that were modelled out of clay at that time are better understood as individuals rather than as representations of a single deity. The interpretation which was posited is that these may have been linked to ancestor cults whose more obvious manifestations are visible in the skull decorating and under-floor burial practices of Pre-Pottery Neolithic Jericho and the Near East (Parker Pearson 1999). Recognising deities in human form in this period before writing is an unwarranted back-projection of religious consciousness from the very different material conditions of much later state societies of the fourth millennium BCE and after. It is only within the context of earlier ancestor beliefs that we can find the seeds of the new supernatural order of human-like deities in the dynastic autocracies of ancient Egypt and Mesopotamia.

The quest for immortality on earth

> When the gods created humankind they appointed death for humankind, kept eternal life in their own hands.
>
> *The Epic of Gilgamesh*

The elevation of certain ancestors to a status comparable with deities appears to have occurred at around 3100 BCE in Egypt and 2500 BCE in Mesopotamia and rather later, around 1400 BCE, in China. In Egypt the 1st Dynasty royal burials at Abydos, beginning around 3150 BCE, are accompanied by hundreds of retainers whose lives were sacrificed for their Pharaohs. The first pyramid, built by Zoser around 2650 BCE, may mark the beginning of a further redefinition of the Pharaoh's relationship to his people in life and in death. Yet pyramid building was a relatively short phenomenon, lasting only a few centuries. Mummification was much longer lasting, being continued, modified and changed as a process for body preservation over 2,000 years, initially for the gods and goddesses who were formerly Pharaohs, and spreading to the nobility, the greater populace and to millions of sacred animals. From the Egyptian pyramid texts and the Book of the Dead we find that the pre-existing deities take human form, or modified versions of human form with animal features, with the newly dead Pharaoh becoming initiated into the pantheon of human-like deities.

Around 2500 BCE in Mesopotamia, the 16 royal graves found at Ur formed part of a much larger cemetery set within the city's sacred walled enclosure in a central area amongst temples (Woolley 1934). The royal graves are complex constructions of chambers entered by sloping passages. Each contains the elaborately decked-out royal corpse laid on a bier and surrounded by a host of grave goods and sometimes the bodies of retainers. These graves are amongst the most spectacular ever found and they bear witness to the absolute power of Mesopotamia's ruling elite, as displayed by their fabulous wealth and their ability to command human sacrifices. By 2300 BCE rulers such as Naram Sin may have been considered deities in their own lifetimes (Postgate 1992: 266). We know something about the link between the Mesopotamians' relationship with their deities and their ancestors from archaeology and from later texts.

A possible explanation of Mesopotamian religion at this time, in the fourth and third millennia BCE, is that it was undergoing a transformation from ancestor worship to the worship of supernatural divinities. Each Mesopotamian city was associated with a particular deity. There were large temple complexes at the centre of each city, whilst individual houses often contained a special altar or place of worship. Written records indicate that adjacent households were related through kinship so that the spatial layout of the city may have formed a map of the kin relationships between the large family lineages which inhabited each of the large courtyard houses. Not only might we see the domestic shrine as a means of worshipping the lineage's ancestors but the individual god of each city may have come into being as the founding ancestor of the people of that city, now deified.

The state on earth was perceived as a mirror and a component of the divine cosmic state. The gods chose who should rule and the king ruled as a mortal but carried a superhuman responsibility which the gods could remove at any time (Frankfort 1948). Dead rulers seem not to have become deities although we have the story of King Urnammu visiting the underworld after his death, presenting gifts to the seven gods, making sacrifices to the important dead, and taking on dead servants appropriate to his position (Ringgren 1973: 46–8). It may well be that the later myths do not relate to the period of the mid-third millennium BCE and thus our interpretation of the royal graves at Ur, and whether they embody notions of living beyond death, must derive solely from the archaeological evidence.

Thorkild Jacobsen considers that Mesopotamian religion went through three stages. In the earliest, in the fourth millennium BCE, the deities were those of grain and the storehouse whilst life, death and rebirth were seen as part of a continuous cycle. In the second stage, in the third millennium BCE, the deities associated with fertility were replaced by ruler and hero gods. They were considered as taking human form and they ruled the heavens like kings. By the third stage, in the second millennium, individuals had personal gods amongst the enormous pantheon of nearly 3,000 deities, to whom they could unburden their problems and ask for forgiveness, as if the gods were supernatural parents (Jacobsen 1976, O'Brien and Major 1982: 139–40).

The remarkable mid-third millennium burials of the early Pharaohs and Mesopotamian elite can be understood as an early state phenomenon. As the Pharaohs built the pyramids, so the pyramids built the state. At the same time, the intention behind the monumentality and excessive destruction of resources was to ensure that the deceased became a deity, a godly ancestor for the successors so that their earthly power might be beyond reproach, god-given. In an exaggerated image of the world of the living, the afterworld also took on a rigidly hierarchical form, shaping and determining the lives of mortals.

The phenomenon of monumental, lavish burials accompanied by human sacrifices has appeared throughout the world in many different places between 3100 BCE and the early nineteenth century (Parker Pearson 1999). The sacrifice of living humans, whether willing or not, is an expression of the supreme power that rulers exercised over the ruled. Even where the afterworld distinctions were not drawn as sharply as those in ancient Egypt, between deified ancestors and other ancestors, the statements of difference amongst the dead are clear and establish hierarchical relationships between and amongst the ancestral dead, in whose light the living bathe.

We may define this phenomenon of building tombs for immortals as cults of deities and heroes. These deity and hero cults are regional and are characteristic of early city states where cities were formed around large temple complexes and where gross social inequalities meant certain individuals wielded the power of life and death over others. The funerary monuments of rulers are elaborate and human sacrifices and copious grave goods accompany the royal dead to the afterworld. Their bodies may be preserved through mummification, jade suits (in China) and other magical means to make possible this transcendence of death. Pantheons of deities are represented as personified individuals whilst certain living individuals have divine or heroic ancestries and personages. Absolute power on earth is translated into, and bolstered by, the eternal rule of heavenly deities. Earthly rulers are their representatives, maintaining the harmony of integration within the cosmos.

The monumentality and pomp of the elite's funerary rites may be matched by representations of individuals in monumental size. In contrast to the small figurines of the Neolithic and Chalcolithic, statues of the third millennium's early states come to dwarf the human scale. Ruler gods, heroes and deities are embodied individually by large statues and imagery – some in human form and some as chimeric part-humans part-animals. In Mesopotamian mythology, statues were not simply representations of people and other creatures but were entities in their own right, made from the same materials as the living. Living creatures are created by mixing dust with water, in other words, from clay. When they die they revert to the materials from which they were made, silt and dust. Statues were considered to be 'raised' or 'given birth' in the same way as living beings. Death was likened to the breaking of a statue, in which the pieces are scattered and strewn in the soil (Cassin 1982: 355–6).

The rise of the world religions

It is broadly in the 2,000-year period of the first millennia BCE and CE that we can identify a new current of human belief about the nature of death and immortality. The earliest beginnings of these myriad new interpretations and reinterpretations of what happens when we die can be traced to the mid-second millennium BCE. According to Hans Küng, '[o]nly for about 5,000 years, since the beginning of the third millennium BCE, were there early historical high cultures and high religions' (1992: 4). The Hindu Rig Veda was in existence by c. 1380 BCE and it reveals polytheist worship of creation, rain and thunder, fire, air, water, the dawn, the moon, sky and faith, in which the correct sacrifices would ensure comfort in the heavens above (Sen 1961, Zaehner 1966). Recent appraisals of the remarkable Indus civilisation cities such as Mohenjo-Daro and Harappa, dating to c. 2500–1500 BCE, have suggested that there are symbolic elements in the architecture and material culture which can be seen to prefigure later Hindu beliefs, such as possible yogic figures and possible representations of the deities Pasupati Siva, Devi (the mother-goddess) and Sakti (the mother image of spiritual power) (Sen 1961, Zaehner 1966, Chakrabarti, this volume).

The exodus of Moses' people to follow their god Yahweh can also be dated to the second millennium BCE, with these early experiences passed down orally before being written down after 1000 BCE (Küng 1992: 19). Within the first millennium BCE we find many of the core elements of the world religions appearing, such as the Hindu *Upanishads* and the teachings of Parsva (Jainism), Zoroaster, Buddha, Confucius, Lao Tzu and Jesus Christ. Latecomers are the emergence of Shinto in the early centuries CE and the prophet of Allah, Muhammad, in the seventh century CE (Insoll 1999, this volume).

There are two questions that should be asked about those groups of religious beliefs that we commonly classify as world religions. Are the 'world religions' qualitatively any different to what came before? Second, are these 'world religions' simply acknowledged as such because they exist today, the survivors of a series of historical conjunctures and contingencies? The world religions can be distinguished from the deity and hero religions through their universal membership. Even with Judaism and Hinduism, where incorporation depends on birth rather than conversion, these are religions which promise salvation or enlightenment for the masses, and not just the elites, regardless of wealth or social position. Most of their prophets and leaders were men who were either from amongst the poor or were princes who renounced their worldly wealth; in contrast to the deity and hero religions, earthly power and wealth are not conducive to successfully achieving transcendence of death.

The origins of these world-renouncing religious movements may lie between c. 600 BCE and c. 622 CE, a period when large states and multi-ethnic empires from Asia to Europe and North Africa established wide-ranging hegemonies over countless ethnic groups, and created new classes of the rootless and the rural and urban poor and dispossessed. At the same time, the emergent world religions also accompanied phases of 'democratisation' or, at least, lapses in autocracy. Initial phases of materialist rejection, after the earliest generations of believers and followers rejected earthly wealth and power, were followed several centuries later by global expansion and massive monumentality in the form of temples, mosques, cathedrals and stupas. For some religions the superhumans who are credited with initiating the way are represented in human form at a whole variety of personalised and monumental scales. For others, such as Islam and Judaism, there is a ban – not always observed – on the representation of the deity or his prophets.

In terms of the contributions that world religions have made to the human experience of death, they have certain characteristics in common which suggest a qualitative change from earlier religions. All are beholden to an all-powerful supernatural entity or worship within a pantheistic monism. A common thread through many is that eternal salvation may be sought through moral improvement and can be realised by supernatural judgement. Monumentality is directed towards the worship of the supreme entity or the transcendent idea. The human body in death is treated with simplicity or is even annihilated. Equally there are contrasts between world religions, such as the degree to which the memory of the deceased is commemorated.

Transcendence of death is possible for all converts or chosen ones. This transcendence is achieved in various ways. Amongst the Abrahamic religions of Judaism, Christianity and Islam, as well as in Zoroastrianism (originating in the seventh–sixth centuries BCE), time is not conceived of in cosmic cycles but focuses on a goal, progressing from creation to an end which promises a universal salvation and everlasting life after the cosmic last judgement (Küng 1992: 17–18, Nigosian 1993: 90–7). In contrast, followers of the Buddha (c. 563–483 BCE) aimed for extinction of the self and release from space and time. Death is not inevitable but a sign that something has gone wrong, caused by Mara 'the killer' who diverts us from the path and from our true immortal selves. By shedding our material attachments, we move beyond death's realm and win relief from an endless series of repeated deaths. By attaining a state of self-extinction (*nirvana*), Buddhists may overcome the error that is death and enter the 'doors to the deathless', 'the gates of the undying' (Conze 1993: 1–8).

The rise of secular beliefs

It is also in the first millennium BCE, in ancient Greece and Egypt and in Confucian China, that we can find the beginnings of the secular religions which ultimately have provided the basis for the broad scientific enquiry into the nature of belief and transcendence which includes archaeology. Secular thought entails either the rejection of the notion of transcendence of death, or the adoption of an agnostic uncertainty, or merely the loss of interest in the possibility of life after death. The search for salvation becomes the quest for solutions in this world rather than the next, whilst people live to moral codes of universal human rights, individualism, common welfare and secular humanism.

And yet the globalisation of world culture and its attendant localisation of ethnicities, interest groups and nationalities appears to be accompanied by great fragmentation of spiritual beliefs. As the world religions shatter into a myriad different movements and Messianic groupings, so the archaeo-cults (goddess groups, New Agers, Druidic orders, witches' covens, shamanic believers), UFO watchers, believers in physical immortality and many, many other cults grow and diversify. The powerful religico-secularist ideologies of the twentieth century – communism, Nazism and fascism – have almost gone, surviving in many areas as small and disparate creeds. Yet the fate of the world in terms of the all-out victory of one of these creeds hung in the balance as millions died in atrocities whose scale was unknown to any previous century. Who can say that everything will not change at the hands of new or resurgent militant faiths before the new century is over? Contrary to some views (Fukuyama 1992), history is not over and ended. Contingency is never predictable.

As the third millennium CE begins, this is perhaps a propitious moment to present this tentative sketch of the 'big picture' context of the world religions. It has very different aims to those of the Victorian evolutionists and it should not be seen in any way as a return to those 'Victorian values' of social evolutionary progress, even if they were the values of destabilising the oppressive institutions of religious intolerance and racialism. It is not the aim here to duplicate the nineteenth-century search for the origins of religious belief. Nor have we sought to find an underlying evolutionary mechanism in the historically rooted changes that have been highlighted. Rather, this has been an attempt at description, to place the origins of the world religions within their broader contexts so that they may be seen as historical products of the religious currents which preceded them, of their settings within large states and emergent empires, and of previous notions about transcending death.

Conclusions

An attempt has been made here to sketch out a series of key stages and transformations in the human experience of death and people's expressed relationships to the supernatural. Such chronological arrangements should not be taken as global prescriptions but as dominant themes within a kaleidoscopic array of different spiritual practices in play at any one time around the world. It is not the intention to state that the concept of deities was invented for the first time around 5000 BP but that the personification of deities in human form was novel at this time; the human-like deity accompanied the concept of the all-powerful ruler on earth. The period before 3000 BCE need not have been devoid of higher divinities – what we would recognise as gods and goddesses – but this author has argued elsewhere that the Neolithic 'little people' modelled in clay may have more human and ancestral meanings rather than being 'deity-dollies' of a notional mother-goddess (Parker Pearson 1999: 157–64). That transition to gods and goddesses in human form in the millennia after 6000 BP is marked in several ways, by the enlargement of statuary to super-human size and by the combining of human and animal forms in single chimeric representations.

Within the exceptionally hierarchical early states which embody these deity cults, the close kinship between rulers and deities is an extension and elaboration of the relationships between the living and their dead ancestors. It is the emphasis which has changed rather than the complete absence of one form to another. Finally, the arrival of the world religions occurred within the context of the deity cults, assimilating many of their aspects and radically transforming and innovating in others. Syncretism was and is a continuous and ever-present aspect of the development and growth of these world religions, not only in their expansions into other belief systems but also in their appropriation of concepts from existing deity cult belief systems. Again, the social conditions which brought them into existence were necessarily different from the ultra-hierarchical early states in regions such as the Bronze Age Near East.

We live in an age when the master narratives of religious myth, of political creeds such as Marxism and fascism, and hegemonic discourses of all kinds are rightfully under scrutiny and attack. For some, the postmodern condition demands incredulity towards such master narratives (Lyotard 1979). Why then has what might be taken as yet another master narrative of how human religious beliefs have changed over 5,000 years been sketched out? Should I not be demolishing rather than building yet another scheme which this time situates a post-religious secular humanism as the ultimate religious state for humankind? The answer is that every demolition involves a rebuilding. Postmodernism is not the end of master narratives but the beginning of a profusion of them (Klein 1995). Gellner points to the paradox of our need for a backcloth vision of history and at the same time the low esteem in which the elaboration of global historical patterns is held (Gellner 1988: 12). Many readers will prefer their own particular vision of the context of the world religions but they need to be aware that the ideas of previous scholars, from Hegel to Marx, Spencer and Durkheim, though derided or unacknowledged are everywhere in use

(Gellner 1988: 12). If archaeologists abandon their efforts to reconstruct the big picture through their own master narratives they will be trampled underfoot by the many others who are far less concerned with honest evaluation of the actual evidence and more determined to impose their politically and motivationally suspect visions of the past and thence the future.

This has been a necessarily brief sketch of the development of religious belief over the last 5,000 years which, owing to constraints of space, has left out much detail. There are three major points with which to conclude. Archaeological interpretations of prehistoric and ancient religion have often unjustifiably assumed certain constants in the evolution of human social life. One of the least supportable but most frequent claims is that people worshipped gods and goddesses in human form prior to the fourth millennium BCE. On the contrary, the spiritual journey of the human species has probably developed and changed far more radically and in a far more complex way than has previously been imagined.

Second, we should question whether there is any certain evolutionary adaptative mechanism behind religious beliefs which make them part of our unchangeable nature (contra Rappaport 1999). The rise of Islam, born-again Christianity and so many New Age 'archaeo-cults' (witchcraft, Druidism, shamanism, earth-mother cults amongst others) within the secularising societies of the twentieth century has been taken as a sign that religion is a necessary component of the human condition. The view of this author is that spiritual beliefs have social and material conditions and, as such, are historically contingent. Organised religion is neither a necessary nor an eternal element of human spirituality.

Finally, over the last 5,000 years developments of religious belief have served to deny the possibility of personal extinction beyond the grave. The world religions provide some of the most complex and subtle self-delusions and negations of death which have helped millions to console themselves within the shadow of death by denying that life really is finite. Within archaeological time, the era of organised religions may be ultimately but a brief phase in the development of human consciousness and spirituality.

Note

Part of this chapter was originally published within Chapter 8 of *The Archaeology of Death and Burial* in 1999. It is reproduced here with permission from Sutton Publishing.

References

Baldwin, J. 1962. Letter from a Region in My Mind. *The New Yorker* (17 Nov.).

Baumann, Z. 1993. *Mortality, Immortality and Other Life Strategies*. Oxford: Polity Press.

Becker, E. 1973. *The Denial of Death*. New York: Free Press.

Bellah, R.N. 1964. Religious evolution. *American Sociological Review* 29: 358–74.

Cassin, E. 1982. Le mort: valeur et représentation en Mésopotamie ancienne. In Gnoli, G. and Vernant, J.-P. (eds), *La Mort, Les Morts dans les Sociétés Anciennes*. Cambridge: Cambridge University Press. pp. 355–72.

Cauvin, J. 1972. *Religions Néolithiques de Syro-Palestine*. Saint-Andrée-de-Cruzières: Centre de Recherches d'Ecologie et de Préhistoire.

Childe, V.G. 1951. *Social Evolution*. London: Watts.

Conze, E. 1993. *A Short History of Buddhism*. Oxford: Oneworld.

Durkheim, E. 1915. *The Elementary Forms of the Religious Life*. London: Allen & Unwin.

Evans-Pritchard, E.E. 1965. *Theories of Primitive Religion*. Oxford: Clarendon.

Frankfort, H. 1948. *Kingship and the Gods: A Study of Ancient Near Eastern Religion as the Integration of Society and Nature*. Chicago: Chicago University Press.

Frankfort, H., Frankfort, H.A., Wilson, J.A., Jacobsen, T. and Irwin, W.A. 1946. *The Intellectual Adventure of Ancient Man: An Essay on Speculative Thought in the Ancient Near East*. Chicago: Chicago University Press.

Frazer, J.G. 1913. *The Golden Bough: A Study in Magic and Religion*. Pt. VII, vol. II. London: Macmillan.

Frazer, J.G. 1925. *The Golden Bough: A Study in Magic and Religion*. Abridged edition. London: Macmillan.

Fukuyama, F. 1992. *The End of History and the Last Man*. New York: Free Press.

Gellner, E. 1988. *Plough, Sword and Book: The Structure of Human History*. London: Paladin.

George, A. 1999. *The Epic of Gilgamesh: A New Translation*. London: Allen Lane.

Godelier, M. 1977. *Perspectives in Marxist Anthropology*. Cambridge: Cambridge University Press.

Hegel, G.W.F. 1956 [1840]. *The Philosophy of History*. New York: Dover.

Heidegger, M. 1962. *Being and Time*. London: SCM Press.

Hendry, J. 1999. *An Introduction to Social Anthropology: Other People's Worlds*. London: Macmillan.

Huntington, R. and Metcalf, P. 1979. *Celebrations of Death: The Anthropology of Mortuary Ritual*. Cambridge: Cambridge University Press.

Insoll, T. 1999. *The Archaeology of Islam*. Oxford: Blackwell.

Jacobsen, T. 1976. *The Treasures of Darkness: A History of Mesopotamian Religion*. New Haven: Yale University Press.

James, E.O. n.d. *The Beginnings of Religion*. London: Hutchinson.

James, E.O. 1957. *Prehistoric Religion: A Study in Prehistoric Archaeology*. London: Thames and Hudson.

James, E.O. 1960. *The Ancient Gods: The History and Diffusion of Religion in the Ancient Near East and the Eastern Mediterranean*. London: Weidenfeld & Nicolson.

Klein, K.L. 1995. In Search of Narrative Mastery: Postmodernism and the People Without History. *History and Theory* 34: 275–98.

Küng, H. 1992. *Judaism: The Religious Situation of Our Time*. London: SCM.

Lyotard, F. 1979. *La Condition Postmoderne: Rapport sur Savoir*. Paris: Les Editions de Minuit.

Marett, R.R. 1909. *The Threshold of Religion*. London: Methuen.

Marx, K. and Engels, F. 1957. *On Religion*. Moscow: Progress.

Morris, B. 1987. *Anthropological Studies of Religion: An Introductory Text*. Cambridge: Cambridge University Press.

Müller, M. 1898. *Anthropological Religion*. London: Longmans, Green & Co.

Nigosian, S.A. 1993. *The Zoroastrian Faith: Tradition and Modern Research*. Montreal: McGill-Queen's University Press.

O'Brien, J. and Major, W. 1982. *In the Beginning: Creation Myths from Ancient Mesopotamia, Israel and Greece*. Chico, Calif.: Scholars Press.

Parker Pearson, M. 1999. *The Archaeology of Death and Burial*. Stroud: Sutton.

Postgate, J.N. 1992. *Early Mesopotamia: Society and Economy at the Dawn of History*. London: Routledge.

Rappaport, R.A. 1999. *Ritual and Religion in the Making of Humanity*. Cambridge: Cambridge University Press.

Ringgren, H. 1973. *Religions of the Ancient Near East*. London: SPCK.

Rowlands, M. 1989. A Question of Complexity. In Miller, D., Rowlands, M. and Tilley, C. (eds), *Domination and Resistance*. London: Unwin Hyman. pp. 29–40.

Schmidt, W. 1931. *The Origin and Growth of Religion*. London: Methuen.

Schütz, A. 1967. *Collected Papers I*. Edited by M. Natanson. The Hague: Mouton.

Sen, K.M. 1961. *Hinduism*. Harmondsworth: Penguin.

Sherratt, A. 1996. Plate Tectonics and Imaginary Prehistories: Structure and Contingency in Agricultural Origins. In Harris, D.R. (ed.), *The Origins and Spread of Agriculture and Pastoralism in Eurasia*. London: UCL Press. pp. 130–40.

Sherratt, A. 1997. Climatic Cycles and Behavioural Revolutions: The Emergence of Modern Humans and the Beginnings of Farming. *Antiquity* 71: 271–87.

Smart, N. 1969. *The Religious Experience of Mankind*. New York: Scribner.

Smart, N. 1998. *The World's Religions*. Second edition. Cambridge: Cambridge University Press.

Spencer, H. 1876. *The Principles of Sociology*. Three volumes. London: Williams & Norgate.

Tylor, E.B. 1871. *Primitive Culture: Researches into the Development of Mythology, Philosophy, Religion, Art, and Custom*. Two volumes. London: John Murray.

Woolley, L. 1934. *Ur Excavations II: The Royal Cemetery*. London: British Museum.

Zaehner, R.C. 1966. *Hinduism*. Second edition. Oxford: Oxford University Press.

Index